CAUGHT IN BETWEEN

ENGAGE YOUR PRETEENS
BEFORE THEY CHECK OUT

DAN SCOTT

Caught In Between
Published by Orange, a division of The reThink Group, Inc.
5870 Charlotte Lane, Suite 300
Cumming, GA 30040 U.S.A.

The Orange logo is a registered trademark of The reThink Group, Inc.

Other Orange products are available online and direct from the publisher. Visit our website at www.ThinkOrange.com for more resources like these.

ISBN: 978-1-63570-066-4

©2018 The reThink Group, Inc.

Author: Dan Scott
Contributing Writer: Jenna Scott
Lead Editor: Steph Whitacre
Editorial Team: Lauren Terrell, Kristen Ivy, Reggie Joiner, Cara Martens, Mike Jeffries, Morgan Brandt, Mike Tiemann, Susan Gaines
Project Manager: Nate Brandt
Art Direction: Ryan Boon
Cover and Interior Design: Five Stone

Printed in the United States of America
First Edition

2 3 4 5 6 7 8 9 10 11

06/20/18

Table of Contents

FOREWORD

Not too long ago, I was sitting in a coffee shop when a pack of fifth grade girls walked in. They were chatty, loud, and moving through the coffee shop like a force. I happened to glance over at the girl behind the counter and couldn't help but laugh at what I saw. She gave the biggest eye roll and let out the largest sigh. She knew chaos was on the way to her counter. And who could blame her. On the outside, these girls looked like trouble. But as a middle school pastor watching from the sidelines, I saw something different.

I caught a glimpse of the space between "little kid" and "teenager." I saw a mix of energy and confidence and uncertainty all at the same time.

These girls were all ready to be grown-up . . . but they weren't quite there yet. I saw the middle before middle school—otherwise known as the preteen years.

Now, you might be asking, "Is a preteen really a thing?" Yes. Preteens are real. But don't mistake them for little kids—because they are not. And don't mistake them for teenagers either. They are a unique group that exist in the most "in between" space in the church. And because they are such a unique group, they require a unique ministry approach to reach them.

When I first read Caught In Between my very first thought was, "I have never read anything like this." This book is dedicated to helping us understand the "in between" space of the preteen years. The pages ahead are filled with an in-depth look at who preteens are, how we can best minister to them within the church, and practical tools you can begin using in your church tomorrow. Dan Scott has created a thoughtful blueprint for building a strong ministry to preteens in the church.

As a middle school pastor, leading the ministry that follows a kid's journey beyond children's ministry, I am grateful for those who are willing to thoughtfully engage preteens. A strong preteen ministry will set your youth ministry up to win and will help kids remain on the trajectory toward a life-long faith.

Katie Edwards
Junior High Pastor
Saddleback Church

How this book works:

The research, ideas, and information we've collected on preteens falls into two major categories:

Who is a preteen?

How can the church help them?

Part 1 is for anyone who wants a clearer understanding of the new challenges preteens face.

Part 2 lays out a dynamic preteen strategy any church can adapt to fit their needs and the steps ministry leaders can take to implement it. These chapters walk you through creating a dynamic preteen ministry at your church.

In NEXT STEPS you'll find a practical guide for how you can start your preteen ministry or take your existing preteen environment to the next level. Included in this section are worksheets and checklists to help you along the way.

When you're ready to get started, turn the page.

PART

1

The Life of a Preteen

Boom boxes. The Bluetooth speaker of the 80's. Where my generation sat for hours waiting to record a song off the radio when our moms wouldn't take us to Sam Goody to buy the single on cassette.

I'll never forget the day the DJ introduced a new single by a band from across the pond by saying, "This new song will change your life."

And then I heard the vocals that really *would* change my life:

"I want to run,
I want to hide,
I want to tear down the walls that hold me inside!"

In that moment, U2 became my favorite band. I pored over their lyrics and discovered their back catalog of music. In the process, fifth-grade me discovered that music was more than notes and lyrics. It was emotion and passion. That was the moment I began to realize how much I loved music. It became an obsession that continues to this day—I make a playlist literally every time I travel. I even created a playlist to write this book!

But what does this have to do with preteens and why is it even important?

Sitting in front of that boom box at age 11 changed the trajectory of my entire life. Because of what's happening in preteens bodies and minds, new ideas and experiences have the potential to set the trajectory for a lifetime.

For me it was music; for others it may have been the first time they touched a soccer ball or put on ballet slippers, held a kitten, or earned their first $20. Whatever happened, while seemingly insignificant at the time, a seed was planted that grew into a lifelong passion. Their preteen years set the course for the rest of their lives.

When I first joined the staff at Orange, I came to the team with a deep desire to address the issue of disengaging preteens both because of my ministry experience and because my own kids were aging into this newly challenging phase. Over the past five years, I have worked with other leaders on the team as well as ministry friends across the country to evaluate what we believe may be one of the most important linchpins for both an effective children's ministry and a thriving youth ministry.

What we're just starting to uncover is that ministries lose kids at every transition. We lose them from preschool to elementary, younger elementary to preteen, elementary to middle school, and middle school to high school, as well as the drop off between tenth and eleventh grades.

What if we've been looking at the wrong numbers?
What if we could stop losing kids and keep them longer?
Is there a way to catch kids before they get lost in transition?

If you've ever wondered about these questions, you're not alone. Children's and youth pastors alike are frustrated, trying to find a solution for engaging preteens.

If you're a children's pastor, you have two choices:

1. Turn a blind eye to the disengaged and dwindling preteen
    population until they make it to middle school (at which
    point you can point fingers at the youth program, keeping
    you and your team blame-free).

2. Set your youth ministry (and preteens) up for success by
    doing something to catch them now.

If you're a youth pastor, you also have two choices:

1. Stay in "your territory" avoiding the fourth and fifth grade
    rooms at all costs (so when you get low numbers on
    promotion Sunday, you can point fingers at the children's
    ministry, proving you weren't set up for success).

2. Cast your net wider and begin to prep the rising youth by
    doing something to catch them now.

With a few shifts in your perspective and programming, you
can easily engage the preteens in your church. You can be sure
they don't fall through the cracks, but instead get caught in
between. Our investment in this impressionable season of a
person's life will have unparalleled influence on their future.

Here are three things to keep in mind as you consider preteens.

PRETEENS ARE MORE POWERFUL THAN WE REALIZE.
Preteens hold unprecedented influence. More than any other
time in history.

By 2020, the United States alone predicts there will be 23 million tweens.

According to a 2016 article, preteens account for $260 billion in direct sales annually.

A 2017 study shared that tweens and teens influence $600 billion in family spending.

Another 2012 study cited that tweens influence 60 percent of their parents' new car purchases.

THE MARKETING WORLD TARGETS PRETEENS.

Marketing executives have created entire agencies focused on attracting and nurturing the influential preteen demographic. They've done their homework. They know the statistics. They monitor the trends.

And with 40 percent of preteens on a smart device, consuming an average of 9 hours of media *per day*, it's more possible than ever for companies to understand their world and influence their decisions.

Is this not alarming?

Look, I'm not a conspiracy theorist. This is our reality. Big data drives the marketplace. Businesses know they'll make a killing when they market to preteens.

Compared to the world in which we grew up, our preteens basically live on a different planet. With a Google search, we can find out all we need to know about what it's like to live on Planet Preteen. While it may take time to wade through it all, the church has much of the same access to the information used by marketing agencies building preteen tribes.

Yet, when it comes to building engaging environments in our churches, we often don't leverage what we know about preteens to affect our ministry initiatives.

The church sometimes operates as if the data on this demographic is irrelevant to the goals we have for the spiritual lives of teens. Yet the goals of corporations and churches are basically the same: life-long engagement. The church just has a more hopeful outcome.

We are raising adults who, we hope, will have a life-long relationship with God and participate in a faith community.

THE CHURCH HAS HOME COURT ADVANTAGE.
Good news.

Not only are you a simple Google search away from knowing everything the market knows about preteens, but you also know something the marketers don't about the kids in your church family.

You have a major advantage the market doesn't have. You already have an established relationship with many of your preteens, several of whom you've known since they were in the church nursery. You might even have some sort of relationship with their parents, peers, or extended family.

How can the church leverage what the market knows and use it to reach this demographic? How can the church build lasting relationships with preteens that will carry on into adulthood?

It starts with knowing the world of preteens.

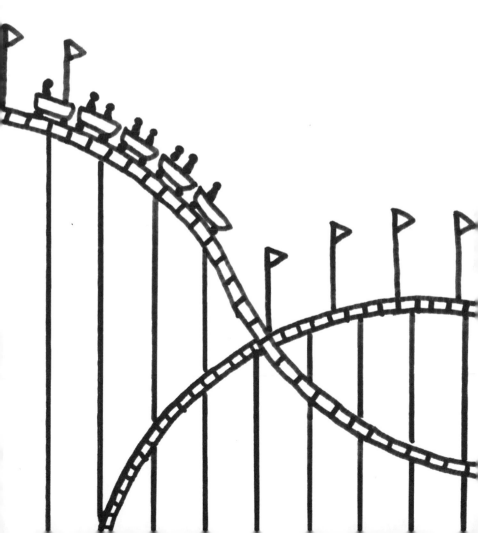

CHAPTER 1

Caught In Between Childhood & Adolescence

We all know preteens love a good fart joke and obsess over YouTube videos. However, defining them is way more complex than just saying they're *anyone who has not yet turned 13*.

In 10-plus years of research and experience, I've yet to find a definitive age range for preteens. Some experts say as young as age 8 (the earliest average-age for hormonal changes associated with puberty) while others simply go with double digits—kids between the ages of 10 and 12. For the purpose of this book, we'll stick to the 10 to 12-year-old range, or somewhere around the fourth grade. While many start their fourth grade year as 9-year-olds, most catch on fairly quickly to what's happening in fourth grade and start acting more like 10-year-olds by Christmas.

The word "preteen" seems dictated by a number, so you may think it's all about the math. But, in order to understand the meaning of the word, it's important to take a deep dive into child and adolescent development.

Rather than assigning an age range, defining the preteen stage starts with a question:

When does childhood end and adolescence begin?

We often think about physical changes in our answer to this question. But the subtle shift into the preteen phase is the result of mental, social, and emotional changes. So a child who is physically a teenager could mentally be a preteen, or vice versa. Fun times.

This question also has challenging ministry implications. Somewhere between childhood and adolescence, we find kids in a highly transitional phase of development. They are realizing that their church experience is exasperatingly too young or too old, too simple or too intimidating. And like Goldilocks, they are searching for something in the middle, something that is "just right" because, after all, they are caught in between.

Preteen kids are a bundle of paradoxes:

Complex and simple
Curious and naive
Abstract and concrete
Physically maturing and acting immature

Preteens are experiencing a unique phase of life where they're caught in between. They're not quite one thing, yet not quite the other. In order to better understand and serve them, we need to deeply understand this phase.

NAVIGATING THE PRETEEN PHASE

The navigation app Waze has changed the game for getting from point A to point B. Not only does it crowd-source from drivers actually on the route in real time (brilliant!), it alerts drivers of future accidents, delays, and trouble spots. It also recalculates another route for you to still arrive at your destination. On time. Unharmed. Unfazed by the obstacles along the way.

When we identify a preteen's struggles, we can use the information to help them navigate from the point A of childhood to the point B of adolescence. And if we're smart about it, we can help them have significantly fewer accidents, delays, stalls, breakdowns, traffic jams or off-ramps along the way.

A few years ago, we decided to embark on a journey to learn everything we could about human development. We were motivated in part by two primary concerns.

1. Churches get theology, but they don't always get child development.
2. Parents love their kids, but they aren't effectively resourced to understand their kids.

We began a research and development initiative that later became known as the "Phase Project." We interviewed teachers, educators, and experts in the child development field for over a year. We collected every significant book written about life stages over the past decade. The effort was designed to give parents and leaders resources to help them understand what is happening at every phase of a kid's life so they can lead and parent better.

Just like every other phase of a kid's life, we believe every preteen is changing in six ways: physically, mentally, culturally, relationally, emotionally, and morally. **However, especially in the preteen phase, each child experiences these changes at different rates. So your uniquely challenging job is to create an environment that appeals to kids who are in different places developmentally.** But before we talk about how you do that, let's sum up a little phase research about these six changes.

WHAT'S CHANGING PHYSICALLY AND MENTALLY

In the preteen phase, girls start to tower over boys. Their rate of growth and change is all over the map. Walking down the fifth-grade hallway is proof that kids experience a wide scope of physical changes. Many are starting to experience the hormonal changes associated with puberty, whether or not they are showing the physical signs. And while it's important to note that kids are changing physically, for the sake of this discussion, we'll focus on the mental changes that preteens experience in this in-between stage.

Elementary kids think like scientists.

In the elementary years, kids are concrete thinkers. Most kids have no difficulty with the world of symbols and objects that can represent letters and words, as well as numbers and math equations. Literal thinking is just that: whatever you say, the younger kids will understand the most literal interpretation of that thought.

If you lead younger elementary kids, maybe you've asked if they want to invite Jesus into their heart forever and been met with confused looks from the audience. It's not that they don't want to follow Jesus. They're just trying to figure out the mechanics of how Jesus gets inside of them. They might wonder if a surgical procedure is required—after all, how else can a fully grown person fit inside a human heart? While this might sound ridiculous, it's a valid explanation of how some younger kids interpret that phrase.

Literal thinking also limits a kid's ability to see the same problem from different angles. Take this math problem for example:

$$x + 5 = 9$$
$$5 + x = 9$$
$$9 - x = 5$$
$$9 - 5 = x$$

You probably took one look at those math problems and answered "4." And you're correct. You know that answering one of the equations actually answers all four of the equations. While that's easy for adults to grasp, not all kids can immediately see how answering one is answering all. Concrete thinkers struggle to see the basic relationship of those four problems. Instead, when things don't look the same at first, they are believed to be different.

Middle schoolers think like engineers.

By the end of the preteen years, middle schoolers and early high schoolers are able to make connections throughout their world. They can see how two different things relate to each other, even holding them in tension with one another. They build on previous knowledge and connect how it relates to what they're learning now. They'd look at the same math problem presented to their elementary counterparts and immediately answer "4" without even thinking about it.

Preteens' thought processes are caught somewhere in between.

Preteens are only starting to move toward abstract thinking

and are just beginning to manipulate abstract ideas. The emergence of new ways of thinking can be overwhelming for some kids, and may even cause anxiety. The mental world of a child has parameters and limited possibilities. But around age 11, the brain starts to awaken to the idea that the world is bigger and more complex than they previously realized.

As their thought processes change, preteens acquire new mental abilities. They transition toward the ability to see a problem from a point of view other than their own. They begin to move from inductive reasoning ("The last three spiders I've read about are black. Therefore, all spiders are black.") to deductive reasoning where they can take a general principle learned in one setting and apply it to an unfamiliar setting ("All spiders have eight legs. A black widow is a spider. A black widow has eight legs.").

Whether your group of preteens is a room filled with upper-elementary fourth graders, or not-yet-teenage seventh graders, working with preteens means working with kids who are in the middle of transitioning not *what* they think, but *how* they think. **Very few of the leaders in either age group are prepared for the inevitable moment when concrete thinking gets in the way of understanding or abstract thinking catches them off guard.**

When you consider the changes taking place, you can be more prepared for the potential hurdles you'll face in communication. Here's something to remember and share with your volunteers: the magic age is 11.

Here's how it works:

At birth, a child's brain has the exact same amount of neurons as a full-grown adult. Yet, as a baby interacts with the world, these neurons make connections that are constantly being trenched deeper with each interaction. By age three, certain connections have doubled or even tripled that of an adult as the young toddler grows into a small child who is ready for school. At this point, they learn patterns that build literacy and help them speak in sentences, and at some point, make so many connections that they can identify words and comprehend what they're reading as they chunk those words into sentences and paragraphs. Along the way, the brain is getting rid of what it doesn't really need anymore, as it's adapting to this new phase of life.

By the time a child turns 8, the brain has tapered off and is back to the original model that looks more like an adult brain. This continues throughout the next few years. This 8 to 10-year-old phase is the golden age for teachers, as kids have plenty of knowledge *and* the ability to engage whatever the teacher throws at them—and they're not snarky yet! Jeff Foxworthy was right that there's no one smarter than a fifth grader. But this golden age only lasts a few years because something big is on the horizon . . .

You guessed it, puberty. Which starts when? Correct again! The magic age of 11!

While 11 might seem young, the average age for a girl to start puberty in the United States is actually 10 years old. For boys it's a bit older. Still, 11 is the second time the brain starts doing all that doubling and tripling of connections. This time it's to get them ready for the rest of their lives. Along with the multitude of connections being formed, all of the information that helped many a fifth grader beat adults on trivia game shows is getting pruned away. What the brain doesn't need in working memory, it either buries deep inside the brain or forgets altogether. This pruning lasts until almost the end of high school.

Don't miss the most important piece. The brain of an 11-year-old is changing at a rate similar to that of a 3-year-old's. That's right, **an 11-year-old basically has the same brain as a 3-year-old.**

It's all starting to make sense now, isn't it?

All joking aside, an 11-year-old's brain is changing fast. In his book *Brain Rules*, David Medina writes, "From a connectivity point of view, there is a great deal of activity in the terrible twos and then during the terrible teens, a great deal more."

It's no wonder our kids seem to be freaking out—they are.
But so did you.
So did I.
So did everyone.

Just remember, preteens are constantly moving with two steps forward and one step back. And, every kid progresses through changes at their own pace. While some kids may be asking deeper questions, others may not. Be careful not to rush kids through their childhood before they're ready. You will walk a fine line as you push the kids who are ready to be pushed while making space for others in the room to play with Legos and draw butterflies.

Mental and physical changes are only the first of what's changing for preteens.

WHAT'S CHANGING CULTURALLY
What happens in the world as a person grows up affects them in ways they can hardly imagine. We don't even have to experience an event in order to experience the way the world changes in reaction to the event.

For example, kids born since 1997 . . .

Have never licked a postage stamp.
Expect unbridled access to broadband Internet and WiFi.
Grew up with Harry Potter.

Use Google as a verb.
Watch television on flat-screen TVs.
Don't remember 9/11 but will learn about it in history class.

> In 2018, preteens were born between 2006 and 2008.
> Thomas Friedman, in his book *Thank You for Being Late*,
> talks about the Age of Acceleration that started in 2007.
> The technological advances that marked that year have
> changed the way we interact with the world.
>
> In 2007 . . .
>
> The iPhone put a supercomputer in the palm of our hands.
> Cloud computing allowed 24/7 access to information.
> Apache Hadoop launched the age of Big Data.
> We landed technology on Mars.
>
> As a result . . .
>
> Preteens grew up with their childhood shared across social
> media platforms.
> Our homes—not just our phones—are smart and allow us
> access to the world from our kitchen table.

Since the 2018 preteens were born, the world has been
changing with unprecedented acceleration. Thomas Friedman
calls this dislocation. "Dislocation" is "when the whole
environment is being altered so quickly that everyone starts to
feel they can't keep up."

When it comes to understanding and surviving in the world at
large, Friedman continues, "There is a mismatch between the
pace of change and our ability to develop the learning systems,
training systems, management systems, social safety nets, and
government regulations that would enable citizens to get the
most out of the accelerations and cushion their worst impacts."

Basically, **the world is having trouble keeping up with the world.** And, let's be honest, sometimes the church struggles with change as well.

We have a reputation for doing things the same way for decades, and in some cases, centuries. We continue to use old solutions for new problems and wonder why nothing seems to work.

Occasionally when someone causes a disruption in the market, we pay attention long enough to see that what we've been doing is now obsolete. But, then sometimes the very word "market" sounds offensive and un-spiritual, and so we continue to masquerade generational preference as tradition or theology.

Every generation is unique. As leaders, we have to realize that what worked to reach one generation may not work for the next. And with the rate of accelerated change in today's world, what worked for your grandparents definitely won't work for the preteens in your ministry today. Of course there are timeless methods for investing in the faith of the next generation. Bible study, prayer, and worship at their core will stand the test of time, but in practice they may look slightly different for a generation who has never asked a question that couldn't be answered without a physical book.

WHAT'S CHANGING RELATIONALLY
The way a preteen values friendships may be one of the greatest transitions of this phase. By around second or third grade, kids begin to notice they don't like everyone in their class equally. Some kids will wonder if that's okay or if they should force themselves to hang out with everyone. By the preteen years, social pressure can feel daunting as most kids will do whatever it takes to fit in with as many people as possible.

Friendships are tricky.

Consider Valentine's Day as an example. In early elementary school, every kid gives a valentine to every other kid in the class. That's just how it is. No one questions it. In fifth grade, if the school celebrates Valentine's Day, every kid gives a valentine to every kid because it's required. But fifth graders see through the every-kid rule. They know who's giving them a card because it's required.

By sixth and seventh grade, no one is giving required valentines. Some club might have a fundraiser where kids can buy candy grams or flowers for each other. So some kids will receive five bouquets of flowers, and others will leave the day empty handed. No doubt about it, that would hurt anyone— but it's especially poignant for preteens who aren't that sure of themselves to begin with.

Most preteens are constantly asking three things:

Do I have friends?
Who likes me?
Who am I?

And don't forget, compounding each of these questions is the primary crisis many kids face throughout the preteen years: puberty. (That's a lot of hormones to add to the equation.)

Most of us should be more thankful that God allows us to have selective memory when it comes to the awkward moments during our preteen years. They can be the worst. If we think about it long enough, we can all remember what it felt like to feel as if everyone was staring at that one tiny blackhead we just discovered behind our right ear. (Oh yeah, preteens can be a little self-absorbed.) Yet as adults, we sometimes forget. We create environments that put mortified preteens on the spot and seem to shine a spotlight on their awkwardness. Think about all the games or activities that call kids up on stage at will. We forget that for some of these kids getting on stage is equal to having a parent affectionately call them "Schmoopy" as they step off the school bus.

As strange and tumultuous as the preteen years can be, you have a unique opportunity to speak truth into their lives and help preteens navigate the changes. Now more than ever, you have an opportunity to make them feel welcome no matter what. Now more than ever, you have an opportunity to help them develop friendships in a faith community.

WHAT'S CHANGING EMOTIONALLY AND MORALLY
Mental and physical changes are fairly linear.
Relational and cultural changes are somewhat predictable.
Emotional and moral changes are neither linear nor predictable.

Think about the best kid in your fifth-grade Small Group. You know the one. The one who sings worship songs at the top of his lungs and asks all the deep questions? That one. Well, he's the perfect kid . . . until he meets the not-so-perfect kid in middle school and BAM! Everything changes and he becomes almost the complete opposite of the sweet child you *knew* would be a pastor someday.

Emotional and moral changes are based on our circumstances as much as what we're learning about our faith and how to love others as God loves us. For some kids, the preteen years are when faith starts to unravel as what they're experiencing conflicts with what they've learned.

For example, many kids learn Philippians 4:4 in preschool. It says:

"Always be joyful because you belong to the Lord. I will say it again. Be Joyful!"

Preschoolers *love* this verse. Be JOYFUL?! Who wouldn't want to be joyful?

Yet, as kids get older they start to realize they don't always feel like being joyful. When they're facing a difficult situation, joy is the last thing on their minds. But that could change when a Small Group Leader explains that Paul wrote that verse while he was in prison. And now, preteens can start to connect the dots that joy has nothing to do with circumstances, but in how we trust God in those circumstances.

Throughout this unique phase of life, we can help preteens discover a few things about God that will lead them to discover more about themselves. The best way to do this is in the context of a faith community. These are the people who will be a shoulder to cry on and a companion to laugh with while helping them work through their faith questions. A preteen's faith community will be foundational for how they experience church for the rest of their lives and hopefully help them to escape some of the downfalls that can happen along the way.

CHAPTER 2

Caught In Between Expectations & Reality

On the surface, it appears that preteens primarily eat (pizza, gum, and anything with the word *sour* in it), sleep (nightly campaigning to push their bedtime an hour later), and go to school (begrudgingly). So, if that's really all they do, why is it their church attendance can be spotty? And why do the ones who show up always look so tired and frazzled?

Days of rest don't really exist anymore. We expect preteens to act a certain way. Maybe because of what we remember about being preteens or because we still see them as little kids. But the reality is that preteens are feeling caught in their schedule, their access to culture, and the pressure to succeed. And the expectations placed on them are often too unrealistic for them to handle.

CAUGHT IN THEIR SCHEDULE

SCHOOL STRESS

Most school systems count the minutes kids are learning. Meaning that from the time they get off the bus until the bell rings at the end of the day, the school has every single minute programmed and optimized for maximum learning.

School districts are also constantly trying to develop new learning strategies to help ease the transition from elementary to middle school.

Fourth graders could be in a self-contained classroom, have team teachers, or begin switching classes throughout the day.

Fifth graders may be switching classes at the top of their elementary school or be the bottom of a junior high school that goes through eighth grade.

Some districts are experimenting with a new environment where fifth and sixth graders have their own building.

Sixth graders could experience those same three options as well.

Regardless of *how* your school district splits grades, you can be sure someone somewhere debated it and made an intentional decision based on how they believe kids learn best. For the most part, all kids in this age group are experiencing:

COLLABORATIVE LEARNING
Collaborative learning allows kids to experience and practice the nuances of group dynamics. Kids start to realize they have influence over not only their grades, but their friends' grades as well. This can make relationships especially tense as kids navigate how to handle peers who don't pull their weight. At the same time, kids get to experience firsthand that success sometimes requires the ability to work well with others. They begin to discover the difference between friends and co-workers. Sure, sometimes co-workers are friends. But, what you feel about someone can't get in the way of working together because if you can't get along enough to finish the project, your grade will suffer.

HIGHER-LEVEL THINKING

Before third grade, schools spend the majority of their time on knowledge of facts with memorization and total recall. Math facts, sight words, reading fluency, and spelling tests are all good examples.

Once kids reach third grade, schools introduce skills necessary for higher-level processing. While they don't expect complete mastery of the skills until the very end of third grade, from the start of the school year kids begin reading for both comprehension and analysis. For example, they may be assigned a work of non-fiction that talks about taking care of dogs. On the flip side of the worksheet might be a fictional story about a family that cares for their pet Labrador. The assignment might conclude with a series of questions in which the student compares and contrasts different aspects of both works. Kids learn how to move beyond basic comprehension to a working understanding of the literature. This might include analyzing, comparing and contrasting ideas, or forming an opinion and having to back it up with the text. For many kids, this is a skill that won't be fully realized until fifth or sixth grade and can be a frustrating journey along the way.

DEDUCTIVE REASONING AND HYPOTHESIS TESTING

As kids get older, they begin to employ deductive reasoning. For example, while taking a multiple-choice test, a fourth-grader discovers she doesn't know the answer. She may be able to deduce that answers A and C are incorrect, and by thinking through the remaining two answers, decide the solution is most likely B.

Fourth and fifth grade teachers may also begin the method of Socratic questioning to enable their students to examine their own thoughts and ideas more deeply. Hypotheses, sometimes competing hypotheses, are introduced to solve problems, and kids learn the value in holding competing views in mind until the best solution is discovered. Through this Socratic questioning and hypothesis testing, older elementary students learn that other people have ideas as equally valid as their own.

These learning theories, along with the brain-power necessary to perform them, are new to the preteen years. At first, they are mentally taxing and our environments should take this into consideration. We need to create a safe place for preteens to think through the possible answers to their faith questions. We also need to be sure that we give them space to rest and rejuvenate from their busy week because school is just one of the factors contributing to their often crazy schedules.

EXTRACURRICULARS
Once a preteen has made it through the school day, the real fun begins:

> A Pew Research survey of US parents revealed:
> 70 percent had kids in sports.
> 50 percent had kids who participated in some sort of music, dance, art, or religious instruction.
> 36 percent participate in after-school tutoring.

Kids spend about 10 hours per week on extracurricular activities, with some reports sharing that more than 3 percent of kids spend 20+ hours in some sort of outside activity *per week*.

At first this seems unrelated to creating an engaging preteen culture at your church, but let's think about a few big ideas.

For many, these percentages overlap. Meaning the same child is participating in multiple extracurricular activities per week, and in some cases, per day. Like the girl in my son's karate class who wore her soccer jersey under her gi because she had to rush from her karate class to her soccer game.

Studies show that participating in extracurricular activities is beneficial to kids' physical and social development. Part of this benefit is for kids to have an outlet to try different hobbies and skills and discover what they truly enjoy. This is exciting but can also be exhausting for kids and parents alike.

I have four children. Soccer has been "the thing" for my oldest from the first moment he touched a soccer ball in first grade. He plays competitively on a travel team, made JV his first year of high school, and hopes to continue advancing so he can play in college. On the flip side, my oldest daughter has gone through ballet, gymnastics, drama, pottery, cooking, violin, piano, and voice lessons. She's landed on voice and has become passionate about it, but what a journey! My other daughter has tried art, tap, jazz, choir, sewing, dog-training and photography. And she's still trying to find the thing she's really passionate about. My youngest has some special needs and everything about his journey of discovering who he is and what he loves is atypical. So, you can see from my family alone that within your ministry, you'll have kids who are all over the map.

Most preteens' calendars rival your church calendar in the number of weekly events. When a fifth grader walks into your environment on Sunday, she might be simultaneously excited about her team's tournament win the day before and overwhelmed with all she has coming up in the week ahead.

On top of being overscheduled with school and activities, many preteens experience complicated family dynamics as well.

> A recent study mentioned that by the time they are 18, 50 percent of all kids in the United States will experience the breakup of their parents.

When you add up all the things happening at school, after school, and at home during a preteen's week, it's not hard to see why a church environment that's programmed for kids to "go deep" feels tedious. I'm not saying we need to dumb down our programming. However, it's important to realize that preteens and the culture in which they live are more complex than we imagine.

What happens throughout their week influences how they interact with your programming on Sunday. This information should impact the sort of environment you create and the expectations you set for student engagement.

Preteens need to be able to take a deep breath and be themselves. They need a space to hang out and escape the nonstop lives they experience outside our walls. (More about that in Part 2.)

CAUGHT IN THEIR ACCESS TO CULTURE

> The brain processes an average of 10,000 incoming messages a day.
> On average, we switch between screens up to 21 times an hour.
> The average attention span is eight seconds.

Preteens spend most of their day filtering through a barrage of information. With the ever—increasing access to mobile devices, most preteens view the world through a window that's small enough to fit in their pocket. Unfortunately, this same access to fashion and music and peers also exposes them to some unwanted content.

Preteens struggle with discernment while navigating the web of information available to them. Everyone has a voice online. And preteens often do not have enough life experience to be able to recognize the voice of an expert from the opinion of a cranky stranger in Nantucket.

> 79 percentage of preteens use a tech device daily
> 90 percentage consume media daily

Today's preteens have more access to what's happening around the world than any previous generation. They no longer need to read a newspaper or watch the nightly news. They see news clips featured on YouTube. News stories often come uncensored. They are raw and real and full of details not always appropriate for growing minds.

The truth is that media and technology are a double-edged sword. Pop culture and the outlets that deliver it aren't going away. We can either lock ourselves up in a bubble, or we can learn to discern how to participate in culture.

Pop culture collides with a kid's world from the moment they see the first image of a Disney princess. Any parent who has spent hours with their preteens looking for just the right cut and color of denim knows the grip trends can have on a kid.

Preteens dive deeper into pop culture as they begin discovering personal favorites apart from their parents. They have favorite brands, favorite shows, favorite YouTube channels, favorite celebrities, and favorite music. And as personal and unique as these favorites are, it's surprising how many of their peers select the same favorites.

That's why we have to do our homework. If we want to effectively minister to preteens, we need to know their culture. We should spend time with the Billboard Hot 100 each week, watch trending YouTube videos, spend time in Barnes & Noble with the tween best sellers and magazines, play the games they're playing, and visit the stores where they buy their clothes and shoes. You don't have to like all of it, but you should know all about it. (Pop culture is part of the language of tweens.)

CAUGHT IN THE PRESSURE TO SUCCEED

Preteens have a hard time separating what they do (see the "overscheduled" section above) from who they are. They often overanalyze their identity with each passing fad, comment from a peer, or new extracurricular activity. It's all a part of the process of discovering who they are.

It's more important than ever to give preteens a place where what they do isn't as important as who they are.

Many preteens find their identity in outside activities and abilities. Then, when they don't perform as desired (or as a parent or coach might have expected), their failure is a heavy blow to their identity. Sometimes these failures are obvious—like losing a game or not even making the team. But sometimes the failure may be more subtle—like a passing negative comment in the hallway. **Whatever the cause, it's important to remember that every Sunday, some preteens will show up feeling defeated by Saturday's identity crisis**.

The opposite is also true. Star performers want everyone to notice them and know all about their success.

And the kids who've yet to discover themselves sit back and watch everyone else grouping up according to their interests and become unsure where (or if) they fit in.

Child psychologist and author Madeline Levine, in her book *Teach Your Children Well,* says that discovering one's sense of self is the primary task of elementary children. By the time a child reaches middle school, they should have a "reliable sense of self and self-worth."

So, by fifth grade, most kids are becoming self-aware enough to recognize what **other** people are good at:

"He's a band kid."
"She plays lacrosse."

But also what **they** are good at:

"I play hockey."
"I'm a dancer."

As preteens, kids are finding their identity both in what they do and what they don't do. And along with the identity found in their activities (or lack thereof), their identity is also tied to grades, friends, and personal style choices. They become more aware of where they fall on the social ladder and start trying on masks to avoid embarrassment in unknown situations.

This growing sense of self generates a lot of tension, as kids vacillate between wanting more grown-up privileges and the fun of staying little for as long as possible. Just walk into the bedroom of a preteen girl and you'll notice stuffed animals sitting next to the nail polish and lip gloss. For a boy it might be the Legos he just can't bring himself to pack up sitting on the shelf below his snapback and sneaker collections.

Preteens are on a journey of discovering who they are and how that identity fits in the world. This search often leads to an identity crisis because they have one version of self that shows up at school, one for home, one for the soccer field, and maybe another for church. The social context defines the identity.

They need an environment on Sunday that allows them
freedom to be who they are that week and helps them feel
comfortable in their own skin.

(Don't worry. We'll cover how to do that in Part 2.
But first, a bit about what preteens need to know.)

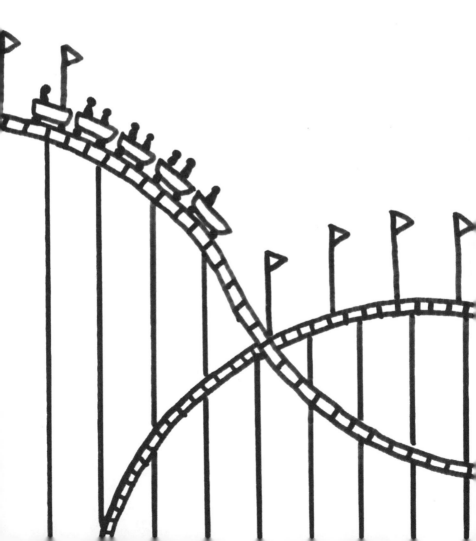

CHAPTER 3

Caught In Between Information & Understanding

So far, we've discussed why you might want to adjust your strategy to better serve preteens, and you may have some questions, like . . .

> WHAT DO WE TEACH THEM?
> AND HOW DO WE TEACH THEM?

WHAT DO WE TEACH THEM?

At Orange, we have spent countless hours working on the first question. We believe it's essential for every ministry leader to have an answer for what they will teach a child in the limited number of hours they have together. In case you haven't done the math, you have approximately 200 weeks with a preteen while he's still a preteen. Then he will never be a preteen again.

Each year, we take another look at what we will teach over the course of a three-year period. We evaluate the Bible stories, the biblical principles, the life applications, and the memory verses. We take very seriously the responsibility of selecting the truths a church will communicate to a preteen in those 200 weeks.

As you consider what you'll teach, remember: **Preteens suffer no lack of access to information about anything, especially faith**. Google "faith" and in seconds a quarter billion articles appear. Our kids can learn virtually everything about anything from anywhere, anytime they want. But do we really want Google answering the tough questions preteens have about faith?

Your preteens don't need curriculum or adult leaders in order to access information about God or the Bible. But they do need a trusted adult like a parent, teacher, or Small Group Leader to help them interpret the information and figure out how it applies to them.

So, if that's true, maybe the most important question is:

HOW DO WE TEACH THEM?

We start by creating an environment where preteens gain . . .

Autonomy to discover more about themselves in light of who God is.
Critical thinking skills to analyze what they discover and wrestle with what they don't understand.
Empathy that connects what they're learning to how it impacts their relationships.
Relevance for how ancient writings connect to their limited but growing life experience.

These are the skills that our kids tend to lack when it comes to processing the multitude of voices vying for their attention. Of course, helping kids gain a working knowledge of material found in the Bible is critically important. But we have to remember that what they know *about* the Bible doesn't automatically translate into living out authentic faith.

If we really want our kids to "go deep" throughout every phase of life, we need to be sure about what that actually means. Paul Tough has written extensively on this subject for several years.

In his book, *Helping Children Succeed*, he says deeper learning is:

"The ability to work in teams, to present ideas to a group, to write effectively, to think deeply and analytically about problems, to take information and techniques learned in one context and adapt them to a new and unfamiliar problem or situation."

Isn't this what we want to do through the church as well?

In the preteen years, we hope kids take the concepts they learn in our environments, wrestle with them, and start to adapt them to any problems or situations they encounter throughout the week.

None of us become better humans or more godly followers of Jesus because of what we know *about* the Bible. We become better at life and grow in our faith because of how we allow the Holy Spirit to transform our lives, this includes using what we know about the Bible to inform our actions and transform our hearts to become more like Jesus.

> Our job is to move preteens from learning facts about the Bible to finding themselves in the Bible.

Remember, most preteens are transitioning from concrete to abstract thinking, and you can help them along that path. To help encourage that transition, share tangible life stories and experiences. Always begin with some tension that establishes

why the content you're teaching matters. And it always helps
to have some fun and games if you want to keep your preteens
engaged.

In the remainder of this chapter, you'll find some concepts that
address the *how* question. They will help preteens understand
what they are learning at church and give them an avenue
to connect it to what they're experiencing in their real-world
settings outside of church throughout the week.

TEACH THEM IN A WAY THAT CELEBRATES THEIR EXPANDING AUTONOMY

What are three words you'd use to describe yourself? Jot them
down in the margin.
How long would you say those words have described you?
If you asked your parents, maybe they would say you've had
these characteristics for as long as they can remember.

My three words are: *music, learner, loud*

I have always been musical.
My family likes to retell the story of me grabbing the mic and
dancing on stage during a Christmas concert as a 3-year-old.

I've always been a learner.
I don't recall a time in my life when I wasn't reading an article
or book or listening to a message that stretched my learning.

And I've *always* been loud.
If I had a nickel for all the times my teachers told me to be
quiet, I could significantly contribute to the redecorating of
your preteen environment on a full HGTV budget.

Now. Here's the question. When did you *realize* what's true
about yourself?

I was 10 when I discovered I *love* music.

I realized around seventh grade that I enjoy learning. And loud . . . Well, I might have realized that during an after-school detention around fourth grade.

I discovered all three of these as a preteen. Sure, I've expanded my self-awareness over the years. I didn't know at the age of 10 what path lay ahead for my loud self. But I did know these traits were part of my identity.

Like we talked about earlier, preteens have an identity crisis. As the adults who lead preteens, we need to create an environment where kids can discover a strong sense of self. As they grow more comfortable with their identities, preteens gain confidence to make wise decisions and will be able to have more authentic relationships. And when they learn how God created them, they will discover ways to use those gifts as part of the church.

Ultimately, a preteen's emerging identity will start driving the decisions they make and impact the direction of their life. And while they don't know that yet, we do.

It's critical that we're prepared to help preteens understand who they are in light of who God is and the role God plays in their personal journey. As people created in God's image, we have the intelligence and intuition that allow us, in light of what we know about God, to make choices about the life we desire to live.

This is autonomy.

Autonomy sounds like a scary word to use in reference to 10 to 12-year-olds. But if autonomy is the end goal for raising a successful adult, we must celebrate any attempts at moving toward independence.

"I love that you're trying a new sport! Soccer was great while it

lasted, but let's see what else is out there!"
"I like the new look! I wish I could still rock some bleached blonde highlights."
"I didn't know you were into hip-hop! I want some suggestions later. My playlists are in major need of an update."

As preteens begin to think about themselves as autonomous, they develop a deeper sense of self. They begin to realize not only their free will, but also the effect their choices have on themselves and those around them. And while it is not until later adolescence when they fully (or finally) realize that just because they *can* make the choice to eat $20 worth of sour gummy worms in one sitting doesn't mean it is a beneficial choice, the preteen years are ripe with autonomous trial and error.

No matter their age, kids try to assert their independence. As kids grow up, they rarely experience the freedom to make choices about their own lives. Rightly so, someone else chooses:

Where they live.
What they eat.
Where they go to school and church.
What they're allowed to wear.
How much time they get to spend with friends.

However, in order to become fully functioning adults, kids must learn to make decisions and take ownership of their lives. It's why we give them work to do. And why, over time, we give them more decision-making opportunities coupled with responsibility for the consequences of those decisions. They might not always make the wise choice, but what better time to make these choices than when they can land safely without threat of life-altering consequences for those mistake?. The younger you start giving kids choices and allowing them to feel natural consequences in age-appropriate ways, the better.

This doesn't work as well if you wait until they can drive, and they haven't exercised their autonomy and learned from their mistakes.

They may no longer want to play the sport they've been playing since they were five.
They may decide they're preppy.
They may start loving rap or country music.

As a preteen moves toward autonomy, they are gradually increasing in independence. Don't expect your sixth graders to carefully weigh the consequences of their actions the same way your co-workers might. Remember. **The preteen years are fraught with tension between who they were and who they will be**.

One week, she'll decide to rock the ripped jeans and leather jacket. The next week, she might look like she's about to take a yoga class.

One minute, he'll tattle on the heckler. The next minute, he'll be the one picking on others.

You can help a preteen cultivate autonomy in how you develop programming, which we'll talk about at length in Part 2. This might look like giving kids a chance to choose how they will interact with what they're learning. When you give kids a choice, you start the process of handing them the ownership of their spiritual growth. You send the message that they are in the driver's seat of their faith journey.

Again, they will not always get it right, but they will feel the responsibility of building an authentic faith. And when they make mistakes or unwise choices, we can respond with grace and truth to provide a safe landing for them to get back up and try again.

TEACH THEM IN A WAY THAT
BUILDS THEIR CRITICAL THINKING SKILLS

Take a minute to think about the following questions:

> What was the first question you had about the Bible?
> How did you find the answer to that question?
> How did the answer to that question impact your faith?

By the fifth grade, some kids may have heard every major story in the Bible. While some fifth graders may not own a Bible or know the Old Testament from the New.

Regardless of a kid's biblical knowledge, life experience will begin to challenge previously held convictions about faith. Life is filled with messy problems. And preteens are ripe to ask questions when . . .

families break up.
natural disasters strike.
kids they know face heartache and pain.

Preteens ask questions that can make adults uncomfortable. Maybe that's why some leaders sweep overly challenging faith questions under the rug, ignore them, or admonish the preteen to have more faith and it will all work itself out.

Sometimes more faith might be necessary. But before we brush aside their questions too quickly, we need to recognize the opportunity to help a preteen apply critical thinking skills to the arena of faith. In a world where preteens can search information at will, it's a privilege for them to select you over Google.

Listen to their question. It's okay to be honest about what you don't know. In fact, it's really the only way you will be able to help kids navigate their questions in a safe environment. When you aren't sure, or even doubt, it sends the message that questions and doubts are okay. They aren't the end of a faith in

God. They are the beginning of an authentic faith.

This is why critical thinking is so important.

Preteens, like adults, have to process doubt as it arises. Kara Powell at the Fuller Youth Institute says it this way: "Doubt isn't toxic to faith. Unexpressed doubt is." Critical thinking allows us to review an idea we once took at face value and decide again whether we still believe that it's true. Critical thinking allows space for our natural curiosity—to process the concepts we find to be complex, confusing, or difficult to believe.

Imagine telling a child about heaven. At first, they love the idea—they get to jump up and down and sing forever. How fun is that?! But then as they grow up, the idea of forever starts to take shape. They understand that forever means every single day and the day after that. Then they sing that line, "when we've been there for 10,000 years," and begin to panic. This is natural for this phase of development, and what they need is a process that helps them understand eternity in the context of now and then. In this case, the goal of talking about eternity is about helping kids understand how believing that we get to spend forever with God changes how we live right now.

That's just one example. The point is: don't let kids wait until adulthood to wrestle with the tough questions. Preteens need a place where they can think critically about concepts that adults now take for granted.

And in all honesty, giving preteens room for questions can be exhausting.
You've already processed their questions for yourself.
You might have an answer you feel pretty good about.
You might feel perfectly okay not having an answer.
But just remember, this isn't about your answer. This is about their process.

Preteens' brains are developing. Their process will take time. But, never underestimate the role you can play in encouraging their critical thinking skills.

Unleashing a preteen to put inquiry and evaluation into practice regarding biblical content might sound like a scary proposition. Yet, if you're really honest, critical thinking probably played a role in your own faith. You might have even had a few questions about Jesus, God, and the Bible along the way. The church should be the safest place for kids to ask questions about their faith. We can either create a place for them to ask these questions now, or allow them to find answers to these questions outside of our influence later.

Kids will feel more comfortable to ask these questions if they have great Small Group Leaders. Check out Chapter 5 for ideas to get the right volunteers for your preteens.

TEACH THEM IN A WAY THAT GROWS THEIR EMOTIONAL INTELLIGENCE AND EMPATHY

There are a few things I remember about sixth grade.

Getting my first day of school outfit at Macy's.
Having my Def Leppard tapes taken away.
All the drama.

Not drama class, but friend drama. In my small school, every day was a friendship gamble. All was well until you said or did something that changed your status, and then you were out. And *out* meant you had few friends, didn't know where to sit at lunch, and weren't sure who you'd hang out with at recess. You were left wondering when you'd be allowed back in.

Today's preteens are navigating the same reality—with texting, social media, and constant connectivity.

Preteens increasingly care about what their peers think—whether it's their shoes, hair style, the way they laugh, or even the way they talk. Research proves that "adolescents spend more time than children or adults interacting with peers, report the highest degree of happiness in peer contexts, and assign the greatest priority to peer norms for behavior."

And because peers influence so much of a child's behavior, peer groups can get a bad rap. But it doesn't start out like this, does it? Toddlers are pretty much the most egotistical people in every room they occupy. Now before you shut this book in defense of preschoolers, please be assured I mean this in the best sense of the word. They can't help it.

Preschoolers can't help but focus on what *they* want. It's who they are. All me. All the time.

If they hadn't already figured some of this out by the arrival of a sibling and sharing Mom or Dad, this trend continues into childhood until sometime after kids start school and realize that—much to their dismay—other people do in fact exist. And *gasp* these other people take attention away from them!

Around second or third grade, kids start to notice that others aren't so bad. Some of those others are actually pretty nice and fun to be around. So much so that kids start modeling the behavior of each other to fit in and forge new friendships.

But suddenly, around fourth or fifth grade, our *social* survival becomes an obsession. And it depends on our ability to model the behavior of peers, choose relationships that feed the right image, and respond according to group standards.

But preteens don't do this consistently, and some can't do this at all. Regardless, all kids feel the impact peers have on their day-to-day lives, which brings us to peer pressure.

As kids enter their preteen years, they are increasingly

susceptible to peer influence because of the lack of a solid personal identity (as discussed in the previous section).

I've watched this happen with my daughters. They get invited to an event but don't really want to go. They feel so much pressure to say yes that they have to work hard to craft an excuse their friends will deem legitimate. They don't want to go but also don't want to suffer the social implications of saying no. There's a vast amount of tension between staying true to their own identity and experiencing the pressure of not letting their friends down.

That's not to say all peer groups are bad, and not all peers who are bad recruit the good kids to join their band of hooligans. Children who are healthy and have a positive self-image do not typically search for groups like that. Most kids seek friendships with peers who are similar to them. If you observe a group of preteen friends for five minutes, you'll realize they all talk the same way, using the same vocabulary, intonations, and catchphrases. They dress alike, listen to the same music, and watch the same shows. Most often those friends selected each other because of those similarities, which only encouraged them to do more of those things as their friendships grew.

In spite of that, adults who work with kids all too often fear the peer group. Parents do everything in their power to control who their kid spends time with. They limit the free time their kid can spend with their peers. They over-chaperone the field trips, parties, and activities, worried that when they look away they'll instantly lose the perceived control they have of their child. They (falsely) assume they can choose their kid's friends, just like second grade playdates, and by doing so save them a lifetime of regret. But the truth is, no one can choose a preteen's friends except the preteen.

Church leaders face the same dilemma. They can't predict successful Small Groups. They can't kick out the "bad" kids.

(I mean, they can, but aren't they the ones we want to reach?) They can't make everyone hold hands around the campfire singing "10,000 Reasons." (Again, they can do all these things, but they don't always work to thwart the potential that exists when putting a bunch of prepubescent humans in the same space for any length of time.)

Peer groups are an inevitable, and very healthy, part of life. We should do what we can to help the preteens in our care to cultivate peer groups where they develop healthy interpersonal skills and begin practicing healthy autonomy.

We want preteens to understand that we need each other. Our lives depend on our ability to interact with one another and work together to get a job done. We must take the risk and create peer-learning initiatives throughout our environments, especially knowing that faith formation happens best in the context of relationships.

Yet part of what freaks us out when it comes to creating peer learning environments is that they're emotionally charged. Kids hardly recognize their own personality types, much less have the consistent ability to recognize the personalities of one another and know how to best work together. This is where emotional intelligence and empathy come into play.

People have written extensively on emotional intelligence (EQ) and empathy in recent years. Simply put, **emotional intelligence** is understanding the consequences of different emotional responses—in yourself as well as others. It is the ability to identify and harness your own emotions in order to have healthier interactions with the world around you.

Empathy—the ability to not only identify but feel the emotions expressed by others—is a foundational skill for enhancing EQ.

Preteens are just beginning to show empathy. And, just like

grown-ups, some are better at it than others. Some are wired to more easily identify the emotions of others and adjust their responses appropriately. While others struggle (even through adulthood) to understand why people always respond poorly to their ill-timed emotional outbursts.

As you encourage EQ and empathy, remember preteens are still caught in between concrete and abstract thinking. They might be able to observe and name the emotions they see in themselves and others, but how they internalize those emotions might still be very black and white.

In other words, when someone . . .

makes a decision they don't like,
doesn't use their idea,
fails to notice or compliment their new shoes,
or any number of negative things that can happen when kids get together,

the preteen emotionally rushes to the extreme assumption that NO ONE LIKES THEM, they have the WORST IDEAS, and NO ONE is their friend.

Sounds harsh, right? But this is how preteens think.

While they are starting to feel abstractly and name their emotions, they tend to view the consequences of those negative emotions in concrete parameters. In other words, they believe if they're arguing with a friend over anything, then they're clearly not friends anymore.

Adults know this is not true. Ideally, most of us understand that healthy disagreements can lead to deeper friendships and better ideas. We know that you can help others pull their weight, or that not every one of our ideas is the best idea.

We've also learned through experience that while negative interactions with others can be awful, we can work through them and come out stronger on the other side.

The preteen environments we create can help model what this looks like through peer interactions and Small Groups.

TEACH THEM IN A WAY THAT IS RELEVANT
Having a strategy for delivering content is great. Thinking about how we communicate to preteens is super-important. But the greatest, most important question when it comes to catching preteens is:

How do we get preteens to stay engaged?

We can create the best environment. But if we can't keep preteens engaged, what does any of it matter?

> Keeping preteens engaged has more to do with what they feel than how they think.

If preteens have some sort of emotional connection to what they're learning, they're more likely to persevere, even in the face of a difficult problem they need to think through in order to solve.

So how does one become emotionally attached to something they dislike or find difficult to understand, such as math or history or church? Combine it with someithing kids enjoy.

A history teacher might use the *Hamilton* soundtrack to teach the American War of Independence.
An economics teacher might use the YEEZY secondary shoe market to explain supply and demand.
A math teacher might use sarcasm and humor to her advantage and win kids over.

In other words, it all comes down to one thing: relevance.

Relevance is actually my job description in one word. One of my primary responsibilities at Orange is to create curriculum that's relevant to a kid's world. Sounds simple, right?

Just make it fun.
Keep it exciting.
Add in some bells and whistles.
. . . and call it a day.

I've learned throughout my time as a children's pastor and curriculum director that relevance has very little to do with fun games, cool videos, and smoke machines. Of course, all of those things can be used to keep kids engaged. But being relevant is so much more than the bells and whistles we add to an environment. Because over time, the brain loses interest in the bells and whistles. This is related to an idea in economics called *the law of diminishing returns*: the point at which the energy invested outweighs the benefits.

Even if you continually try to one-up yourself with bells and whistles, kids will eventually lose interest. It's how the brain works. A preteen's ability to stay engaged is directly related to their level of interest in and perceived importance of the environment they are in.

The first time you walk into a room you've never been in before, your brain lights up with excitement. Bright orange couches! Flashing signs! Exposed brick! But as time passes, the couches are just couches, the signs fade into the periphery, and you learn to steer clear of the exposed brick after scraping your gangly shoulder on it one too many times.

Every time you walk into that room, your brain does the same thing. Only as time passes, your brain will notice that nothing or very little has changed. As a result, your brain won't pay as much attention because it feels like there's nothing new to learn. Once your brain no longer thinks what's in the room is important, you'll lose interest and stop paying attention.

So how do you keep a preteen engaged week after week?

Completely change your environment during the week! Swap out the neon couches for hanging egg chairs! Replace the flashing signs with original paintings inspired by your ministry's last gathering! Cover the exposed brick with whatever the latest HGTV show is featuring! Invest in MORE light rigs and fog machines.

(I mean, what else does a church staff have to do Monday through Friday?)

OR keep the environment you set up to grab the attention of preteens the same, and let it do just that: grab attention.

THEN connect to what's true, what matters most in each preteen's life right now by building authentic relationships with the kids in your ministry. And instead of growing bored with the bells and whistles, your preteens will stay engaged with growing relationships and truths they carry with them between Sundays.

The truth is being relevant is not creating Justin Timberlake's world tour stage in your preteen environment. Rather, being relevant, as Reggie Joiner puts it, "is simply connecting to the matter at hand."

In other words, being relevant on Sunday means answering the question:

How does what we share impact the rest of their week?

In order to help kids answer that question, we need to make some effort and discover their world, which is actually easier said than done. Most often when we communicate with kids, we assume two things:

They are like us now.
They are like we were at their age.

Neither one of those assumptions is true.

As we've mentioned previously, kids think differently than we do. They're on their way to thinking with their whole brain, but they're just not there yet. They don't make the same connections we do. When we communicate to them and try to be relevant yet miss that important fact, it won't matter what we're saying—they won't be able to automatically connect how what we're saying connects with their life.

Kids are also not how we used to be. Me as a 10-year-old

listening to music on my boom box is light years away from kids having access to 40 million songs on their Apple Watches. The world has changed, and childhood has changed right along with it.

If we want today's preteens to connect with the ancient truth of Scripture, we need to engage them where they are. That will take some homework, but the work you invest into understanding current youth culture will have a huge return: preteens staying engaged in church.

When it comes to communicating God's truth to preteens, there's one simple rule.

> The Bible story isn't over until a preteen has the tools to know what to do with it.

Kids should be able to understand how what they're learning impacts their day-to-day life. Preteens are just gaining the ability to do this on their own and see how something learned in one context impacts another context. In the meantime, we can start discussions and help them make those connections.

Our goal is to emphasize how the Bible relates to today while honoring why the passage was written in the first place. It's possible to do both. We can give kids a solid foundation for experiencing the power of God's Word while helping them see how the original context connects to life in the 21st century.

Creating a Preteen Strategy for Your Church

B efore you start dreaming about what your preteen environment will look like, you need to know what you want your preteen ministry to accomplish.

The goal of a preteen strategy is to create an environment intentionally designed to help preteens navigate faith as they transition from childhood to adolescence.

Preteen environments give kids their first taste of owning their own faith in a way that offers them an opportunity to learn something about God that connects with their life. The environment offers preteens the tools they need to move forward with their faith into adulthood.

In general, the goal of family ministry in the church is simple: to influence parents and leaders to give kids the tools needed to make wiser choices, have stronger relationships, and have a deeper faith.

As church leaders, we make plans and scope out the 18 years of a child's faith formation. We are often tempted to program as if spiritual development happens on a linear trajectory. And while some aspects of child development are linear from infancy to adulthood, much of what happens in life that impacts faith formation doesn't happen in a straight line.

Faith development is more like a roller coaster.

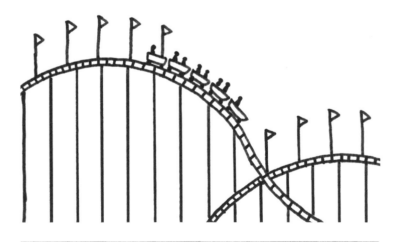

Ups and downs.
Twists and turns.
Over and around again.

Rarely does the path even out and allow time for the car to coast along the tracks. And if it does slow down throughout the ride, the slower speeds only indicate that something big is about to happen and give you time to mentally prepare for it.

You're riding along, and then you see it—the biggest, most thrilling, most frightening of all the loops on the track. The whole coaster was designed with this loop in mind. The engineers planned to get the riders in and out of that loop without derailing or skyrocketing into orbit.

> Parents and leaders are helping kids navigate through the twists and turns of growing up. And like the roller coaster, the giant loops kids face throughout their faith development are the most treacherous and require thoughtful preparation. In faith formation, these giant loops show up throughout the transitions from one phase of development to the next. If we aren't careful, kids could fly off in any number of directions as they exit the loop into whatever is on the other side.

Until the preteen loop, parents or immediate caregivers tend to control how kids navigate through the loop. But during the preteen years, kids transition and start taking hold of the steering wheel. They have more control over the outcome of the loop than ever before, and how we guide them through this can make or break what happens on the other side in their next phase of faith formation.

The church has a unique opportunity to offer not only guidance but also a community where preteens can find positive voices from peers and mentors, as well as offer help to parents and caregivers who aren't quite sure what is happening to their child. This is where preteen ministry becomes important.

If we want kids to experience a growing, authentic faith, we need to consider how we help them do that. We tend to feel this pressure to pass on the sort of faith we experience as adults.

Since preteens fall somewhere on the continuum between concrete and abstract thinking, our words can either be a foundation or a confusion for how they'll think about God as they mature in their faith. **The best foundation we can offer gives them simple answers to complex questions while introducing ideas that won't begin to crumble when they are able to understand complex answers.**

Take King David, for example. Preteens need to know that David was a man after God's heart even though he wasn't perfect. However, preteens don't need to know the sordid details of David having an affair with Bathsheba, then arranging to have her husband killed once he found out she was with his child.

One is correct and introductory. The other is correct and too mature for the age group.

When it comes to learning about God, kids and adolescents learn differently. Kids learn from experience, while adolescents have the potential to learn from reflection. But like we've been saying, preteens are in between. A unique environment provides a safe place for them to be who they are as preteens, both giving them new challenges to experience while not introducing too much too soon.

Take time to consider some ideas for how your church can implement a preteen strategy that does just that. One that offers kids and families a solution to make sure they don't get lost in the transition from childhood to adolescence.

CHAPTER 4

Catch Them with a Unique Environment

THE GREAT DIVIDE

Preteens are changing so quickly, they think anything that doesn't adapt as fast as they do is dated, stale, or for little kids. But you're now a preteen expert, so you won't take it personally when kids (especially the ones who have been in your ministry since birth) start to react against children's ministry as boring or babyish.

The good news is, you're reading this book, so you're one step ahead of them!

And the first step to creating a preteen environment is giving them their own space. Even if you can't create an entirely separate space in your building, reformatting how and where in the room you place your preteen attendees is key. Before you start tearing down walls, though, you have to figure out how your ministry will be structured.

How will your church divide the different age groups? Unfortunately, there's no easy answer and no hard and fast rule, but there are some things to consider.

The first place to start is the natural break between local elementary and middle schools, which varies from state to state or even county to county.

While what school districts are doing is a determining factor in how you will mirror what you do in your student spaces, it can't be the only factor as you consider what you know about your kids. You also have to think about critical mass.

Critical mass is that subjective, magic number of kids needed to make your programming work. For example, hosting a rock concert for 100 people at an arena that seats 20,000 would make for a terrible show. It would feel vacant and empty and the music would bounce all over the room.

It's very tempting to group kids of all ages together for the sake of critical mass, but in the long run, it will not give you the results you want. Don't let a lack of supposed critical mass stop you from creating a unique environment for preteens, or for any age group. **The more tightly you can target your audience, the better chance they have of understanding and applying the message.**

Many churches start with a kindergarten through fifth grade environment. When the fifth graders start to check out, many move them to middle school for a fifth through eighth grade environment. This isn't ideal, but if this is your only option, get creative and figure out how to divide them into two groups. Consider that the average fifth grader is 10 years old when they enter school and may not turn 11 until after Christmas break, while the average eighth grader is 13 or 14.

A lot happens between ages 10 and 14. These groups need different things from a ministry environment. Putting them in the same environment does a disservice to both. Giving each group a space of their own allows you to craft messages and Small Group materials that target their felt needs in their unique stages of development.

A SPACE OF THEIR OWN

This should be the first place where kids see a difference in how they experience church as preteens versus elementary kids. A preteen space should speak to their culture and what they enjoy. This doesn't have to be elaborate, but it does need to be something they own. It's a tangible, obvious way for them to see that you care about them and what they like. They will immediately feel important because you've dedicated a space that's just for them.

Preteens live in a fully customizable world. They can change the background on their mobile device, pick what they want to wear, even design their own shoes and backpacks. More and more, their teachers give them opportunities to choose how they demonstrate their understanding of material, which also allows them to display their skills and personalities.

It can be hard for a church to replicate that level of personalization for several reasons like:

- Multipurpose rooms that must remain generic so they can house multiple audiences
- A lack of space
- Aging buildings
- The only available room being a dark basement
- Portable or temporary environments that require setup and teardown
- Multi-site campuses striving to achieve environmental consistency at each location

Challenges, yes, but not impenetrable barriers to creating preteen spaces. You may have to think outside the box to allow kids some ownership in a preteen space they can call their own.

In one preteen environment I helped design, we decided to allow kids to graffiti the Small Group tables. We didn't care if they looked messy; it was part of the urban aesthetic. Kids loved being able to draw and write on the furniture. And 99 percent of the time, the art was copacetic. The other 1 percent? We addressed it, covered over it, and gave kids a fresh surface to mark up. This is just one simple, fun way for kids to customize their preteen experience. You could also try:

- Allowing kids to vote on the games for the game cabinets.
- Creating a graffiti wall where preteens can write their names, draw something fun, or take selfies with their friends.
- Encouraging Small Groups to build group identity by coming up with team names and even logos to display.
- Taking music requests/suggestions for the walk-in playlist.
- Asking kids to help choose furniture style or decorations for the environment.

Most churches need to share spaces. That's not a deal breaker. Be strategic about which spaces you share with which part of your ministry. If the student ministry has a space they don't use on Sunday mornings, consider using that space for your preteen ministry. However, don't use everything the student ministry space has to offer—intentionally save something for when kids get into student ministry. Getting to use that space gives them something new, but also builds anticipation for what's coming in the next phase.

This is a great time for the children's and student ministry leaders at your church to work together and plan how this new environment will transition kids from one environment to the next.

IDEAS TO THINK ABOUT AS YOU CREATE YOUR ENVIRONMENT

Room

When you choose a room to use as your preteen environment, think through how you'll outfit the room. Fire-code numbers are based on kids sitting in chairs in rows. For preteen environments, there's a good chance kids will want to be on bean bags, couches, or at tables and chairs. Just because a room says it can fit a certain number of kids doesn't mean it will actually fit that many once you start using it a certain way.

In some cases, your space might not actually be a room. One portable church created a preteen "space" at one end of a hallway using pipe and drape. They decorated with Ikea furniture and lamps, and had a laptop hooked up to a TV for their teaching slides. Get creative with how you define a "room" to figure out an amazing space for your preteens.

Room Décor

Whatever year it is outside the walls of your church should be what it looks like inside too. Invest in a few larger pieces that will get a big bang for your buck. Try technology like flat screens connected to video game systems. "VIP sections" with couches and soft seating for Small Groups can be fun!

Don't spend a lot on paint, as it will get dinged up and can always be repainted. Posters can always be replaced. The trendier items will be more temporary, so don't spend a lot of money on them either. Chalkboard and whiteboard walls are a great way to decorate, as kids will continually be drawing and writing on them. You can also use them to highlight themes, big ideas, or bottom lines. Your decorations don't need to be elaborate, but should reflect what today's preteens like.

Stage Design

As you build your set, consider ways to adapt it each month to incorporate the new message series. You might want to create a set design that mimics an environment such as a garage or café, but these are hard to update throughout the year. The elaborate set has great wow-factor at first, but over time you'll experience diminishing returns as the brain no longer sees it as exciting and new.

One of my favorite environments had a skate park vibe. It used chain-linked fence as the focal walls of the stage. It was simple to decorate with standard skate park decorations like street signs, skateboard decks, and rails. It was both a great set that would stand alone, but also allowed flexibility for series-specific decorations. Hooks and carabiners made it easy to change decorations and add interest throughout the year.

As you start out, you may not have the resources to build an elaborate stage. Don't get discouraged! All you need is a focal point to draw attention to the Large Group Communicator. This can be as simple as a 6-inch platform, a TV monitor, and computer. As you grow, so can your stage area.

Lighting

Lighting plays a huge role in how preteens will respond during their time in your ministry. Fluorescent lighting can be harsh on the eyes and not conducive to creating a good atmosphere for conversation. Try soft lighting and use stage lights to focus attention during Large Group. You can hang fun chandeliers throughout your room and connect them to your lighting board to control how bright they are during Large Group and Small Group.

Music

Music adds a lot of energy to an environment. Each month, create a playlist you can play as preteens are walking in and hanging out. You can publish these on Spotify so kids can listen to them with their parents throughout the month. You can also publish playlists of the songs you sing throughout the year so kids can hear them outside of Sunday morning.

Events

Events do not need to be expensive, elaborate getaways. Plan something out of the ordinary at the church or at a local park. The goal of events is to build Small Group relationships. That can happen anywhere. Start small and build upon what you learn. In general, be as cost-effective as possible to make it easier for more kids to attend, and figure out a way to scholarship those who want to come but cannot afford the event.

Snacks

Some preteen ministries provide snacks as part of their programming. This can be a fun way to build anticipation for preteen ministry. Keep in mind, when you think about preteens, what's the first thing that comes to mind: fruit or donuts? Exactly. Don't worry about healthy when you're considering snacks for Sunday morning. Consider hosting a contest each quarter to stuff the pantry with things preteens like to eat. Work with the parents of the kids with allergies to figure out a plan to make sure they also have favorites to eat.

Remember, having a space of their own is more important than what the space looks like.

However you decide to decorate your preteen environment, keep in mind that there's more than just the physical space.

Creating a unique environment also includes creating a unique experience. And the key to keeping the experience unique and exciting is not to give away too much too soon.

AN EXPERIENCE OF THEIR OWN

Think through your entire family ministry. How does each environment build upon the last? What is new and unique about each stage? How do you build anticipation as kids experience each successive phase of ministry? This starts with filling in the blanks to this statement:

Kids get to _____ when they are in _____ grade.

For example, we created a fourth-grade environment horizontal rock wall. Third graders couldn't wait to graduate to the room with the rock wall, while middle schoolers wanted to come back to see if they could still climb.

Not every preteen environment needs a rock wall. You can scale this principle to the size of your preteen ministry. Maybe preteens get access to a game room or donuts as they enter your environment. Maybe they can check themselves in instead of getting dropped off by their parents. Maybe they get to use a limited part of the student ministry space until they achieve all access once they are in student ministry.

The same concept of scaled experiences applies in many areas of your family ministry. Take worship music, for example:

PreK – Preschool worship songs led by middle schoolers singing along to videos or full-mix tracks.

Lower Elementary – Age-appropriate worship songs led by high schoolers singing along to videos or full-mix tracks.

Preteen Ministry – Age-appropriate worship songs led by

> high schoolers or adults singing to background tracks with live lyrics.
>
> **Middle School Ministry** – Worship music you might hear on the radio led by a live band.
>
> **High School ministry** – Worship music you'd hear on the radio led by a live band with live lyrics and a light show.

Worship is just one example of how you can build upon what kids experience throughout their years attending your family ministry environments, changing things up just a bit to keep them engaged. Whatever you plan for your physical environment, be sure you capitalize on where kids are now, but also build anticipation for where they're headed next.

Environment also extends to the unique experiences preteens get to enjoy throughout their time in your ministry. What happens on Sunday is important, but you can go deeper with Small Group relationships with events that happen outside of Sunday morning.

It's important for preteens to see the value in having wise voices speaking truth into their lives. This happens most naturally at events developed to strengthen the Small Group.

Camps
Retreats
Adventure Courses
Bowling Parties
Arcades or Laser Tag
Parties

If done right, these can be powerful ways to build relationships. Prioritizing concentrated time with Small Groups can exponentially increase how preteens relate to each other, which prayer requests they share, and how open they are about what's going on in their lives.

Special events should also include service projects that allow kids to put their faith into action. Consider local organizations that will both open the eyes of preteens to the needs around them and give them a chance to meet those needs.

Your environment will depend on several factors, from space to budget to personnel. As long as you are intentional about the environment you create, your preteen will feel like you care enough about them to create something unique for them. That feeling will encourage on going participation in your ministry.

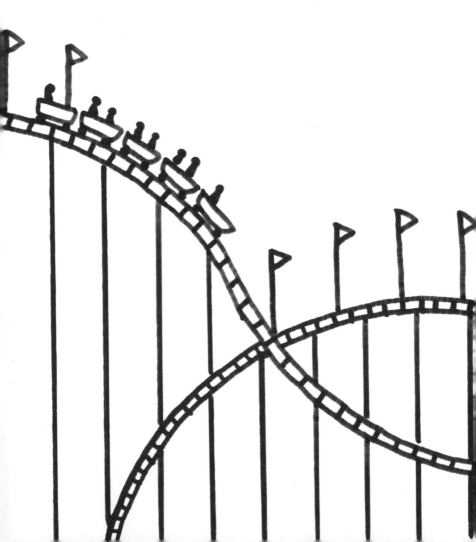

CHAPTER 5

Catch Them with Consistent Volunteers

While the physical environment you create for your preteens is important, **the relationships you encourage through that environment are what matter most.** Finding the right people to invest in your preteens might take some time. But, trust me, it will be worth the effort.

Volunteers are the secret sauce to engaging preteens in your church. If your preteens ever get tired of your programming, the strong relationships they form with Small Group Leaders, people on stage, and Communicators will encourage them to keep coming back. So as you start filling these roles within your ministry, consider how you think about their job descriptions. Let's talk about the specific types of volunteers you'll need to make your preteen ministry happen.

FOUR SHIFTS FOR THINKING ABOUT VOLUNTEERS

SHIFT FROM THE HOST PLAYING A CHARACTER TO BEING AN EMCEE (MC).

In children's ministry, kids enjoy being regaled by a larger-than-life Host who morphs every month and takes on a new persona related to the current series. This works great for younger kids who'll go along for the ride because the Host is fun. But preteens see this whole shtick differently. They're moving into abstract thinking and know their Host can't possibly have a total personality makeover every month. They don't buy it, and it's not long before the heckling begins from the back of the room.

For a preteen environment, the Host should serve less as a character and more like an event MC, making sure everyone knows what is going on and is having a good time. A preteen Host can still lead kids in a game and connect them to a series theme and why they should pay attention. But the Host is doing this more as a fellow participant with the kids instead of being an all-knowing character who is pretending to be someone they're not.

Most MCs warm up the room, add energy, and make everyone feel at ease. Think of this like a late-night TV show monologue, connecting what's happening at church to what's happening in the world by humorously mentioning appropriate sporting events, viral videos, and preteen trends. It should feel more like a conversation than a memorized script.

Following the welcome, the MC should lead the room in some sort of game that breaks the ice and gets kids excited to be there. These can be games where preselected kids come on stage and the audience cheers on their favorites, or you can have everyone participate in the game. Make sure the opening activity ties to what kids are learning later on during the Bible message.

> Example: Bible story of Isaac digging wells
> Game: Every Small Group gets a large bucket of sand with several buried objects. The first group to dig around and find all of the items wins several bottles of water and a box of donuts to snack on during Small Group time.

Anything the Host can do to prime the pump without giving too much away helps preteens pay attention during the Bible story. The Host doesn't need to be overt about connecting the game to the Bible story, because the preteen brain will automatically connect the dots once the kids hear that the Bible story is about digging for water in sand.

Something to keep in mind as you plan games is that bringing preteens on stage can be fun, but it can also cause major anxiety for the kids you choose. Instead of picking random participants from the audience and putting them on the spot, preselect kids and give them a heads-up of what to expect. Let them opt in or out. This will help sort the kids into those who would love the chance to be doused with chocolate pudding on stage and those who would consider changing schools if called out in front of a crowd.

Overall, the Host is the initial relationship on stage that captures kids' attention and ensures they're having fun. After all, fun is the currency of preteen attention spans. If kids are enjoying themselves, you've bought yourself more time to help them connect with God.

So who makes a good Host for a preteen environment?

A preteen Host should be a person who is naturally fun and has no problem making a fool out of themselves in front of others. They should be the type of person who's never met a stranger and can make anyone feel like they are the most important person in the room. Kids should see this person on the street and immediately want to run up and give them a high-five or a fist-bump.

The Host should be able to engage preteens from the moment they step on stage. So when you're recruiting new Hosts, the first thing to consider is their personality. They must have the ability to balance having fun while maintaining control of the room.

This sounds like it might be an impossible person to find in your church. But think about the people you know who always seem surrounded by people hanging on every word to whatever story they're telling. If they can tell great stories and get people having a good time, chances are they'll be great in a preteen environment. Talk to them first and see if they're interested. You can also look to your high school or college students and see if one of them fits the criteria. One of my best Hosts started when she was a sophomore in high school, and now she's on staff at the church in children's ministry working with Large Group volunteers.

SHIFT FROM STORYTELLERS TO COMMUNICATORS.
In their book *It's Just a Phase So Don't Miss It*, Reggie Joiner and Kristen Ivy outline the three dials we constantly need to turn up in a child's life to help them interact with God and connect them to a growing faith.

Wonder – This is a child's introduction to the awesome love of our creator God.
Discovery – This is how children learn to love life and see their place in God's story as they follow Jesus.
Passion – This speaks to how a child lives out their faith in relationship to how they love others around them.

When children are young, Storytellers help first connect them to the wonder of God. The stories that they hear in your children's ministry are their first introduction to the Creator.

They incite awe about the God of the universe, who—out of His love for us—set the world in motion. The God who didn't leave us to fend for ourselves but continued to interact with His creation. The God who sent Jesus to save us. While a Storyteller's main focus is turning up the wonder dial, they start to amplify the discovery dial as well. They paint a picture and cast vision for how God created each and every one of us to play a role in the world. Children's ministry Storytellers engage their audience with a story that connects beyond the story itself to the deeper meaning the story wants to communicate. They do this through heightened expressions, physical movement, theatrical props, costumes, or object lessons. Sometimes, they even use the audience as participants in the story.

As kids grow into their preteen and adolescent years, the Storyteller gives way to a Communicator who cranks up the discovery dial. **Communicators speak from a place of having wrestled with the content and come through on the other side with some sort of understanding to impart to the audience.** They engage the audience through personal stories, props, object lessons, or audience participation through discussion. Rather than a pure Storyteller, they are more of a guide—an older peer who's just a bit further along on their faith journey.

So who makes a great preteen Communicator?

Great preteen Communicators are . . .
Humorous
Dynamic
Likeable
Authentic

Finding all of these characteristics in a single person is like finding a unicorn.

Dynamic refers to how engaging a person is—how they use their voice and non-verbal cues to connect with an audience.

The voice is the Communicator's primary instrument to engage kids. They use pitch and volume to cue kids to what's important. They slow down or speed up the pace of their voice to help kids engage. And while a person can learn to be more dynamic, some people have a natural affinity towards using their voice and movement to keep an audience connected to their message.

Likability is totally subjective. Often, we can't predict who a kid will like and connect with. However, kids find it easier to get along with some personalities than others. Often, likability is tied to surface-level characteristics like age and personal style. This doesn't mean an older person can't make a great preteen Communicator. It's just a bit more challenging. Regardless of those surface characteristics, likability is often tied to the fourth characteristic, authenticity.

Authenticity means that the person on stage is *real.* I don't mean real in the sense that they aren't playing a character. I mean they're not trying to be someone they are not. You can't fake authenticity. In any preteen environment, authenticity wins the day. **If preteens can tell you mean what you say and believe it, they'll follow along with you.** Whatever your Communicator is saying should come from a place of having wrestled with this content themselves.

Don't let "difficult to find" stop you from even trying to find people who could serve as Communicators for your preteens. These people are out there. I've recruited them and trained them. They exist, and they are phenomenal. It just takes patience and a bit of work to find them.

SHIFT FROM A SONG LEADER TO A WORSHIP LEADER.
For preschool and younger elementary kids, worship time is more about getting kids excited about God and expressing that excitement through movement and singing. The person leading worship doesn't have to be the best singer in the world—their

excitement and ability to get kids dancing to music is often all it takes to lead kids. For younger kids, the lyrics they sing can be foundational to what they come to believe about God, but worship is often less about the words and more about the fun of singing great songs. Often the worship you do see from kids is what they mirror from those great, excitable Worship Leaders.

Preteens need something different. As they are beginning to understand more about how they can worship God with their life, they need people who are closer to adult Worship Leaders. The concrete thinkers in the room will need some help understanding the poetic words to the songs. A Worship Leader can guide them in how to connect their lives to the message of the lyrics.

As we've said, preteens are also self-conscious about how they look in front of their peers. They may think that singing along and engaging with these worship songs may make them stand out. When they have someone on stage they can look up to, they are more likely to sing along.

Recruit Worship Leaders who are strong role models for this group. Fifth and sixth-grade boys are much more likely to feel comfortable singing along with a "cool guy" Worship Leader than a grandma borrowed from the choir. Fifth and sixth-grade girls need powerhouse females to look up to. Try to get a good mix of young, relatable leaders on stage for worship.

So who makes a great preteen Worship Leader?

Start with your student ministry—teenagers who are just a few years ahead of them. Work with the youth pastor to find fun, engaging guys and girls who would be great at leading preteens in worship. They don't have to play instruments, but singing on pitch would be a plus—especially since preteens are much more critical of what they like or don't like. Have them sing along to background tracks and get the kids excited about worshipping God, while helping them see what authentic faith can look like in the context of worshipping their Creator.

SHIFT FROM ACTIVITY DIRECTORS TO FACILITATORS.
If they've grown up in the church, kids up until their preteen years have been part of kids' ministry programming where someone has been tasked with leading their Small Group. It could be called any number of things from Sunday school teacher to Small Group Leader, but the task is generally the same: Direct kids through a planned-out curriculum focused on a Bible story or verse, with activities that lead towards some predetermined end in mind.

Yet knowing what we know about how kids learn, the role of Small Group Leader (SGL) should adapt to the different needs of a preteen.

Preschoolers need activity directors to guide them from station to station and help them with the messy crafts and activities that inspire learning as concrete thinkers.

Younger elementary students need a director who leads them to a destination. Leaders may not be quite as hands on with the materials, but they are definitely directing the group towards a clear message.

Preteens need something different. Preteens are looking for their SGL to be a facilitator.

To help pay my way through seminary, I worked at a Christian ministry where one of my responsibilities was as a work team facilitator. Here's how it worked. I met with the team leader and sketched out an agenda for a meeting. This would include what needed to get accomplished throughout the meeting and how we might go about accomplishing those goals. I was trained with an arsenal of ways to go about accomplishing those goals, such as brainstorming techniques, how to handle rabbit trails, and ways to build consensus. Once the meeting would start, the team leader would sit back and participate in the meeting while I ran it and helped the team arrive at their destination— with everyone feeling like they had a voice and were able to participate.

While a corporate work team and a Small Group aren't an apples-to-apples comparison, there are enough correlations that we can draw valuable insights to help transition Small Group Leaders into this new role of facilitator.

> A preteen SGL should be a facilitator who helps bring about an outcome by providing indirect or unobtrusive assistance, guidance, and supervision.

I'm not suggesting the SGL should take a back seat in the group. They are still the leader and are tasked with getting something accomplished during group, but how they go about doing that changes during the preteen years.

If we want preteens to own the process of a growing faith, they need opportunities to discover faith on their own. Small Group is the perfect chance for this to happen. The Small Group Leader knows the intended outcome for the discussion but doesn't give it away at the start of group. Instead, they lay out the plan and give preteens the opportunity to make decisions about how they'll put that plan into action. When SGLs act as facilitators, they can step in with strategies as preteens need help navigating their questions or figuring out what to do next.

What makes a great preteen Small Group Leader?

Interestingly enough, the four words used to describe an ideal Large Group volunteer are the same words I'd use to describe a great Small Group Leader: humorous, dynamic, likable, and authentic. And for many of the same reasons. They are leading and motivating a group of kids to grow in their relationship with Jesus. Kids should want to connect with their Small Group Leader each week.

The biggest difference between a Large Group and Small Group volunteer is where they fall on the introvert/extrovert continuum. Natural introverts have a way with conversations. They are thoughtful, ask great questions, and often make great listeners. Find people who are caring and treat everyone like they're a best friend. When leaders are authentic and show interest in others, they're keepers. Don't let them get away.

FINDING THE PERFECT VOLUNTEER

As you're finding the perfect volunteers for your preteen environment, here are a few things to keep in mind:

Don't settle. Finding volunteers seems urgent. And on some level it is. Sunday is always just around the corner and you want people in every available spot. However, sometimes in our rush to fill volunteer gaps, we end up placing someone in a role they're not fit for. While this helps us out in the short term, it might prove detrimental in the long term. Over the years, I've found it's often better to go with no volunteer than the wrong volunteer. I'll find someone to fill the gap for the upcoming weekend, but I'll also be upfront that this is a temporary solution as we search for the best person to fill the role.

It takes time. You may not fill all the roles you need right away while waiting for the perfect volunteer. You may try people in many different roles before finding their sweet spot. Have patience and wait for the perfect person. The results will be worth it.

Diversity is not an option. Preteens need to hear from

diverse voices to gain a richer perspective on life. This not only includes people from various cultural backgrounds, but also male and female Communicators. Today's preteens are growing up in the most culturally diverse time in history. We need them to experience this same diversity within the walls of the church. If your church is not culturally diverse due to where you live, consider Communicator videos that offer these perspectives as part of your regular cast of speakers.

Mix it up. You might be the best person to fill a volunteer role in your preteen ministry, but you should also work at building your bench with other great options. This is especially true for who you put on stage. When kids hear from the same person week after week, they're only hearing one person's faith journey. And the kids who don't naturally connect with that person will check out. Replicate yourself and use your skills to train others to become great Communicators as well. This will allow you to recruit and care for leaders while your volunteers care for the preteens.

CHAPTER 6

Catch Them with Effective Programs

Kids construct a faith foundation throughout childhood. Parents and church leaders connect what a child has been taught about God to what they experience in the world. In turn, kids build a foundation for what they personally believe about God. But then something changes.

At some point, kids become aware of the abstract nature of faith. They start to notice when their personal experiences no longer seem to line up with the faith of their earlier years. When that happens they start kicking against the foundation they've built.

I can trust God no matter what . . . but He still let my dad get a job in a different state.
Jesus wants to be my friend forever . . . but I still feel lonely.
I need to make the wise choice . . . but the wise choice isn't always clear.

It's not that parents and church leaders mislead younger kids about what faith looks like. It's simply the way a child's brain works . . . at first. Eventually, questions start to pop up as preteens develop a better understanding of abstract ideas and move beyond their initial beliefs about God to a more mature and authentic faith.

For many preteens, these questions can cause anxiety, especially when the answers aren't as concrete as they'd hoped. Preteens need a safe place to turn and find reassurance that they're not crazy and that God still loves them through this process of growing their faith.

If we've helped kids build a solid foundation, it should remain strong and carry the weight of the demolition and renovation as they attempt to make sense of faith with their new-found ability for deeper thinking. This is a process that starts as kids enter their preteen years and may continue well into adulthood. Preteens, however, have the potential to gain a clearer understanding of foundational truths that will actually add a thicker layer of mortar to strengthen their foundation.

This is part of what it means to live a life of faith. A person must—like most other things in their life—wrestle with the truth in order to make the truth their own.

So much is at stake, and doing nothing or playing it safe is no longer an option. We've already talked about the importance of finding the right volunteers to work with preteens. Along with having the right people on our teams, there is a short list of programming shifts that will help provide a safe atmosphere and ensure preteens don't get caught in between.

1. ELEVATE QUESTIONS.

When I was growing up, my Sunday school teachers, pastors, and Christian school teachers told me the church was the best place to find all the answers. So, I figured if I had a question about God, Jesus, my faith, or life in general, I'd discover the answer at church. Which was great, until I asked a question that didn't really have a cut-and-dry answer, or at least an answer that made sense to me. When that happened, I felt like my lack of faith or some misguided belief stood in the way of my understanding. At times, I was even told I was asking inappropriate questions and should just have more faith. Other times, I was encouraged to pray about it and allow God to answer it. But then He didn't, at least in a way that I could understand. And then where did it leave me? Well, questioning the validity of *everything*.

I often wondered, if church was the place where I should find all the answers, why I couldn't ask all the questions.

As I talk to church leaders around the country, I hear echoes of the same story. Church was not a place they could ask hard questions. Hard questions were met with condescending looks and wagging fingers, reminding the question-asker that if they really believed, they wouldn't doubt.

Thankfully, many family ministries have started to see how difficult questions are a crucial part of a growing faith.

As preteens become aware of the complexities of life, questions will start to surface:

Are these stories really true?
Is my friend's religion just as true?
Why would God send Jesus as a baby?
Why won't God heal my sick friend or family member?
Why would God allow my parents to separate?
Why do mean people succeed and good people struggle?

The list goes on and on. And the questions could get more and more difficult to answer, depending on the asker. So instead of following the rabbit holes, remember:

Not all questions have answers.
No single human knows all there is to know about God and how God works.

Often the best answer you can give is, "I don't know."
The best way to process these questions is through a discussion
that leads back to what we do know about God.

One of the best things you can do for preteens is start your
programming from a place of questions. When you start with
a question, you communicate that questions are part of a
growing, authentic faith.

Help your Large Group teachers to land the message on a
question kids can keep thinking about as they head to Small
Group. Train your Small Group Leaders how to handle the
tough questions and how to ask good questions in return.
After all, the role of a Small Group Leader really is not to give
answers and check boxes but rather to ask questions and help
kids process their faith.

When Small Group Leaders ask questions that go beyond
regurgitating the details of a Bible story, they model for
preteens that asking questions is normal and never goes away.
We set kids up for success when we show them how to ask
good questions about the Bible and their faith.

Always reassure kids that their questions and doubts are valid.
Questions and doubts are not an indication that they've lost
their faith. Rather, when we encourage kids to ask questions,
we normalize them and get the chance to remind them that
God is bigger than any question they have.

2. MAKE A BIGGER DEAL ABOUT SMALL GROUPS.

For the most part, what kids have experienced throughout their
time in children's ministry has been great, and hopefully they've
responded well to it. However, now that the preteen switch has
flipped in their brains, what they previously saw as fun they may

now find annoying and childish.

Large Group is the time when your audience gathers around for fun games, corporate worship, and an applicable message from God's Word. Large Group can include ice breakers, object lessons, games, worship music, sketches, and Bible teaching. But we often put so much energy into Large Group production that Small Group becomes an afterthought, even though Large Group is meant to enhance the Small Group experience.

Preteens may not remember the details of what they learn in church each week, but they will remember how they felt and the positive relationships they developed. That's why it's more important for preteens to have a consistent person looking for them, noticing when they're gone, and remembering the details of their lives, than it is to have an engaging Bible Storyteller.

The most important environment you can create in your church is a relational environment where kids feel like they have value and are active participants in what they experience. This starts with making sure they are in the right Small Group with a leader who cares for what's happening in their life and who models for them what it means to live out authentic faith.

Small Groups help make sure the truth you're communicating through Large Group will stick in the everyday lives of preteens.

3. FOCUS ON LANDING PLANES.

So Large Group is no longer the main dish. Therefore, instead of wrapping up the message with a neatly tied bow and sending the kids off with a Bible story complete with full resolution, a Large Group Communicator needs to land the plane.

Landing the plane indicates that the journey isn't finished. When a plane lands at the airport, you get off the plane, hop into an Uber, and continue until you reach your final destination. The same is true of a Communicator who introduces questions and sends kids into a Small Group environment.

When it comes to communicating, knowing the difference between tying bows and landing planes is critical. If your audience needs to wrestle with the material following Large Group, tying the bow on the talk—telling preteens exactly how the Bible story can be applied to their lives—hinders their thought process heading into Small Group. Their brains conclude that all that needs to be considered has been said. Landing the plane, on the other hand, provides just enough closure for kids to know where they're headed while remaining unsolved enough to spark wonder about further possibilities.

4. DON'T IGNORE ACTIVITY-BASED LEARNING.

When we start our programming with a question, one might assume that Small Groups will only use discussion questions to talk about the material. Yet, for many preteens this will fall short. Just because we start our programming with a question and send preteens to Small Group for further discussion, doesn't mean all a preteen wants to do in Small Group is philosophize.

One of the biggest misconceptions of preteen ministry is that preteens no longer want to engage in Small Group activities and prefer only discussion-based learning. While that might be true for some kids, most preteens still need some sort of concrete activity to connect abstract ideas and connect them to real life.

While it's true that discussion questions are important to introduce at this age, how we introduce them is equally important. Discussion questions shed light on multiple sides of an argument, helping preteens to consider further options that may impact what they believe about something. However, this is an emerging ability, and not all preteens can think like this consistently. When you start with discussion questions, one week you may have great Small Group conversations while other weeks it's like a room full of crickets. This inconsistency is why you need more than discussion questions to successfully lead a preteen Small Group.

Preteens need some sort of concrete activity to give their brains a foundation for abstract conversation. And while the fact that activities can feel like craft projects in disguise might cause some preteens to feel angst, activities in general engage more learning styles. Activities that get preteens moving or manipulating objects engage kinesthetic learners. Activities that use images and pictures and drawing engage visual learners. The most effective Small Group activities engage multiple learning styles, helping the brain retain more of what was discussed.

Often, we default to discussion questions because they require very little preparation. We can show up on Sunday, listen to the message, and ask some questions. We can make it up as we go along. But before we let this become our mode of operation, we need to remember that we're adults who've been thinking like adults for some time. Discussion questions are something we've done for many years and are second nature to how we learn.

For preteens just learning the art of having good conversations based on discussion questions, they need a hook to help ground them in the topic and build a bridge for their brain to understand why they should care about it. Once they have that, ask away. They may still need some prompting and reframing of the questions, but they should be able to engage with the discussion.

These four ideas will focus your programming towards an experience that will engage your preteens and give them the tools they need for building authentic faith.

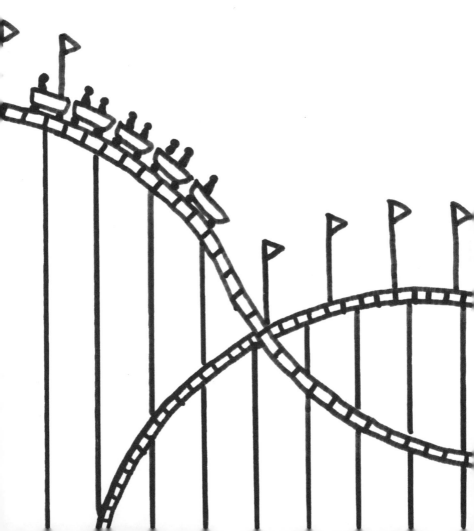

CHAPTER 7

Catch Them with Intentional Parents

Most of your preteens are still part of an elementary school, and their parents feel an intense pressure to prepare them for middle and high school when parents know they will soon take a backseat to peers. For church leaders, this feels like the last chance to help parents be intentional before they check out. It's time to turn up the volume on helping parents be connected, engaged, present, aware, and confident in how they interact with their preteens.

At every age and stage, what kids learn in church should have an impact beyond Sunday. This is especially true in the preteen years.

But like we've mentioned, preteens live hectic lives. Their brains barely have enough processing capacity to make it through a day at school or home, not to mention what we are throwing at them in church. This isn't to say what happens at church isn't important. It is arguably the *most* important. But between Sundays, kids have to be ready for quizzes, games, projects, and friendships that require their full brains. The urgency of the now outweighs whatever truth was taught on Sunday.

On top of that, *parents* of preteens live hectic lives. They work and have responsibilities around the home on top of chauffeuring kids to and from after school activities. Even if there was enough time for a parent to focus on faith formation throughout the week, many parents feel like the church expects them to be formally trained Bible teachers on top of their daily routines. So how do we ensure our message has an impact beyond Sunday?

PARTNER WITH FAMILIES IN A WAY THAT ACKNOWLEDGES THEIR DAY-TO-DAY LIVES.

The church has to make faith formation easy for parents and kids. **A great home strategy for families uses the time they already have together to instill the importance of faith in their kids.**

The preteen years can be especially difficult on parents who are navigating their kids through this highly transitory phase alongside their child—especially their first time around.

With all that's happening to their kids, parents may begin to freak out. They've lived with these tiny humans for so long and have come to expect certain behaviors from them. One morning, they wake up to a child who seems nothing like the kid they tucked in bed the night before. I've experienced this with my own kids when, for hundreds of nights in a row, they would come in and give us hugs before heading to bed. Then one night, they didn't. They might call down from upstairs and told us good night, and eventually they didn't even do that. At first this upset me or made me feel sad about them growing up, but then I realized that I did the same thing as I grew into my teenage years. It's just part of growing older.

The more I talk with student ministry leaders, the more I hear how partnering with parents of middle and high school students often feels like an insurmountable task. However, I hear the opposite when talking with leaders of preteen ministries. Preteen parents are still quite involved in the lives of their kids. They are interested in everything their kid experiences from school to home to church.

This is a pivotal time to lean into parents. You can not only help them understand what's happening to their kids, but also cast vision for how to stay engaged throughout the rest of the adolescent years. Even if parents have been through this before, each child is different and will travel a unique path through adolescence.

Assure parents that while they may feel like their influence with their preteen is fading away, the influence they have in their child's life actually never ends. But the way parents influence their children does go through seasons. If parents understand how that influence changes, they can anticipate how they can proactively parent their child through the preteen years and ease into adolescence. The church should be the best-stocked resource center to help guide parents through every phase of their child's life.

Here are some ways to leverage technology to build community among your preteen parents:
- Host an annual parent orientation to help them understand what's happening at each phase of their child's life.
- Create a private Facebook group where parents can talk about what's happening at home.
- Regularly email and share what your ministry is doing, along with helpful articles.
- Live-stream or post training videos to meetings they can't attend in person.
- Post what kids learned on Sunday and include questions to continue the discussion at home.
- Use Instagram to remind parents what kids learned about on Sunday and advertise events coming up in the year.
- Suggest Bible reading plans families can use throughout the week that get the whole family reading God's Word.

Don't overwhelm the parents in your ministry! They're already overwhelmed trying to raise their kids—they only have so much time. Maybe try one or two ideas, see how they land with your parents, and adjust as necessary.

Regardless of what you try, start with the assumption that parents want the best for their kids and want to help their kids grow in faith. Employ a good dose of empathy and choose the approach that best resources parents to take ownership of their kids' faith formation.

When it comes to parents, remember that you can learn from them too. As a leader, you may be the expert when it comes to creating church environments, but parents are the experts on their kids. They know what is happening at home, who and what is influencing certain behaviors, and the struggle areas of their kids. Ask parents about what it's like to raise preteens and use their insights to influence the sort of environments you create.

Use your Small Group Leaders to create a bridge to your families. Small Group Leaders are on the front lines with these kids and have the potential to invest deeply into families as they start to feel comfortable and trust one another.

PROVIDE PRETEENS WITH RESOURCES THEY CAN ACCESS IN THE HOME.

While any age is great for helping kids understand how they can practice their faith, the preteen phase is a perfect time for them to own this process as they learn faith skills they can build upon for the rest of their lives. But remember, kids are motivated by fun. **It's okay for how they practice their faith to look more like fun and games than hard-core Bible study.** We want preteens to engage with God's Word and start to practice faith skills without feeling like it's homework or a chore to spend time with God.

Understanding a week in the life of your preteens allows you to have realistic expectations. Don't expect daily anything. They don't really do anything daily that they aren't required to do (besides eat and shower . . . and sometimes not even that!).

Set realistic goals to help preteens start practicing their faith at home. Try guided Bible reading plans, age appropriate devotionals, worship music in the car, and opportunities to serve their communities both with their Small Groups and their families.

Not all kids enjoy reading and writing out answers in a devotional. Be creative and do something like publish a Spotify playlist with the worship music you sing throughout the year. Encourage kids to connect with God through nature, offer a prayer or service challenge, or dare them to invite a new friend to church.

It's Not
Too Late

Next Sunday, walk through your children's ministry environment and observe the third graders. I imagine they're still enjoying it, engaging with their leaders and each other, and wanting to return week after week.

While these third graders may love attending your church right now, they are merely months away from their preteen years.

They're currently in the roller coaster car headed up the giant hill, just about to crest the hill and drop into the preteen loop.

And though they're climbing the hill, they haven't hit the peak.

It's not too late. You still have time.

What you do RIGHT NOW to help preteens connect . . .

To their faith
To a consistent Small Group
To a relevant Large Group
To each other
To their parents
To your church

. . . will have a direct impact on whether or not they fall through the cracks between the important transition from childhood to adolescence.

No matter what your church looks like, you have a chance to influence the future of preteens by making sure to catch them before they start dropping out. You can create a meaningful experience for preteens that has the power to transform how they see God, Jesus, the church, and other people for the rest of their lives.

It will take some time. Making changes isn't always easy. But it will be worth it when, years from now, you see . . .

More preteens inviting their friends to experience what they love about your church.
More kids entering your middle school ministry than ever before.
More students graduating your family ministry than you've ever thought possible.
More young adults returning and stepping up to serve in the church.

The stakes are high.

It's worth it to do the work. Make sure your preteens get caught in between.

You might be thinking to yourself, "This is great and all, but how do I make this happen at my church?"

That's a great question, and one that we'll help you answer.

In the following section, you'll find everything you need to plan your church's preteen environment and make it a reality.

And be sure to check out the worksheets and checklists at the back of the book to help you organize your ideas.

Next Steps and Worksheets

Next Steps

I can be impulsive. I've been known to buy concert tickets, mountain bikes, and puppies on a whim because they sounded like a good time. And every so often this would happen as a children's pastor. I would get inspired in a creative meeting or from a book or something I'd watched, and immediately I'd be off to the races.

During one such impulsive moment, someone on our creative team came up with this amazing idea for a Christmas script. Santa and his family were like mob bosses who went around the world "Christmasing" everyone and spreading the joy of the Christmas season. The script was hysterical. I knew it would be a hit.

But it wasn't. Because in my excitement for this amazing script, I didn't really think through all of the implications of putting Santa on stage at a church Christmas program. Maybe I should have thought that all through as people got up and walked out the MOMENT they saw Santa on stage. They may have even asked that the person responsible be removed from staff . . . but thankfully, that didn't happen.

Lesson learned.

Jesus > Santa.

Don't do that again.

Or at least talk to someone in leadership before making a decision like that.

The same lesson can be applied to starting an entirely new ministry within your church.

When starting a new ministry initiative in your church, it can be easy to get so excited that you move from inspiration to execution without thinking through everything from all angles. Often the first step is communication. Overcommunicate the plan every step of the way. No one should ever feel caught off guard by something you end up doing as you launch the ministry. This is especially true if you try to make the change before explaining why you're doing it.

It may take some convincing. Some may need their own space to pause, pray, and ruminate. Others may need to hear your reasoning two or three times before it resonates. Most churches have a children's ministry and a youth ministry. Many may wonder, *why create something to serve kids who, on paper, are already being served by one of those two environments?* An effective game plan will help decision-makers understand what you hope to accomplish through a preteen ministry.

I know this can sound overwhelming. But don't worry, we'll walk through it together. Before we get started, let me give you an overview of where we're headed. We're going to walk through three steps: PLAN, PREPARE, and LAUNCH.

PLAN

This is when you'll . . .
do your homework,
clarify your vision and goals,
gather a team around you,
and sort out the details of your budget and resources.

PREPARE

At first, PREPARE might look a lot like PLAN. But PREPARE is when you begin communicating beyond your inner circle of leadership and high-capacity leaders to your broader church community.

In this step, you'll connect with . . .
your cheerleaders,
your volunteers,
parents,
and, of course, preteens.

LAUNCH

It's finally time! In the LAUNCH phase, you'll fine-tune . . .
the environment,
volunteer training,
and all the logistics.

And if that still feels overwhelming for you based on the size of your church or the resources you have available for a preteen ministry, you can still do something unique for your preteens that will go a long way to catch them in between. Look for some tips at the end of this section.

For now, let's get started with creating your plan.

PLAN

Although it would be amazing to flip a switch and—VOILA!—a brand-new preteen ministry appears, I have yet to hear of that actually happening. Once you've determined to begin a preteen ministry, you'll need to talk with your church leadership and get their blessing to move forward.

Before you do that, take time to pray and ask God to give you the insight you'll need to capture the imagination of church leadership and help them see why a preteen ministry is important and worth the time, energy, and resources it will take to accomplish.

Then start gathering information. As with any meeting to pitch a new idea, come having already thought through the questions they might have regarding a preteen environment. Have your research ready—have answers, statistics, charts and graphs, potential roadblocks and challenges.

Does it sound like I'm telling you to prepare for the big pitch?

Well, I kind of am.

Why?

Well, not because I think church leaders don't want to help advance the spiritual well-being of kids. But because change is hard—and it seems that for some reason change is exponentially harder within the church!

Once you've done your homework, have an initial conversation to let your direct report know that starting a preteen ministry is something that's been on your heart. Share gaps you've noticed as you've been working with the kids and students in your church. Don't ask for a decision right a way, but schedule a time when you can sit down together and talk through the details of your ideas. Once they fully understand why the change is so important, you'll have a chance to lay out your heart and vision for an effective preteen ministry strategy.

VISION, MISSION, AND GOALS: WHY IS THIS IMPORTANT AND WHAT DO YOU HOPE TO ACCOMPLISH?

If you want someone to understand something new, figure out a way to put it into a story. Vision is all about answering the "why" questions. These "why" questions are often best answered through stories. Consider what you're noticing about the kids in your ministry. How are you seeing them check out of church? Are you watching as your own attendance numbers decline? Have you talked with those families and discovered the reasons why their kids no longer want to attend your children's ministry or have never connected with your youth ministry? Use those anecdotes to cast vision for why this is important for the kids in your church.

If you share the story of a boy or girl who now thinks church is for little kids, end with, "Imagine if instead of feeling like church was a place for little kids, preteens felt that they had a place of their own. Instead of feeling talked down to, they felt empowered to build a faith of their own."

Or if your sixth graders are getting lost in the shuffle as they transition into your student ministry environment, creating a preteen environment could help them realize their leadership potential as the oldest kids in the group. They may enter student ministry with a better understanding of how God has gifted them to lead and serve the church.

Think through your stories and use them to share why a preteen ministry is important. Connect those stories to what you can accomplish through this ministry.

List out your goals, and be able to articulate how you think this ministry can accomplish those goals.

> Your goals might look something like this:
>
> To grow in the number of preteens kids invite to church throughout the year. (Create and invite opportunities throughout the year where kids come to have fun)
>
> To provide service opportunities for preteens. (Work with local ministry partners to create service projects throughout the community. Find opportunities for kids to serve with adults in your preschool ministry.)
>
> To connect kids with consistent Small Group Leaders. (Recruit leaders for the whole school year, train them, and resource them.)
>
> To create an environment of their own. (Give them their own name. Create a logo and a T-shirt. Decorate the room with preteens in mind.)

WHO WILL HELP YOU CREATE THIS ENVIRONMENT?
Think through the people you can enlist to help you. Most of the time when we think through the team we need to create an environment, we think about the volunteers such as Small Group Leaders, Communicators, tech crew, and welcome team. However, also think about the influencers and champions you will need throughout your church to help encourage you, as well as talk to others about what you're hoping to do through this new ministry.

Having the right people on the bus is important. Consider the exact people you will ask to be part of this initiative, what they'd do, and why they would be the best people to have on your team. You will need to staff several roles with either paid staff or volunteers. Like any role in the church, some require more from a volunteer than others. During the launch season, however, you can expect to need high-capacity leaders who share your vision for preteens and are willing to go the extra mile to create this ministry.

Consider implementing the following roles throughout your preteen ministry:

Small Group Coaches to lead the team of Small Group Leaders. This helps you carry the load of caring for volunteers. Coaches can help fill in the gaps, gather supplies when they run out, and help find last-minute replacements.

Small Group Leaders to lead groups of kids. These should be every-week leaders who have a consistent group of kids they serve. This helps facilitate growing relationships between kids and leaders. You should shoot for about eight to 10 kids per Small Group Leader.

Stage Hosts to welcome kids into Large Group and lead games to get them excited about being there.

Bible Communicators to present Scripture with energy that grabs kids' attention and keeps them engaged throughout Large Group.

Worship Leaders to lead kids in singing.

Tech Operators to run sound, lights, and on-screen presentations.

Curriculum Coordinators to gather supplies and prepare what is needed for the lessons each week.

Welcome Team to welcome kids into the environment and help with check-in and security.

TIMING: WHEN DO YOU WANT THIS TO START?
WHEN WILL IT MEET?
Creating a new initiative is a big undertaking for any church.
Consider how much time you'll need to do it right. You
have one chance to make a first impression on a kid who is
already questioning if they want to come to church or not. So
make sure that your launch week is far enough in advance to
complete the task list and create an unforgettable experience
for the preteens.

You may want to consider different phases for your launch.
If you're pressed for time, think through the bare minimum
you need to get up and running, and then consider what a
phase two would look like combined with how and when you'll
accomplish that phase.

The best time for your preteens to meet is when their parents
are already going to church. Sunday mornings are ideal for a
preteen environment. However, due to facility needs, Sunday
mornings may not work. If that's the case, you'll have to
think through the second-best option for your church. As you
consider those options, think through a week in the life of your
families. Make it easy for them to make this a priority. Families
will always have scheduling conflicts, but attempt to find a time
when they'd have the fewest.

FACILITY AND RESOURCES: WHERE WILL THIS TAKE PLACE
IN THE CHURCH? WHAT WILL YOU NEED TO MAKE THE
ROOM READY AND BE PREPARED EACH TIME THEY MEET?
Think about the rooms you have available in your building.
Which would make an ideal space to create your preteen
environment? When you're looking for the right room, think
about what you need out of the space. (For more on this, check
out Chapter 4.)

Large Group and Small Group space. These could be in the
same room. Our preteen environment was self-contained for

Large Group and Small Group, meaning that both happened in the same room. We had a stage up front, but plenty of room for kids and leaders to spread out on carpet circles or at small tables throughout the room.

Technology needs. Be sure the space you have in mind can accommodate any tech needs you have for Large Group. These can include audio and visual equipment such as TVs or video projectors and screens, computers, presentation software, Internet access, microphones, and speakers. Think through a typical service and consider what you'll need to run smooth Large Group and Small Group environments. Make note of what you already have on hand that you can repurpose for the preteen ministry and what you'll need to purchase for launch.

Multi-purpose rooms. It could be the best space for your environment is already being used by another part of the ministry. If that's the case, consider how you could switch things around to make the ideal room a possibility for the preteens, either by providing an alternate space for the ministry currently using the room or how you could make your preteen environment portable to set up each week.

Curriculum. At this point, the to-do list is growing. And we haven't even talked about what you'll teach throughout the year! Since your primary role is to care for volunteers and preteens, you need a curriculum that makes it easier for you to pull off a preteen strategy. Finding a curriculum that "gets" the transition from elementary to middle school is going to make it easier for you to implement and execute for your preteen strategy.

Preteen curriculum should include:

> Content that highlights the tension of the Bible passage
> and allows preteens to work through the tension in a way
> that connects what they are learning to their life outside
> of church.
>
> Large Group experiences that include fun games
> and engaging Communicator scripts that consider
> the developmental needs of the kids in their approach
> to learning.
>
> Video components that support Large Group and offer
> an alternative to Large Group teaching in place of a
> live Communicator.
>
> Small Group lessons that create concrete experiences that
> launch meaningful discussion without feeling like a day at
> school.
>
> Home pieces that give parents tools to encourage faith in
> their kids and offer preteens a way to practice their faith.

Even if you have to tweak the curriculum to fit your
environment, it's better than starting from scratch, which takes
valuable time away from focusing on your volunteers and
preteens.

Along with the curriculum, you will have on going supply
needs. What will those be? Create a list of items that you'll
need throughout the year, including technology, Large Group
props and game supplies, Small Group resources for activities,
and games and extras that you'd want in the room for kids to
play with or use during hang time as they get dropped off. Be
sure that wherever you meet has enough room to facilitate your
storage needs for your ongoing resources, or gain access to
existing storage space within the church.

BUDGET: HOW MUCH WILL IT COST?

Let's be honest for a moment here. Not many people love creating a budget. I'm not the most detail-oriented person, and budgets can make me go cross-eyed. However, if you want to get buy-in from the leadership in the church, you'll need to sit down and plan out how much money this new preteen initiative will cost.

Be realistic with the amount of money it will take to build your preteen ministry. Often you can find ways to save money along the way, but think through the worst-case scenarios to ensure you don't go over budget during the process. Think about what it will take to run this ministry. At first, you may not be able to hire new staff and will need to staff your preteen ministry with high-level volunteers. But be prepared with what staff positions you will need as the ministry grows.

The people in leadership that will be most concerned with budget will want this part of your presentation organized. Consider using a spreadsheet to categorize and itemize what you'll need, along with the cost of each. If spreadsheets are not your strong point, ask for help from someone who would be able to quickly create an organized layout for this part of the conversation.

When you're seeking to get the green light to start a new ministry, the more questions you've thought through and are able to answer, the better your chances of helping others see the vision for why preteen ministry matters.

PREPARE

Once you have permission and a plan to start your preteen ministry, it's time to get others on board with the plan. This includes casting vision and building momentum. It's important for others to catch your heart for all that's possible with a preteen environment.

CHAMPIONS: WHO WILL BE YOUR CHEERLEADERS?
Throughout every church, for one reason or another, you have people who are influencers. Maybe they are leaders in several parts of the ministry or they're well-respected throughout the congregation. These influencers should be some of the first people you meet with once you have the green light to create your preteen environment. Host a lunch after church and personally invite them to attend. Create a presentation that allows them to hear your heart for why preteen ministry matters. Invite them to be part of the launch team to talk about the new initiative with the people in their circles, help build and staff the environment, or invite families outside the church who could benefit from a preteen environment.

When I was a children's pastor and we were opening our new ministry, we had a champion like this. She didn't serve as a volunteer, but she showed up to pray. She talked about what we were doing in children's ministry with other parents in her circle of influence and invited them to be a part of what we were doing. She brought us snacks as we were working. She'd send us thank you notes that encouraged us to keep pursuing our goals for the ministry. Her family even allowed several of the staff a free week of vacation at their cottage on the lake. We needed volunteers for sure, but we also needed people like her to encourage us behind the scenes and help others see the value in what we were building.

Find people like her in your church. They may not be able to come serve every week, but they will be a sounding board, a voice of encouragement, and a champion of your ministry to other families in the church.

VOLUNTEERS: WHO WILL HELP YOU EACH WEEK?
Start with the volunteers you need in the key roles discussed in the previous section. In the beginning, you may personally need to fill one of these roles, but as you're staffing your volunteer base, also think about who would replace your role as well.

Depending on the size of your ministry, you will not need all of these roles right away. However, they are good to think through as you create your preteen strategy.

Find your Small Group Leaders first. They are the most important for the success of preteen ministry. Work towards a ratio of eight to 10 kids per Small Group Leader. This is a good starting point to be sure you don't lose your quieter kids in the discussion. Look to the Small Group Leaders in the third or fourth grade and make note of which leaders would move up with their kids into preteen ministry.

Next, find the volunteers who will run the sound and lights. This is a great role for high school students who often know computers like the back of their hand. Most likely they'll be able to figure out the presentation software on their own and train you.

After you find the people to run tech, find your welcome team to help with attendance and greet preteens as they enter your environment. These are warm, inviting people who make kids feel like a million bucks and help them feel like you want them there. These volunteers can also serve throughout the hour as a security team or resource team to help prepare the lessons for the following weeks.

Finally, find your on-stage volunteers to lead games and

communicate the message. This role could also be filled by you or your church's youth pastor for the short term until you find permanent volunteers who can share the responsibility. Finding these volunteers last might seem backwards. However, many preteen curriculums now offer excellent Communicator videos to help churches tell the Bible story. As you're looking for great Communicators, you can serve as a Host and use videos to do the heavy lifting for the Bible lesson.

PARENTS: HOW CAN YOU GET PARENTS EXCITED ABOUT THE NEW ENVIRONMENT?

Many parents have probably felt the pushback from their preteens each Sunday morning as they attempt to get them in the car and bring them to church. These same parents might have even expressed their concern to you. But anything new is often met with questions . . . lots and lots of questions:

How will this be different from what they had before?
Is this youth group?
What will they be learning?
When will it meet?
Can they check themselves in?
When are the special events?

Getting parents on board is one of the most important things you can do as you build momentum for your preteen ministry. Here are several ideas to help you communicate to your parents and get them excited about your preteen environment:

1. Host several parent meetings to cast vision and share the details of what you hope the preteen ministry will accomplish. Not all parents will be able to make this, but if you host two—a lunch after church and an evening dessert on a weeknigh—most parents will be able to make it to one. Continue sharing stories and casting vision for how this ministry could impact their kids.
2. Create a private Facebook group and invite preteen

parents to join. Use this not only to cast vision for your new environment but also to communicate dates and times, as well as to share information that would be helpful for parents as they raise their kids in faith.

3. Create a page on your church's website with a Frequently Asked Questions section. This can serve as a quick reference guide for the basic questions parents will have about the environment. You can also attach this as a PDF to your Facebook group.

4. Use a communication app to use text messaging to communicate with parents. Many parents already use these apps for school communication. They can add your preteen group and receive information where they're already looking each day.

5. Get kids excited about the new environment! If you do, they'll be sure to tell their parents about it.

KIDS: HOW CAN YOU GET THE KIDS EXCITED ABOUT THE NEW ENVIRONMENT?

The kids are the real reason you're doing any of this. Not only do you want to make sure they know about what you're planning, you also want to help them get excited about it and show up that first Sunday!

You'll want to make a big deal about this new environment. Announce that they'll have a new preteen environment soon, and post pictures of the progress as you create the environment to build anticipation of what to expect. Show them one photo each week. Don't give too much away. Teasing them with the one image will get their brains wondering what else they can expect.

Kids love getting physical mail in the mailbox. Create a fun postcard invitation that announces the launch date and invites them to an open house where they can get a sneak preview of the new environment.

When we were building our new environment, we got permission to take our kids on a tour of the construction site before the crew put up the drywall and laid the carpet. We gave the kids Sharpies and had them write their names on the cement floor throughout the room. We encouraged them to write their favorite Bible verse or something they hoped would happen in those new rooms. Reading their thoughts and prayers brought tears to our eyes as they wrote about wanting to build friendships, hoping people would come to know Jesus, getting to sing really loud, and growing in their relationship with God. We took time to pray over those rooms and everything that God would do in the years to come. This immediately gave the kids ownership. These were their rooms where they could connect with God. They couldn't wait to come back when construction was finished.

Building momentum is all about helping people anticipate the exciting possibilities of the new space. Everyone involved should catch the fever for all that's possible when you focus your energy on building something that could have so much impact on a group of kids. As people get excited, they'll pass it on to others. You'll be ready to launch with everyone on the same page, working towards the same goal, with the same level of energy to get it done!

LAUNCH

You planned and prepared, and now it's time to pull the trigger. Choosing a launch date can be tricky based on how your church schedules throughout the year. However, we've found it's best to start something new when families are already starting something: the beginning of the school year.

This gives you the summer to hammer out all of the details, finish the environment, and get the kids excited about the new space. The first Sunday after kids start school can be your first Sunday in the new environment. This works particularly well if you're creating a fourth to sixth-grade environment. Instead of moving on to your middle school environment, rising sixth graders can head to the preteen space.

The other option is to use a natural break in the school year, such as Christmas break. This works well if you're starting your preteen ministry with only fourth and fifth graders. When they come back from Christmas, they get a brand new space that's just for them. This also works in creating a soft launch where you continue building momentum for a full-blown launch the following August or September. At that point, the rising sixth graders can stay in the preteen environment as you add the rising fourth graders.

You have several options to consider. Be sure to work with your children's and youth ministry teams to make sure that everyone is okay with the decision and will help make the transition a great experience for the kids.

Once you have the launch date finalized, you'll need to work on the logistics of getting everything ready by the time the kids show up, excited for something new and just for them.

FACILITY: WHAT DO YOU NEED TO GET THE ROOM READY?
Work backwards from your launch date to make sure
everything is finished on time. You don't want kids to show up
to a half-finished environment. By this time, you've worked
hard to build momentum, and not finishing could result in
disappointment and kids not really feeling like they want to
come back. You might need a project manager to keep things
organize and keep the renovations moving forward. This may
or may not be you. Personally, I'd be awful at this. I'm just not
that detail-oriented. I'm great at seeing what needs to be done
and casting vision for what it could look like, but I need lots of
help getting it to the finish line. You might be the same way.
Don't take on jobs that don't fit your strengths or skill set. Ask
for help! I'm sure you can find someone in your church who'd
love to manage this process for you.

Work enough time into the schedule if you need any
inspections or want input along the way. Because this is a
public building, you'll need to work with your county and
get the right inspections and signatures to be sure the room
is safe for people to use. This shouldn't be an issue if you're
not changing the structure in any way, but definitely ask
your church's facilities team to be sure what you're doing to
the room doesn't change anything that would require new
inspections.

As you're creating your environment, it's a good idea to get
feedback along the way from the people you trust. Don't
surprise anyone with, wall-to-wall orange shag carpet. Run
ideas past decision-makers and make sure there are no
surprises. This helps build trust for other things you might want
to do in the future.

As the room is getting ready, there are some other things you
can be working on as you prepare for launch day.

TRAINING: WHAT DO VOLUNTEERS NEED TO KNOW?
Even if people have served in children's or youth ministry before, holding preteen ministry-specific trainings is a must. Help volunteers know what to expect as they work with these kids. You can use the material in the first half of this book to give them insight into a day in the life of a typical preteen. This can be eye-opening and can help leaders know how to relate better with the kids.

You may need to schedule multiple opportunities to attend these volunteer training events. Consider holding one on Sunday after church and one on a weeknight. This allows people to work with their schedule and make sure they get to an event. You can also record these and post them to your private Facebook group for your volunteers to watch at a later time.

Volunteer trainings can be full of information that isn't always fun by nature. We always made these meetings into a bit of a celebration, with food and decorations. We handed out T-shirts for the year and got everyone excited about what God would do through them.

Of course, there is information you need to cover. This event is your chance to run through any legal information they need as they work with preteens, as well as any requirements you have for them through the church. Once you get the general information out of the way, divide the volunteers by their different roles and give them a chance to get specific training in their area. For this, you may need to enlist some help to make sure everyone can be trained simultaneously.

For Small Group Leaders, help them understand how their role has changed from activity director to facilitator and mentor. Give them simple ideas of how to have great conversations with the kids, as well as how they can connect with their group outside of church.

For Hosts and Communicators, train them how to prepare each week and how to best engage preteens with God's Word. Teach Hosts how to lead games from the stage. Talk to Communicators about vocal dynamics, stage presence, and how to capture attention with a personal story.

For Worship Leaders, rehearse new songs and cast vision for how they can help preteens connect with God through singing. For tech volunteers, make sure they know how to use the equipment in the room.

For the welcome team, help them learn how best to connect with all sorts of families that may come to church each week.

Volunteers will feel more comfortable in their roles if they know what's expected of them and are set up to succeed. You can support them throughout the year with ongoing training. But having an initial training allows you to communicate an overall vision and mission to all of them, as well as focus on what's needed for their individual roles.

LOGISTICS: HOW CAN YOU KEEP THE NEW ENVIRONMENT ORGANIZED?

A new environment might mean that you need to update your attendance roster, as well as how families register their kids and check them in each week. Do this in advance, with enough time for a test run to make sure you're capturing the information you need. Then, as preteens register for your new environment, begin placing them into Small Groups.

If you haven't already, now is the time to split groups by gender. With the average age of puberty being 10 in girls and 11 in boys, many kids are experiencing new hormones and physical changes that both guys and girls are learning to navigate. Dividing groups by gender helps make this time less awkward. This also allows kids more freedom to talk about what's going on in their lives without becoming embarrassed by who might be in the group.

If you don't know how to start building your Small Groups, consider grouping them first by gender, then grade, and finally school district. It might help preteens feel more comfortable if they see people in their Small Group that they see at school throughout the week. This isn't always possible with kids who attend private schools or are schooled at home, but it does help with building initial groups you can add kids to as they register. If you only have a few kids, starting a guys' group and a girls' group would work perfectly.

Publish and advertise your launch date. You will want to over-communicate this. Often it takes several times before a date like this registers in a person's mind. Along with your launch date, you may want to consider holding an open house where families can check out the environment before the first official Sunday. This can be especially good for introverts to become familiar with the space before they show up.

Give Small Group Leaders their Small Group roster at least two weeks in advance of launch date, so they can contact their kids with a personal invite to their group.

For the first Sunday, you may want to have a dress rehearsal with all of your volunteers. Consider not only doing this for your Large Group presentations, but also for your welcome team and Small Group Leaders. Having a run-through of the hour gives them a chance to see how it all works together without the pressure of having kids around.

Help put volunteers at ease, knowing what to expect and that everything works according to the plan. Of course, you may find during this run-through that not everything goes according to plan, but at least there won't be any surprises that first Sunday. After your run-through, take time to pray as a group for all of the kids who will show up on launch Sunday and throughout the year. Ask God to do great things in these kids' lives throughout their time in your preteen ministry. Believe that

God can build an authentic faith that they'll cling to throughout the rest of their lives.

After all is said and done and prepared and prayed over, you have to press play. You have to launch. You've done all you can do. Rest in the truth that God can take our efforts and do exceedingly more than we can imagine! Work hard, but also watch as God does what only He can do—as He meets preteens and changes their lives forever.

Tips for Small Churches

If you don't have resources or volunteers to create a full preteen environment, here are some simple ways you can still make a big deal about preteens and catch them in between.

Small Group: Even if you have two or three preteens, put them in the same small group. This will be a way for them to connect to the content on the same level. If you have one preteen, invite her to help you lead a Small Group of younger kids. This will help your preteen think about the content in a deeper way as she helps others understand.

Large Group: Try to give the few preteens you have a unique Large Group experience. This can be as simple as watching a preteen video teaching on a tablet before they start their Small Group activities.

Leadership: Involve your preteens in leadership roles. Task them with serving on your welcome team. They can greet people coming into the building and help them feel welcomed. Invite your preteens to lead worship for your preschoolers or younger elementary kids. Use them on stage to help with the Bible story. Whatever you choose, get them involved with *being* the church.

Events: Create an event for preteens and their parents to experience something together. This can be as simple as hosting a dinner or taking everyone bowling. Create a way for the parents to connect with each other and build their own community while their kids have fun at the event.

Home: Purchase devotionals for your preteens and follow up with them throughout the week to see how they're doing. You can talk about these during Small Group. Have extras on hand for when a new kid starts coming.

Worksheets
& Checklists

GOAL WORKSHEET

What is your church's goal for family ministry?

_____

_____

_____

_____

_____

_____

_____

_____

_____

Who are the people who decide the direction for
family ministry?

_____

_____

_____

_____

_____

How can you work together to build a preteen environment?

_____

_____

_____

_____

_____

_____

_____

_____

_____

_____

_____

_____

_____

_____

_____

_____

_____

Name three things you hope your preteen ministry will accomplish:

1. _____

2. _____

3. _____

Write down three initial ideas for how you will do that. (Don't worry, it's okay if they change along the way. You just need to get started thinking about how you'll accomplish your goals for ministry to preteens.)

1. _____

2. _____

3. _____

ENVIRONMENT WORKSHEET:

Preteen grade range:

_____

Approximate number of kids:

_____

Ideal room options:

1. _____

2. _____

3. _____

Room design ideas:

_____

_____

_____

_____

_____

_____

Pinterest board:

_____

Stage design ideas:

_____

_____

_____

_____

_____

_____

_____

Pinterest board:

_____

Tech needs:

_____

_____

_____

_____

_____

Walk-in playlist ideas:

_____

_____

_____

_____

_____

_____

_____

Spotify account:

_____

Ways kids can personalize the environment:

_____

_____

_____

_____

_____

_____

_____

Who can help design and build the environment:

1. _____

2. _____

3. _____

4. _____

5. _____

6. _____

VOLUNTEER RECRUITMENT WORKSHEET

Possible Hosts:

_____

_____

_____

Possible Communicators:

_____

_____

_____

Training ideas for Hosts and Communicators:

_____

_____

_____

_____

_____

_____

_____

_____

_____

Possible Worship Leaders:

_____

_____

_____

Training Ideas for Worship Leaders:

_____

_____

_____

_____

Potential Small Group Coaches (People who can lead Small Group Leaders):

_____

_____

_____

Possible Small Group Leaders:

_____

_____

_____

_____

_____

Team Building ideas for Small Group Leaders:

_____

_____

_____

_____

_____

_____

_____

Small Group Training ideas:

_____

_____

_____

_____

_____

_____

_____

PROGRAMMING WORKSHEET

Curriculum options that incorporate Large Group and Small Group environments:

_____

_____

_____

_____

_____

How can we highlight the importance of questions in our preteen environment?

_____

_____

_____

_____

Stage games to play with kids:

_____

_____

_____

_____

_____

Songs kids enjoy singing:

_____

_____

_____

_____

_____

Ways we can help promote Small Group relationships:

_____

_____

_____

_____

_____

_____

_____

_____

_____

Team building ideas for small groups:

_____

_____

_____

_____

_____

_____

_____

Possible small group events outside of Sunday:

_____

_____

_____

_____

_____

_____

_____

_____

_____

HOME WORKSHEET

Social Media to connect with parents:

Facebook group:

_____

Instagram account:

_____

Text Message App:

_____

Ideas for using social media to connect with parents:

_____

_____

_____

_____

_____

Training ideas for parents:

_____

_____

_____

_____

YouVersion reading plans for families:

_____

_____

_____

_____

_____

Devotionals for kids:

_____

_____

_____

_____

_____

Incentives for kids to build faith skills:

_____

_____

_____

_____

_____

_____

PLANNING CHECKLIST

- ☑ Initial conversation

- ☑ Schedule meeting

- ☑ Meeting Date:

- ☑ Homework to gather details of preteen ministry strategy for your church

- ☑ Collect stories from kids and families who would benefit from this ministry

- ☑ List out your needs:
  - Environment
  - Technology
  - Resources
  - Staffing

- ☑ Formulate your budget based on what you'll need (see Budget Worksheet on the next page)

- ☑ Create a presentation (formal or informal based on the sort of meeting that is scheduled)
  - Keynote or PowerPoint
  - Handouts for leadership

BUDGET WORKSHEET

Environment Updates: What will we need to do to the physical environment to make it ready for the preteen ministry?

* Paint for walls, or to create a chalkboard wall
* Carpet or flooring
* Carpet circles for Small Groups to sit on
* Furniture such as chairs, tables, couches, bookcases
* Decorations for the walls
* Games and activities for kids to play while they're hanging out
* Stage construction or updating
* Room lighting
* Optional construction of a featured wall or item in your preteen environment such as a rockwall

Technology: Does any of the audio/visual equipment need to be updated or purchased new?

* Sound equipment such as a sound board, microphones, speakers, speaker towers
* Visual equipment such as TVs, projectors, screens, TV stands or mounting brackets
* Computer to run presentations or play videos, connect to the internet for music or YouTube videos
* Computer presentation software for slides and videos
* Optional video game consoles, controllers, and games for kids to play as they're hanging out
* Technology for check-in
* Optional stage lighting and a lightboard to operate the stage lights

Resources: Will the preteen ministry require extra supplies for Large Group and Small Group?

- Bibles
- Paper, pens, pencils, markers, glue sticks, etc.
- Clipboards to use as a flat surface for writing
- Whiteboards, dry erase markers, and dry eraser
- Tissues
- Props and/or costumes for Communicator
- Miscellaneous supplies for Host-led games
- Optional snack budget if you decide to offer snacks

Staffing: As the ministry grows, think through the roles you'll need to fill with staff or volunteers.

- **Preteen Ministry Director**: Leads the team of staff and volunteers throughout the preteen ministry. Casts vision and sets direction for the preteen ministry and ensures that the environment is accomplishing the goals for the ministry.
- **Small Group Director:** Recruits, trains, and organizes Small Group Coaches and Leaders. Help coordinate Small Group curriculum and organize kids into Small Groups.
- **Large Group Director**: Recruits, trains, and schedules Hosts and Communicators. Coordinates the Large Group curriculum and produces the weekend Large Group experiences, making sure that all the presentations, props, and supplies are ready to go for each service.

PREPARING CHECKLIST

☑ Talk with influencers and champions:

_____

_____

_____

_____

_____

_____

_____

☑ Parent communications:

- Email
- Facebook post
- Schedule meetings
- Create presentations for meetings
- Hold meetings
- Gather feedback and answer questions

☑ Volunteers

☑ Recruitment Sundays:

_____

_____

_____

- Schedule volunteer interviews
- Complete volunteer interviews
- Follow up with volunteers
- Place them in roles

☑ Kids:

- Write Sunday announcements
- Schedule Sunday announcements in kids' ministry
- Create invitations
- Send invitations

LAUNCH CHECKLIST

☑ Launch date:

_____

☑ Open house date(s):

_____

☑ Environment:

_____

☑ Project manager:

_____

☑ Volunteers:

_____

_____

_____

_____

☑ Work days:

_____

_____

_____

_____

☑ Volunteer training:

_____

☑ Training dates:

_____

☑ Training topics:

_____

☑ Small Group Leaders:

_____

_____

_____

☑ Hosts and Communicators:

_____

_____

_____

☑ Worship Leaders:

_____

_____

_____

_____

☑ Tech operators:

_____

_____

_____

☑ Welcome team:

_____

_____

_____

☑ Logistics:
  - Update attendance software
  - Place kids into Small Groups
  - Publish rosters for Small Group Leaders
  - Create postcards for kids
  - Small Group Leaders write postcards
  - Send postcards from the church

☑ Run-through date:

_____

FIVE BIG IDEAS
EVERY SMALL
GROUP LEADER
NEEDS TO KNOW

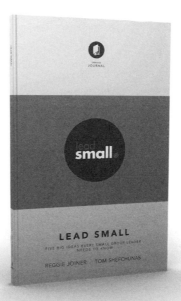

Lead Small, **BESTSELLING BOOK**
for volunteers and leaders who
work with kids and teenagers

ORANGEBOOKS.COM

What Leaders Are Saying

"There is a new movement today to shift worship away from its indebtedness to the cultural narrative and to re-situate it in the divine narrative. Gerrit Gustafson's *Adventure of Worship* puts worship, thankfully, where it belongs—in the story of God."

Robert Webber, Myers Professor of Ministry, Northern Seminary

"When Gerrit talks about the adventure of worship, he is not talking about something he learned in a book. It is his life's message, and he has been living it ever since I have known him."

from the foreword by **Don Moen**, president, Integrity Label Group

"*The Adventure of Worship* is nothing less than the story of worship fused to your own story. It is a personal, Bilbo-esque journey through the God-territory of not only Old and New Testaments but the testament of the now—the work of God in your own life. Gustafson's conversational narrative will illuminate your mind about what worship is and does. But its real brilliance is the hunger it will create in your soul."

Sally Morgenthaler, Sacramentis.com

"Gerrit is a worshiper, and his book challenges all of us to become just the same. This book is important and timely for the entire Church. In an age of many opinions about real worship, Gerrit makes it simple and clear. I highly recommend this book."

Chris Tomlin, worship artist; songwriter

"Comprehensive yet readable and inspiring, this book will take you on an amazing journey into wholehearted, biblical worship."

Stuart Townend, worship leader; songwriter
("How Deep the Father's Love," "In Christ Alone")

THE ADVENTURE OF
WORSHIP

DISCOVERING YOUR
HIGHEST CALLING

GERRIT GUSTAFSON

Chosen

Grand Rapids, Michigan

© 2006 by Gerrit Gustafson

Published by Chosen Books
a division of Baker Publishing Group
P.O. Box 6287, Grand Rapids, MI 49516-6287
www.chosenbooks.com

Printed in the United States of America

Library of Congress Cataloging-in-Publication Data
Gustafson, Gerrit.
    The adventure of worship : discovering your highest calling / Gerrit Gustafson.
        p.   cm.
    Includes bibliographical references and index.
    ISBN 10: 0-8007-9394-3 (pbk.)
    ISBN 978-0-8007-9394-4 (pbk.)
    1. Worship. I. Title.
    BV10.3.G87 2006
    248.3—dc22   2005027163

To Himmie, my wife and my closest companion in the Great Adventure. I had no idea what an incredible adventure was beginning that day when I first saw you at the Koinonia House. You were then, as you are now, *beauty abandoned in worship*.

CONTENTS

FOREWORD

The subject of worship needs to be separated from the trends, personalities, marketing and hype that so often attach to it. What we read, hear and see is usually pretty hyped up. Too often it seems we are trying to make things bigger than they are. Do you ever wonder whom are we trying to sell? We may be able to sell people by the way our worship looks or how it sounds, but we have to ask, Is it pleasing to God?

That is why I believe this book will be an important one for you: It is about the kind of worship that transcends trends, personalities and hype. The following definitions, stories and convictions that Gerrit shares will give you insight and focus to help you engage in authentic worship. The impact of this book will be even greater, I believe, if you could better know the man behind the book. That is why I am excited to be writing this foreword.

I had the privilege of working and traveling with Gerrit for several years. In fact, when I moved to Mobile, Alabama, in 1988 with my family, we stayed with Gerrit and his family for several weeks while we looked for a house to buy. I saw him up close with his children and with his wife, Himmie, before I knew him as a teacher or an author. This is important because it gives credibility to what he is teaching in this book. When Gerrit talks about the adventure of worship, he is not talking about something he learned in a book. It is his life's message, and he has been living it ever since I have known him.

Over the years, the words I first associated with Gerrit—transparency, character, authenticity and honesty—still describe him and his ministry. In our travels—I am thinking about Denver; San Francisco; Starkville, Mississippi; and Destin, Florida—I would introduce him then just as I would introduce him today: "The truth you are about to encounter can change your life, for it is coming from the throne of God through someone who lives it."

I read the other day a comment by Eugene Peterson (*The Message*) that he likes "books that marry Scripture and life—not Scripture imposed on life and not life that uses Scripture as a spiritual commodity—but God's revelation and human living all tangled and mixed up so it's hard to tell one from the other." I do, too. And if you do as well, you will love reading Gerrit's *The Adventure of Worship*, as I have.

For Gerrit and Himmie, "God's revelation and human living" are "all tangled and mixed up so it's hard to tell one from the other."

Enough from me. Read on! A great adventure awaits you.

Don Moen
President, Integrity Label Group

INTRODUCTION

THE CALL TO WORSHIP

O that with yonder sacred throng
We at his feet may fall!
We'll join the everlasting song,
And crown him Lord of all.

Edward Perronet

Jesus declared, ". . . A time is coming and has now come when the true worshipers will worship the Father in spirit and truth, for they are the kind of worshipers the Father seeks."

John 4:23

When Bilbo Baggins met Gandalf in Tolkien's *The Hobbit*, he did not think he wanted an adventure. For, you see, Bagginses are not the adventurous type.

But the wise Gandalf knew Bilbo better than Bilbo knew himself. He had known Bilbo's mother, Belladonna Took, and Bilbo's grandfather, the Old Took, and was very much aware that, among hobbits, the Tooks were quite adventurous. Whether he knew it or not, Bilbo Baggins was just the one for the adventure Gandalf had in mind.

Like Bilbo, you may not be looking for an adventure, but in a very similar way, there is a part in an amazing story that has your name on it. It is an ancient story—one that stretches back to the beginning of time—and you have an important part to play in it.

Called to Worship?

What is this grand story in which you were meant to participate? It is the story of the ages, the meaning behind your life, the purpose for which you were born: You were made to be a worshiper—not to be just a religious person, or even just a believer, but someone who actually worships, someone whose life is a daily sacrifice in the hands of an unseen Priest. You were made to be a fragrant offering presented with joyful abandon to serve a history-changing purpose much greater than that of your own well-being.

Are you interested? Then listen in with me on a conversation between a man called the Son of David and a woman who was drawing water from a Samaritan well on a hot and dusty day many years ago. You will see how someone else was enlisted into this life of worship.

"Good morning," the man says. "Would you mind drawing some water for Me?"

"You, a Jew, would request a favor of me, a Samaritan woman?"

"I would. But I have something even greater to give you, something that can satisfy your most profound thirst. Go get your husband; we'll talk some more."

She looks down. The very word *husband* brings to mind the painful realization that she has not done so well with her decisions regarding men. "I'm not married," she replies quietly.

Now watch the look on her face as the man responds to her admission. "You're right. You have been married five times, and the one you are living with now is not your husband."

The pain intensifies on her brow, but now it is mixed with wonder. And if you look closely, you will see just a hint of hope. *How did He know that?* she thinks. *Why would He remind me of that? Who is this man? Is He some kind of a prophet? Does He really have something to give me?*

Pause for just a minute and realize something important: This is not just her story—it is our story, as well. She once had dreams just like you and me. She once believed that her life was special, that it would count for something. But after years of disappointments, unexpected turns and careless choices, she wrapped up her dreams, packed them away and forgot where she left them. Ever since, she has been slowly settling in to living on the surface with minimal expectations. But this man whom she is talking with today seems to know something about who she is and how her life might make sense again. This same man also knows something about who you are and how your life can begin to make sense.

Back to the well. "I don't know who You are, but that 'most profound thirst' You said You could satisfy . . . I don't think it's just about being a better wife; I think it has more to do with how I connect with God. Do You know how that's supposed to happen? Can You tell me? So many people have such different ideas."

"It is your time, woman, and the time for many others to know: God is looking for worshipers—those whose worship is fueled by God's own Spirit, and is expressed in utter truth and reality. I'm telling you, that is your deepest desire. And I am here to open the door for you to become such a worshiper."

Stop. Rewind . . . let's hear that again: "God is looking for worshipers." That is it. That is the one-liner that I am

13

hoping will be with you for the rest of your days: *God is looking for worshipers.* Those words define the very mission Jesus was serving that afternoon in Samaria—gathering worshipers for His Father.

When the Samaritan woman signed on, she was so excited that she left her water pot behind. When you grasp what Jesus is saying to you, you will forget what you thought was so important, too. The woman went and bragged on the Lord to everyone who would listen, and eventually her whole town believed and spoke His praise. Finding that woman proved to be a good day in Jesus' mission of gathering worshipers.

But there is much progress yet to be made, even today. The goal is that a great multitude—more than the stars in the sky—from every language and culture will broadcast God's goodness throughout every sphere of influence available.

And that is why I am so glad you picked up this book. We need you. And there are many non-worshipers out there who need you—in fact, you will probably meet some of them today. As your paths cross, look at them in a new way: They are all potential worshipers. Under your breath, ask yourself, "What would it take for him or her to become a real live worshiper?" One of the great worship fathers saw people in this way. The great King David sang, "Let everything that breathes praise the Lord." Are they breathing? Then they should be praising. That is the heart of David.

What is this call to worship? It is an invitation to a deep-level conversion in which you give up *you* as your life's center, and instead begin to live around the true Center of the universe—an invisible King who sits on an invisible throne. It is an offer of transformation in which being blessed is incidental to being a blessing to your Creator-Redeemer and to others.

This call to worship is a summons to share in the coronation process of the magnificent King of the Ages whose rule thrives in an atmosphere of praise. John saw it clearly and wrote about it in Revelation 5: The King's throne, from which He reigns, is surrounded with songs. His rule, the exercise of His liberating power, is saturated with worship.

You may be thinking, *Who would refuse such a call?* But before you sign on the dotted line, consider the next few thoughts. There is a disturbing, even dangerous, aspect to this call to worship. Truth in advertising requires that I tell the whole of it. The call to worship is also an invitation to war. It is conscription into holy subversion.

Not only are you going to see the true Heir enthroned, but you will also be involved in deposing a treacherous phony who, through an international scam involving a massive network of puppet pretenders, has convinced much of humanity to value and worship what is actually worthless. As you begin to route increasing quantities of worship toward God's throne, you will be removing it from this jealous imposter and inspiring a rage that can only be understood by knowing the twisted passion of his heart: to supplant God as the ultimate object of worship. (Later in the book you will be briefed on the global contest between the worship of the beast and the worship of the Lamb.)

In This Book

For those who are taking up the gauntlet to be the worshipers God is seeking, this book offers support. Even with the dangers, there is most surely a band of worshipers today who are joining that "yonder sacred throng." The unflagging, eternal procession is marching through our neighborhoods and its captivating pulse draws us in. As we see it more clearly, we are stirred to realize that our time has come to be one of them, to be out there with them.

In these pages you will learn of the epic drama we could call "Worship Lost, Worship Found." You will understand that God's quest for worshipers, like other epic dramas, combines exhilarating heights of hope and promise with tragic depths of failure and dismay.

The heights include the reality of the eternal song—it is not just figurative—and how worship once filled the skies. I cannot wait to tell you about the singing stars, which provided music for God as He was working on creation. There were the primal expressions of worship that God counted as acceptable (Abel's offering and Noah's altar) as well as those that were unacceptable (Cain's offering, for instance).

Among the worship heroes is Abraham; he will lead a lesson on how costly worship can be. We will also learn about priests and how they do what worshipers are called to do—offer sacrifices.

You will grapple with the tragic significance of Israel's refusal at Sinai to become a kingdom of priests, and David, the worshiping king, will tutor us in the areas of priorities and passion. His son, Solomon, will teach us that beginning well in worship does not necessarily ensure that we end well. We will sit in the stands of the Super Event of Elijah's day—worship versus worship—and the national reform it prompted.

You will see that it was a worship failure that led to the seventy-year captivity of the Israelites. But also from Isaiah, Jeremiah and John, you will hear of a time when praise will spring up internationally and reigning worshipers will be too numerous to count.

Once you are persuaded to join the procession and live as a worshiper, the next task is to find out exactly what kind of worshiper God is looking for. I hope it does not sound strange to you that He does have certain preferences concerning worship, but in John 4:24, Jesus used the word *must* to describe how to worship ("in spirit and in truth").

There are some fundamentals, some imperatives and some "non-negotiables" in this glorious adventure of worship. Learn those early on—it is all just part of the training—and you will be amazed at the variety and creativity that God not only allows but loves.

Central to this book are the "Twelve Convictions of True Worshipers." These are identified and offered, not to load you down with a list of external dos and don'ts to keep you in line, but to help you recognize the from-the-inside-out workings of the Holy Spirit as He forms and shapes our lives of worship. These twelve convictions are the basics, the fundamentals involved in being true worshipers. They are the essentials we work on until they become part of us.

You may be wondering, *Where is God finding worshipers these days? Who else is joining the procession?* Before you finish this book, I want to introduce you to some of the others. But I need to warn you: They are not all going to look just like you. When our leader chose His original twelve disciples, there was considerable variety among them. He chose a zealot, who was definitely anti-establishment, and a tax collector, who was definitely pro-establishment, to be on the same team.

Today it is no different. You will discover that your fellow worshipers come from many different backgrounds and perspectives. Among the true worshipers, some are busy with an assignment to work on recovering the radical nature of worship; others may be working on relevance in worship . . . or rootedness . . . and so on. Through the "Five Fingers of Worship," you will come to appreciate that the wondrous tapestry of worship that God is creating is much bigger than the particular aspect of it you are working on yourself.

My Story

I told you about how the Samaritan woman heard and responded to the call to worship. Now I would like to tell you how someone else was apprehended as a worshiper—me. My story does not begin on a hot and dusty day by a well in Samaria but rather in a meeting room in a bank building in Tallahassee, Florida, in 1968. I was a sophomore at Florida State University working on a music degree in theory and composition.

The year before, I had become a Christian through the testimony of my roommate, Bob Sutton. Because of my involvement with Campus Crusade for Christ, I was learning the importance of anchoring my faith and experience in Scripture. In fact, we liked to have a chapter and verse for everything.

There must have been 150 to 200 people in the meeting room that day. I do not remember much about the speaker's message, but what I do remember is that after he had finished, one of the leaders of the meeting said something like, "Let's just lift our voices to God in praise." I was completely unprepared for what followed.

After we sang one of the current popular choruses—I don't remember which one; they were all new to me then—there were some moments of silence. Then gradually there arose the most beautiful, captivating singing I had ever heard. There was not just one single melody; rather, there were many melodies being sung simultaneously. It sounded like an orchestra tuning up with voices instead of instruments. The volume would swell and then subside, and then swell again, as if everyone were watching an unseen Conductor.

Though I had not yet learned of what John and Luke both described as "a sound from heaven" (Revelation 14:2–3; see Acts 2:2), I instinctively knew that this sound was not of this earth. I had not yet done a study on the presence of God, but I was experiencing it firsthand.

The word *captivating* is the best way to describe the effect this music had on me. I was seized, captured and taken in by its irresistible appeal—*Gladly!* I remember saying

18

to myself. *I do not ever want to be very far from this sound.* I enlisted, then and there. Or maybe I should say, Someone enlisted me.

For me, it was like a second conversion. I had been intellectually converted the year before when I agreed to the facts of the Gospel, but this conversion penetrated into my spirit as I encountered the phenomenon of God's presence.

Years later, a conversation with a Nigerian pastor helped me make sense of this. When I asked him to compare Christianity in America with Christianity in Nigeria, he first made sure I wanted an honest answer, and then he said, "In America, you believe; in Nigeria, we worship." Before my second conversion, I was a believer; now I think of myself as a worshiper.

Since then, I have had a growing awareness of heaven's worship and how God plans for it to affect the worship on earth. The reality of God calling our generation to join what Edward Perronet called "the everlasting song" has become increasingly clear to me. In 1988, I wrote the following words in a song entitled "I Hear Angels." Its picture of a symphony of praise arising is the governing vision of my life, and the reason I hope you will accept this call to worship, as well.

> I hear angels singing praises,
> I see men from every nation bowing down before the
>   throne.
> Like the sound of many waters,
> Like a rushing wind around us, multitudes join the song.
> And a symphony of praise arises,
> Tears are wiped away from eyes,
> As men from every tongue and tribe all sing:
>
> Holy, holy, God Almighty,
> Who was and is and is to come.
> All the angels are singing praises
> To the Lamb who sits upon the throne.

I see One who's filled with wonder,
Eyes of fire and voice of thunder, shining bright, His
    Majesty!
All the colors of the rainbow
Circle Him and fill His temple. So beautiful, this is to me!
And a symphony of praise arises,
Tears are wiped away from eyes
As men from every tongue and tribe all sing:

Holy, holy, God Almighty,
Who was and is and is to come.
All creation is bringing glory
To the Lamb who sits upon the throne.

There is a call to worship—do you hear it? The Samaritan woman heard it by the well. I heard it in a bank building in Tallahassee. If you have not heard it already, I pray that you will hear it as you read this book.

When Bilbo ended his initial conversation with Gandalf, it did not seem that he would accept his part in the story, but Gandalf stood outside the door chuckling quietly. Then he made a mark on Bilbo's front door and went on his way. The adventure had begun.

PART 1

DEFINITIONS

The love of Jesus, what it is, none but his loved ones know.

Bernard of Clairvaux

1

DEFINING WORSHIP

Worship is the act and attitude of wholeheartedly giving yourself to God—spirit, soul, mind and body.

Introduction

Because you are reading this book, I am going to assume you have a desire to be God's worshiper. But I am also guessing that somewhere in your mind is a question like this: *Okay, I want to be a worshiper, but what does that really mean?* Or if you are a hard-nosed, somewhat skeptical, you-gotta-convince-me type of person (like me), you are probably wondering, *What's this guy going to tell me about what it means to be a worshiper?*

It does not bother me if you are the kind of person who reads the label carefully before swallowing something. It says to me that when you do let something through the gate, it is yours—you own it. It also says that you will be a persuader of others. So, welcome aboard.

23

Convincing reasons for believing something are important to me, too. And I have found there are two levels of convincing that I need: the objective and the subjective. That is why, to explain what it means to be a worshiper, I will use both definitions and stories.

Definitions are like code used in computer software: If you build the assumptions and relationships correctly, the functions that follow are reliable. Stories, on the other hand, affect us even more deeply. Tell me a story of a hero's courage against the backdrop of corruption and cowardice, and my desire to live courageously for the right is deepened.

In these next two chapters, you will find foundational definitions on which we will build throughout the rest of this book. You will learn first what worship is. You will find lots of challenging implications here for you and your church. You will then learn the definition of a worshiper, what it means to be a priest and the significance of sacrifice. These key definitions will prepare you to understand your priestly history and help you apprehend your prophetic destiny—becoming a part of the functioning kingdom of priests. I hope you will learn these definitions so well that they sink deep into your heart.

Following these definitions, I will take you into an imaginary theater in which you will experience the "Story of Worship," from the singing stars in Genesis to worship's final showdown in Revelation. And all along the way, you will be reminded that this is *your* story—it is about your ancestors, your relatives. But the story does not come to you and stop. It invites you, your family and your church to join the procession and even shape its outcome.

How Simple Is It?

In some ways, it may seem simple to just lay out the reasons, both objective and subjective, for every human being to become a hearty worshiper of God, and—*voila!*—the

Church should immediately have a great harvest of worshipers. Explain it well and communicate the adventure of it all, and who could resist diving in with reckless abandon? Unfortunately, it is not that easy.

I think back to the challenge I received from a history professor at Florida State as I was considering becoming a Christian. I had read about all the alleged historical inaccuracies of the Scriptures, and I figured that this thoughtful Ph.D. and outspoken Christian could help me work through the problems. He did, but his help had a sting to it—a sting for which I will be forever grateful.

When I told him that I had certain intellectual and philosophical problems with the Bible and the claims of Christ, without hesitation he said, "Gerrit, you don't really have an intellectual problem; you have a volitional problem. It's not that you *can't* believe; it's that you *won't* believe." And even though it took me several weeks to agree, he read me right.

Jesus said it like this: "If anyone chooses to do God's will, he will find out whether my teaching comes from God or whether I speak on my own" (John 7:17). In other words, "If you are willing to *do*, then you will *know*." Most of us would like to think that we must know before we can choose to do. But as Dallas Willard says, "Our thoughts and feelings have a crucial dependence on our will, on our choices. . . . What we think is very much a matter of what we wish and seek to think, and what we feel is very much a matter of what we wish and seek to feel."[1]

I talk regularly to church leaders about the difficulty of seeing transformation come into a church's life of worship. My teacher's bent wants to respond: "Just inform them, and transformation will happen." While it is true that thoughts and feelings inform the will, ultimately we must choose to be the worshipers God is seeking *before* we will know what it means to be those worshipers.

So before we begin to engage these definitions and stories, I invite you to take a *selah*, a personal "pause-and-consider" moment. Take a deep breath . . . in the words of the old hymn acknowledge that we are all "prone to wander" . . . and whisper, from the deepest part of your being:

> Here's my heart, O take and seal it,
> Seal it for Thy courts above.

Add to that Tim Hughes' more recent words of commitment:

> Here I am to worship, here I am to bow down,
> Here I am to say that you're my God.
> You're altogether lovely, altogether worthy,
> Altogether wonderful to me!

Pray with me as we begin: *Here we are, Lord, learners wanting to know what it means to be worshipers, beginning by giving ourselves without reservation to You, the worthy and wonderful Lamb of God. Amen.*

Count the Worshipers

If someone asked, could you explain what worship is?

Ask some folks if they are worshipers and you will likely hear something like this: "Well, I don't play an instrument, and I sure don't sing very well. . . . No, I guess I'm not." If the pastor announces a worship conference taking place in the church, these "non-musicians" will probably think it does not apply to them.

We suffer from a lack of clarity as to what Jesus said His Father is seeking—true worshipers—and as a result, we falter in fulfilling our greatest mission. If you are a pastor or church leader, ask yourself this question: *What percentage of those I lead are worshipers?* If you are an evangelist, try this: *Are those who are coming to Christ through my ministry becoming worshipers?* Parents, are your children worshipers? And when was the last time someone described *you* as a worshiper? God is looking for worshipers.

The problem is that it is hard to quantify worshipers. You can count the number of attendees, the money collected and the number of professions of faith or baptisms, but how in the world do you count the number of worshipers? Because we are uncertain about what qualifies someone to be called a worshiper, we seldom use the term to describe one of the faithful. But that is in contrast to the Scriptures.

One of those listening was a woman named Lydia, a dealer in purple cloth from the city of Thyatira, who was a worshiper of God.

Acts 16:14

Then Paul left the synagogue and went next door to the house of Titius Justus, a worshiper of God.

Acts 18:7

True worshipers will worship the Father in spirit and truth, for they are the kind of worshipers the Father seeks.

John 4:23

"Go and measure the temple of God and the altar, and count the worshipers there."

Revelation 11:1

I would like to suggest an assignment to help us recover the word *worshiper*. My eighth-grade English teacher told us the secret of acquiring a new vocabulary word: "Use it three times in a day, and it's yours." As you begin to understand what it means to be a worshiper, begin to consciously use the term to describe your worshiping friends. Set aside the other terms for a while—*Christian, believer,* etc.

27

They are good terms, but we already know them. When the word *worshiper* becomes a regular part of your natural conversation, then you can go back and use the other terms, too.

This assignment—and I hope you will really follow through with it—will actually revive and *fill up* the other terms. The term *believer*, for instance, was never meant to be separated from the response of worship. We will talk more about this in the twelfth conviction, "Worship and the Good News," but, for now, here is an appetizer: Abraham, the father of faith, being "fully persuaded," was "strengthened in his faith and gave glory to God" (Romans 4:20–21). When he truly believed, he worshiped. We, too, when we believe, will worship.

So, what is a worshiper? Simply put, *a worshiper is one who really worships*. The follow-up question would be: What is worship? Here is the definition of worship that I believe will help us "count the worshipers":

> Worship is the act and attitude of wholeheartedly giving yourself to God—spirit, soul, mind and body.

When I conduct a Worship School, I have everyone at this point repeat the definition. So, if you do not mind, say it aloud: *Worship is the act and attitude of wholeheartedly giving yourself to God—spirit, soul, mind and body.* Because you never know when you might have a pop quiz, learn it well.

This definition is based on two key Scriptures: Paul's definition of worship in Romans 12, and the greatest of all commandments, found in Mark 12: "Therefore, I urge you, brothers, in view of God's mercy, to offer your bodies as living sacrifices, holy and pleasing to God—this is your spiritual act of worship" (Romans 12:1); "Love the Lord your God with all your heart and with all your soul and with all your mind and with all your strength" (Mark 12:30).

The *What* and *How* of Worship

There is a *what* and a *how* in this definition of worship. Paul wrote that the essence of worship—the *what*—is utter self-giving, the presenting of ourselves as living sacrifices. And *how* should we give ourselves? Wholeheartedly. That is, with *all* that we are—spirit, soul, mind and body—withholding nothing.

The following is a corny story, but it illustrates what sacrifice is. A chicken and a pig were walking down the road together when they saw a homeless man who looked as though he had not had a good meal in weeks. The chicken, moved with compassion, said to the pig: "Let's help him out and offer him a nice hot bacon-and-egg breakfast."

The pig quickly responded: "That's easy for you to say. For you, it's just an offering. For me, it's a *total sacrifice.*"

Being a worshiper, when it is rightly understood, is about total sacrifice. A soldier told me that in order to deal with the fear of battle, he was taught to approach his enemy in combat "with reckless abandon and utter disregard for personal safety." Our definition of worship points in the same direction: total abandonment and disregard for protecting oneself.

Sometimes I feel that many people are "riding the brakes" when they worship. Many of us are tentative and cautious, maybe even more concerned about what those around us think than what God thinks. The Scriptures call this the "fear of man." It is peer pressure, which adults battle against

29

just as much as teenagers. And when it becomes the governing force in our lives, something besides Jesus has become
our lord. Not good.

So, worship is essentially self-giving. Notice that worship is *not* essentially singing. It includes singing, but it is
much bigger than that. Fundamentally, worship is the act
of giving ourselves to God and His purpose. If there is no
self-giving, there is no worship . . . even if you are singing
all the really great songs.

Years ago I had an experience with my son Brent that
helped me understand self-giving. At the time, my office
was in the basement of our home. Brent, who was probably about ten years old at the time, came in while I was
working and asked me if I wanted to shoot some baskets,
which we often did.

I was involved in some project—I can't remember what—
and was torn between doing something with my son and
finishing my work. But after a brief debate with myself—*A
good Christian dad would spend time with his son* versus *Yeah,
but work is important, too*—I went out to our driveway with
him to play basketball. Well, to be honest, my body went
out there, but the rest of me was still down in my office
working.

After about ten minutes of playing what probably felt to
him like a one-sided game, Brent said, "Dad, if you have
something else to do, we don't have to do this." I was
embarrassed and quickly called the rest of me out of the
office to join us. I *gave myself* to playing with my son, and
the activity turned out to be a lot more enjoyable—for both
of us.

For days after that experience, I knew God was writing
something on my heart about self-giving. (When God
is teaching me something, I never *get it* all at once; it is
always a process.) Here is what I came to understand:
If a ten-year-old boy knows when his dad's heart is not
in what he is doing, you can count on the fact that God

is surely aware when you and I are just going through the motions. God knows exactly how much of us is really involved in our acts of praise. And He expects us to give it our all.

In one of the few times Jesus commented on worship, He said this: "These people honor me with their lips, but their hearts are far from me. They worship me in vain" (Matthew 15:8–9). Just going through the motions equals unacceptable worship.

If worship is total self-giving, how many worshipers did God count last Sunday in your church?

Some Acts of Worship

Back to the definition of worship. Now that we understand *self-giving* and *wholeheartedly*, what is this *acts and attitudes* phrase about? This is where we begin the important process of integrating our hearts, minds, souls and strength. If the resolve to give ourselves to God in worship is genuine, it will inevitably affect our actions and attitudes.

The title of one of Robert Webber's early books, *Worship Is a Verb*, is perfectly to the point. To worship is to do something. Worship is interactive. You do not just listen passively—you engage actively. Even though church leaders often lament passivity among their followers, their church's worship service may be actively reinforcing that inaction. For many people, church is characterized mostly as an exercise in sitting and listening. The worship movement is catalyzing participation and expression.[2]

In contrast, Hebrew worship was much more action-oriented than our worship today. I see God at work in today's emphasis on worship as a recovery of biblical worship, in which our minds and hearts and bodies are more involved and less divided.

31

Let's look at some of the biblically prescribed acts of worship through which we give ourselves to God—spirit, soul, mind and body. Measure your own expression by these tokens of worship. Some of these you will be comfortable with. Some may cause you to reply: "You don't mean we should do *that* in our worship, do you?" It is the ones to which you react the most that you should probably pay the most attention to.

- Thanksgiving: "Give thanks in all circumstances, for this is God's will for you in Christ Jesus" (1 Thessalonians 5:18).

If you practice this act of worship regularly, it will become a habit. But forming this habit of giving thanks—in all circumstances—is a challenging, deep-level reorientation. Every day you live on this earth, you face hundreds of moments in which you can either give thanks or complain and murmur.

Regularly giving thanks is to our spiritual health what regular walking or running is to our physical health.

- Declaring praise: "Through Jesus, therefore, let us continually offer to God a sacrifice of praise—the fruit of lips that confess his name" (Hebrews 13:15).

Similar to giving thanks, declaring praise is a distinctive act of worshipers that involves our mouths. I do not know if you are like me, but at first it was hard to speak out loud what I felt toward God. For some reason I felt that, because God knows our thoughts, it was unnecessary to have to say it aloud. I would have rich thoughts of the greatness of God, but meager words.

When I learned that God designed a close connection between my heart and mouth (see Psalm 116:10; Matthew 12:34; and Romans 10:10), I realized that I was actually diminishing the power of His truth in my life by not declaring praise. Now David's habit is becoming mine: "His praise will always be on my lips" (Psalm 34:1).

- Acts of kindness: "And do not forget to do good and to share with others, for with such sacrifices God is pleased" (Hebrews 13:16).

Along with spoken praise is the praise of service to others. Think of it like this: When the Good Samaritan gave assistance to the helpless man along the side of the road, God heard worship. When you go the extra mile for someone—even by doing something seemingly insignificant—you are worshiping.

Just as some churches are strong with their spoken praise, others worship more with acts of kindness. But we should not practice *either* one *or* the other; we should practice *both*. (For more on this, see the ninth conviction, discussed in chapter 16.)

- Prayer: "The four living creatures and the twenty-four elders fell down before the Lamb. Each one had a harp and they were holding golden bowls full of incense, which are the prayers of the saints" (Revelation 5:8).

The commingling of worship and prayer is found throughout Scripture. Certainly, one of the acts of worship is prayer. As you are praying for your friend at work, God is receiving worship. He loves the fragrance of intercession—it is like incense before Him. The sixth conviction (see chapter 13) is all about the relationship between these two priestly ministries.

- Singing: "I will praise God's name in song" (Psalm 69:30).

Even though worship is not primarily made up of sing-ing—worship is essentially self-giving—the song is still a huge part of worship. As your heart becomes full of the desire to glorify God, your mouth will be filled with song.

Years ago, the Holy Spirit filled my friend Bob Visser with a new love for God. After this experience, Bob, who was a hard-working Dutch farmer in Colorado, an ex-Marine and hardly a musician, attended a family reunion. He told me later that his older brothers were amused at how heartily Bob sang the hymns at church. New hearts overflow with new songs.

- Instrumental music: "Praise him with the sounding of the trumpet . . . with the harp and lyre . . . with tambourine . . . with the strings and flute . . . with the clash of cymbals . . . with resounding cymbals" (Psalm 150:3–5).

When your heart is bursting at the seams with God's praise, it is not strange to want to use every musical sound available to glorify Him. Bring on the guitars; find those in-teresting sounds in your synthesizer; let's hear the cymbals. King David, who had such a heart to make God's praise glorious, actually created musical instruments to magnify his nation's praise (see 2 Chronicles 7:6).

- Lifting of hands: "My lips will glorify you. I will praise you as long as I live, and in your name I will lift up my hands" (Psalm 63:3–4).

If you are not used to doing this, give it a try. You prob-ably already do something similar at an exciting basketball game.

Last weekend in Maine, in a Baptist church I was vis-iting, a 72-year-old man, who had been a member of that church since he was ten, asked, "Do I have to lift my hands?"

I answered: "No, you don't have to—keep them down as long as you can."

Think of it, though, as simply increasing your worship vocabulary. Maybe you already kneel down to pray, giving evidence of humility. In the same way, lifting your hands to God in prayer or worship is an outward and physical way to express your inner heart. In this case, it expresses exultation, surrender and even yearning.

- Bowing down: "At the name of Jesus every knee should bow" (Philippians 2:10).

Throughout Scripture, kneeling, bowing, lying prostrate and even falling down are instinctive responses to God's presence. Years ago, in San Pedro, California, I visited Larry Christensen, a leader in the Lutheran renewal. It impressed me that in his office, along with his library and desk, was an altar where he would kneel and pray. I am also impressed that kneeling is a regular part of worship for most liturgical churches. Evangelical and charismatic churches can learn from this biblical pattern that the liturgical churches have preserved.

- Dancing: "David . . . danced before the LORD with all his might" (2 Samuel 6:14).

You may be thinking, *Dancing . . . uh-oh. We're not really supposed to do that, are we? In our church?*

But before you dismiss the idea of dancing and go on to the next item, bear with me a moment. When I first found this in the Bible, I was probably more uncomfortable with it than you are. I thought that perhaps the verses calling us to praise God with dancing—Psalm 149:3, for instance—were meant for the people in Bible times. Or maybe the translators got their words mixed up. Or maybe God meant that we were to dance only in a figurative sense—as in dancing before Him in our hearts.

Eventually, however, I submitted to the fact that God is smarter than I am, even in this matter. And I came to understand that all of us, but especially people like me who can talk ideas and concepts all day long, need to be exercised in the area of physical and emotional expression. So I dance. And if I can, you can, too. God is not expecting you to be Fred Astaire or Ginger Rogers (my own dancing is more like Tevye's in *Fiddler on the Roof*)—He simply wants your body to express your heart.

- Clapping and shouting: "O clap your hands, all ye people; shout unto God with the voice of triumph" (Psalm 47:1, KJV).

Why is it that the expressions of shouting and clapping are normal and legitimate at your child's soccer game, but they are somehow abnormal in church? True worship involves giving ourselves to God wholeheartedly—and shouting and clapping should be a part of that. Not only will these demonstrative acts help us be more integrated physically and emotionally, but there is something even greater at work here, a power in these expressions that causes results. Jericho's walls collapsed at the sound of Israel's shout (see Joshua 6:20), and when the Ark of the Covenant was brought back to Israel, the roar actually caused the ground to shake (see 1 Samuel 4:5).

Who knows what might happen today if the shout were restored to our worship? In my own life, I have discovered that the shout is God's antidote for depression. If you do not believe me, try it out for yourself. If you find yourself battling depression, get a good worship CD with some energetic praise songs, put it in your car's player, go for a drive out on the interstate, turn the music up loud and shout out the high praises. Those spirits of depression will flee in terror.[3] It is like cleaning out cobwebs from your soul.

- Offerings and tithes: "The gifts you sent . . . are a fragrant offering, an acceptable sacrifice, pleasing to God" (Philippians 4:18).

Giving money, like the other acts of worship, is meant to be symbolic of our giving our very selves to God. In my experience, I have found that worshiping churches are almost always generous churches. The same heart that is truly generous to God in praise will usually be generous in giving to the needs of others

- Any act of obedience to God in faith: "To obey is better than sacrifice" (1 Samuel 15:22).

Our acts of worship are meant to reflect hearts that are devoted to God. And our devotion is proven by our discipleship—by our hearing His voice and obeying His will. There is really no way to separate lives of worship from lives of obedience. The one confirms the other.

Jesus is our example here. He "humbled himself and became obedient to death—even death on a cross!" (Philippians 2:8), and so He offered the perfect sacrifice. Although His sacrifice is unique—He alone atoned for the sins of the whole world—our sacrifices, too, should spring out of lives of grateful obedience.

This list of the acts of worship is certainly not comprehensive. It is just a start. But the most important thing is to actually begin to practice these simple ways of communicating your love to God. In our relationship with God, these expressions are a lot like hugs and kisses in our families—they are acts of love expressed in affection.

Some Attitudes of Worship

Not only are there acts of worship through which we give ourselves to God, but there are attitudes of worship, as well. Think about what David said: "The sacrifices of God are a broken spirit; a broken and contrite heart, O God, you will not despise" (Psalm 51:17). Humility is a disposition of the heart in which God takes great pleasure.

There is a fascinating truth about attitudes: God can see them just as you and I can see a blue sweater that someone else is wearing. "Man looks at the outward appearance, but the LORD looks at the heart" (1 Samuel 16:7). We tell a friend, "I love how you're doing your hair." God says, "Your compassion for those three children who lost their dad is just beautiful." We see suntans; He sees stubbornness. We think the music is out of tune; He loves the simplicity. We think the music is awesome; He sees pretension.

Here are some of the attitudes that God commends in worship:

- Dependence on the Spirit: "True worshipers will worship the Father in spirit" (John 4:23).
- Truthfulness: "True worshipers will worship . . . in . . . truth" (John 4:23).
- Gratitude and reverence: "Let us be thankful, and so worship God acceptably with reverence and awe" (Hebrews 12:28).
- Purity: "Give me an undivided heart" (Psalm 86:11).

- Joy: "Rejoice in the Lord always" (Philippians 4:4).
- Love for justice: "Away with the noise of your songs! . . . But let justice roll on like a river" (Amos 5:23–24).

Of course, there are also attitudes people have during worship that displease Him: impatience, stubbornness, unforgiveness and so on. In 1 Timothy 2:8, He says to "lift up holy hands" (the act) "without anger or disputing" (the attitude). God wants our acts of worship to be connected to the proper attitudes of worship, and so at times we may need to adjust our attitudes and then come back and present our offerings before Him.

I have often imagined that when God looks down at us, He sees something like a spectrum of colors surrounding us. Red might be compassion, white might be the fear of the Lord, blue might be joy. And perhaps these colors have certain sounds that accompany them. When we come before Him and worship, He may take pleasure in the kaleidoscope of beautiful colors or sounds. Or perhaps there are missing colors that He wishes He would see.

The good news about having the right attitude in worship is that God knows we learn in increments. He reveals to us progressively the things He wants to change in our lives. He does not pull the dump truck of His truth up to our lives and pull the lever: "So glad you decided to follow Me. Here, take this." Instead, He gives us little capsules of truth—"little by little" as He says in Exodus 23:30. I am so grateful for His patience with me in every area of my life.

Now let's check on how well you are learning these important definitions. Can you answer these two questions?

1. What is worship?
2. On which two Scriptures is this definition based?

If you need help with the answers to these questions, feel free to review this chapter until you feel comfortable with your knowledge of these concepts. In the next chapter, we will enlarge this definition of worship by discovering more about what it means to be a worshiper.

2

THE CALLING
OF A WORSHIPER

In precise terminology of the law, a priest (*kohen*) is one who may draw near to the divine presence.

Merrill F. Unger

When you become a worshiper, you become part of an emerging company of worshipers from many different nations and many different eras of history—past, present and future—*the kingdom of priests*. You really will not understand what it means to be a worshiper without learning about this incredible family of worshipers. So, let's turn our thoughts to this great company we are joining.

There are two words whose definitions we need to consider: *priest* and *sacrifice*. There are also two principles: the *God-answers-sacrifice principle* and the *power-to-bless principle*.

What Is a Priest?

Here is our working definition of the word *priest*:

> A priest is a worshiper who draws near to God, offering gifts and sacrifices, and who represents the needs of others.

Few truths have had more impact on my life than the connection between being a worshiper and being a priest. I knew that I loved to worship, and I was aware that somehow when I worshiped I actually went through invisible gates and entered God's very presence. But it was not until I realized that a worshiper is a priest and a priest is a worshiper that I began to understand the incredible significance of the current emphasis on worship.

I am not a language scholar, but thanks to Bible dictionaries I learned of the close relationship between two Hebrew words: *kohen*, meaning "a priest," and *qarab*, meaning "to bring, present, offer, draw near or approach." As I was studying this one day, my eyes fell on these words from *Unger's Bible Dictionary*: "In precise terminology of the law, a priest (*kohen*) is one who may draw near to the divine presence."[1] I know that sounds dramatic—telling you that *my eyes fell on these words*—but it was true. And it changed my life, just as it could change yours.

Every good worshiper knows Psalm 100:4: "Enter his gates with thanksgiving and his courts with praise." How many times have we sung those words? But now, Dr. Unger has come along and told us that we who are drawing near to God in worship are priests.

That is why this worship movement is so significant. In our day, the Church is to become an activated priesthood, fulfilling the ancient passion of God's own heart. A priest is one who draws near and presents a gift. A worshiper does the same: He draws near to God and presents a gift.

Draw near to worship. In the New Testament, there is a word that carries the same meaning: *proserchomai*. In Hebrews 10:1, it is translated as "those who draw near to worship." So, the essence of being a priest and being a worshiper is the same. That means that if you are a worshiper, you are a priest. Mentally acknowledge this truth: *I am a priest.* Now say it out loud using your own name: (*Your name*) is a priest. Now go tell your wife or husband or best friend: "I am a priest."

Spend some time with this thought, because this is a profound component of your own identity and destiny. This realization links you with your own unknown spiritual ancestry. The impact on your life may well be similar to the orphan's discovery of his biological parents and his lineage. It can help to explain the things that are stirring deep inside of you.

There is another major element in understanding what a priest is (and who you are): Priests do not only draw near to God for their own enjoyment; they also do so to represent the needs of others. We will develop this more thoroughly when we get to the sixth conviction and learn how entering God's presence in worship allows us to extend His purpose in prayer (see chapter 13). But think about this: On the high priest's breastplate, which he wore when he entered God's presence, were twelve precious stones with the names of the twelve tribes of Israel engraved on them. Near his heart were the names of those he represented as he went before God with his sacrifices. My fellow priests, that holy task is yours, too. God has already given you a sphere of relationships and a circle of concerns. Wear them near your heart as you enjoy God's presence. It could change history.

Priests Offer Sacrifices

To become those worshipers God is seeking, we must understand sacrifice. I think you will find this to be more of an exciting subject than it sounds. Simply put:

> A sacrifice is a unit of worship.

Scripture says that no one is to appear before God empty-handed (see Deuteronomy 16:16). Heaven's protocol is that we enter His presence with a gift. You can still see this today in some cultures, in which gift-giving is an essential expression of honor between guests and hosts. It is certainly meant to be an integral part of a worshiper's access to God. The gifts we bring are sacrifices, and sacrifices are tokens of giving ourselves. King David said it like this: "I will not sacrifice to the LORD my God burnt offerings that cost me nothing" (2 Samuel 24:24).

Think of a sacrifice as a unit of worship, just as an inch is a unit of distance or an hour is a unit of time. At some points in our history the units of worship were bountiful, and other times they were meager. Contrast the priests under King Solomon, for instance, with the priests under King Ahaz. Under Solomon, the sacrifices were so many they could not be numbered (see 2 Chronicles 5:6). But under Ahaz, "They did not burn incense or present any burnt offerings at the sanctuary to the God of Israel" (2 Chronicles 29:7). What followed? In the early years of Solomon's reign, God's presence filled the Temple, and the nation experienced the pinnacle of its greatness. But under Ahaz, God's anger fell on Judah and the people became an object of scorn and a conquered nation. *May the worship in our churches be like that of Solomon's reign rather than that of Ahaz's reign.*

When our sacrifices are meager or improper, it is as if we are an engine that needs a tune-up; we are simply not working as we were designed to work. I pray that God will raise up a host of "worship counselors" who will intelligently advise the leaders of our churches, and even nations, of the whys and hows of regularly honoring God. To get a vision of what could happen—both in our churches and nations—read about the "worship tune-ups" that took place under Hezekiah and Josiah (see 2 Chronicles 29–31 and 2 Chronicles 34–35:19, respectively). As you do, translate the Old Testament "shadows" of sheep and cattle and burnt offerings into the New Testament "realities" of worship in spirit and truth. In both cases, national renewal began with restoring sacrifices.[2]

But Doesn't the Bible Say . . .

Many of us mistakenly have a vague theological notion that sacrifice is really not that important to God. We may call to mind verses like Psalm 51:16 ("You do not delight in sacrifice") or Hebrews 7:27 ("He sacrificed for their sins once for all") and we conclude that the sacrificial system is over.

Let's look more carefully at these passages so that we do not maintain any underlying reason to minimize the importance of sacrifice. In Psalm 51, David was making the same point that Jesus did when He said in Matthew 15:8–9: "These people honor me with their lips, but their hearts are far from me. They worship me in vain." Both were saying that external expression without heart connection is empty and meaningless. God gets weary of such worship.

David better defined sacrifice when he went on to say: "The sacrifices of God are a broken spirit; a broken and contrite heart, O God, you will not despise. . . . Then there will be righteous sacrifices, whole burnt offerings to delight you" (Psalm 51:17, 19). Or to paraphrase: "God does not delight in outward acts of worship alone, but in sacrifices that are vitally connected with humble hearts; when our hearts are right, then our outward acts of worship are pleasing to God."

With regard to the "once-for-all" sacrifice of Jesus, we must distinguish between a sin offering and a thank offering. Jesus did offer the final sacrifice for our sins. The solution for human sin is not pending; it is finished. But that awesome act of love should be met with volcanic sacrifices of praise. In fact, the writer of Hebrews—the same one who described Christ's once-for-all sacrifice—went on to exhort us to offer sacrifices of praise continually (see Hebrews 13:15).

There is a huge difference between the sacrifices in the Old and New Testaments. There is no longer any need for the high priest to make annual sacrifices of animals to atone for our sins; Christ has taken care of that. But although animal sacrifices are now obsolete—they were simply foreshadowing greater, more costly sacrifices—the New Testament never implies that the time of offering sacrifices is over. We are now to offer different sacrifices, as the following passages suggest: "I urge you, brothers, in view of God's mercy, to offer your bodies as living sacrifices, holy and pleasing to God—this is your spiritual act of worship" (Romans 12:1); "They [the financial gifts] are a fragrant offering, an acceptable sacrifice, pleasing to God" (Philippians 4:18); "Through Jesus, therefore, let us continually offer to God a sacrifice of praise—the fruit of lips that confess his name" (Hebrews 13:15); "And do not forget to do good and to share with others, for with such sacrifices God is pleased" (Hebrews 13:16).

The new sacrifices we are to offer are lives laid down in utter submission to God, spoken praise, generosity and acts of kindness toward others—all of which were meant to accompany even the Old Testament sacrifices.

In fact, offering sacrifices is fundamental, not incidental, to the Church's existence. It is our *teleological nature*, meaning that it has to do with our inherent design or purpose. First Peter 2:5 declares, "You also, like living stones, are being built into a spiritual house to be a holy priesthood, offering spiritual sacrifices acceptable to God through Jesus Christ." We are being built together for the purpose of offering acceptable sacrifices to God.

How I hope that you begin to approach this subject of sacrifice devotionally rather than just academically. I once heard Francis Frangipane distinguish between *teaching* and *training*. Teaching, he said, is the process of imparting the information; training is the process in which the Holy Spirit brings us into the experience of what we were taught.

Pray with me: *Holy Spirit, take these facts about sacrifice and let them become governing truths in our lives. Open the heavenly closet and take out the priestly garments of praise. Help us wear them frequently so that we can function as priestly worshipers in Your kingdom. Amen.*

The Power of an Acceptable Sacrifice

There is more ground yet to cover before we leave the subject of sacrifice, and it, too, is exciting. Here is the first principle in capsule form:

God answers sacrifice.

There is a clear correlation between acceptable sacrifice and God's intervention. Here are some examples:

- *Abram's sacrifice.* In Genesis 15, Abraham questioned the promises given to him by God. God then directed him to prepare a sacrifice. When he did, God renewed His word to Abram and punctuated it with a flaming torch that passed between the flayed animals. It is a story of sacrifice and divine response.

- *Moses' sacrifice.* In the last few verses of Leviticus 9, Moses and Aaron were offering sacrifices in the Tent of Meeting. The glory of God appeared, and "fire came out from the presence of the Lord and consumed the burnt offering and the fat portions on the altar" (verse 24). This is another story of sacrifice and divine response.

- *David's sacrifice.* A plague had struck Israel because of David's sin, and seventy thousand people died. Stricken, "David built an altar to the Lord there and sacrificed burnt offerings and fellowship offerings. Then the Lord answered prayer in behalf of the land, and the plague on Israel was stopped" (2 Samuel 24:25). Again, acceptable sacrifice, divine response.

- *Solomon's sacrifice.* We find a similar story of sacrifice and divine response in 2 Chronicles 7: "Fire came down from heaven and consumed the burnt offering and the sacrifices, and the glory of the Lord filled the temple" (verse 1).

- *Elijah's sacrifice.* In 1 Kings 18, in the "Showdown at Mount Carmel," we can see a contrast between the results of the unacceptable sacrifices of the prophets of Baal and the acceptable sacrifice of Elijah. Regarding the first, "there was no response; no one answered" (verse 26). But when Elijah offered his sacrifice, "the fire of the Lord fell and burned up the sacrifice," and the whole nation of Israel cried out, "The Lord—he is God! The Lord—he is God!" (verses 38–39). And "the god who answers by fire" answered (verse 24). I was challenged one day when the Lord seemed to ask me, *Which is more typical in today's churches: "No one answered" or "The fire of the Lord fell"?*

- *Paul's sacrifice.* One more story—this one in the New Testament, Acts 16:22–32—shows the principle in dramatic fashion. It was midnight, and Paul and Silas were prisoners in the inner cell of a Macedonian jail. Although they had been stripped and "severely flogged," they were not complaining. Instead they were "praying and singing." That is what I call apostolic faith. Every true sacrifice is precious to God, but there is something about the sacrifice of praise offered in the midst of suffering that touches His heart deeply. What was God's response this time? An earthquake opened the prison doors and caused the jailer to know the reality of God. That night he and his whole household became followers of God and were filled with joy.

These are just a few of the many stories that illustrate the principle that God answers sacrifice. Once you understand the principle, you will see it throughout the biblical record—and in your own life.

I first began to see the implications of this principle in an Episcopal church in Destin, Florida, around 1989. Don Moen and I were conducting a worship renewal weekend, and on Sunday morning, I enjoyed seeing how their musicians led in worship, mixing historic worship hymns with fresh new worship songs. But what really gripped me was the simple practice they had of waiting for God to respond after their worship.

When they waited, God answered. After a time of quiet expectation, an older gentleman stood and spoke with obvious authority: "I believe the Lord is saying to us that . . ." (a word of specific direction and emphasis followed). Later there was prayer for the sick, and they expected the Spirit to quicken healing just as He had inspired prophecy. I learned that there was a long list of miracles this congregation had experienced because they frequently waited on

God to respond. They worshiped, they waited expectantly and God responded.

Most churches do it differently. Just after worship, just as the Holy Spirit is about to move and fill the Temple with His glory, someone will pop up to let us all know that the annual men's pancake breakfast will be at 7:30 in the fellowship hall this Saturday instead of 7:00.

In the story of Elijah's sacrifice, God's prophet confronted the prophets of Baal. Elijah told Ahab that God was going to answer his prayers by fire. So what do you think he did after he prayed? It is not recorded, but I think he backed up! "Lord, is this far enough? Maybe another fifteen yards? How's this?" Suddenly—*FFWHOOOOOSH!* (That is the sound of fire falling.) It is always wise to make room for God to move.

What would happen if our churches really began to believe that it is still standard procedure for fire to fall when acceptable sacrifices are offered? I believe we would begin to make room for God.

Now, I certainly hope that we will not degrade this truth and turn it into a gimmick to try to get God to do whatever we want. The fact is, you cannot manipulate God, no matter how hard you try. It did not work for Mrs. Zebedee, who came to Jesus and tried to use her worship to win her sons' spiritual promotion (see Matthew 20:20–21, KJV)—and it will not work for you, either.

It always bothers me when I hear church leaders say that they want to use worship as a means to "grow their churches." Worship is not a means to do anything. It may affect the growth of your church, but you should worship God because He is worthy. Period.

When we do worship Him for who He is, He is delighted to reveal His glory, His intervening power. His own Word assures it: "He who sacrifices thank offerings honors me, and he prepares the way so that I may show him the salvation of God" (Psalm 50:23). Our Spirit-led worship creates an atmosphere that accelerates His Kingdom activity in and around us.

When Is Worship Unacceptable?

Can worship ever be unacceptable to God? If so, what determines a sacrifice to be *acceptable* or *unacceptable*? Follow me on this. According to Jesus, Spirit and truth are the two pillar qualities of true worship. (We will consider this further in chapter 9, regarding the second conviction.) So, we could say:

> An acceptable sacrifice is an offering that is pleasing to God, in harmony with His Spirit and in accordance with His truth.

And the converse:

> An unacceptable sacrifice is an offering that is offensive to God, violating either His Spirit or His truth.

The obvious fact is that not all worship is acceptable. We see this from the very beginning of the Bible (Abel's worship was acceptable; Cain's was not) to the very end of the Bible (the worship of the Lamb in contrast to the worship of the beast).[3] The idea that any old offering will do just does not jibe with the record. God has specifications for worship. Let's look at some further examples and see if we can tell what He does not like.

Here are four categories of unacceptable worship:

- The worship of false gods.

The first two of the Ten Commandments make this perfectly clear—no other gods, and no worshiping of idols (see Exodus 20:3–6).

- The worship of God mixed with the worship of idols.

Not an outright denial of God, this behavior may be harder to recognize because God is still being worshiped. With our culture's value of tolerance and celebration of pluralism, this may be one of the Christian's most easily overlooked temptations. We see it in Scripture: "Even while these people were worshiping the LORD, they were serving their idols" (2 Kings 17:41).

- The worship of the true God in a wrong way.

Here is a verse from 1 Chronicles. Can you tell if the worship was acceptable or unacceptable? "David and all the Israelites were celebrating with all their might before God, with songs and with harps, lyres, tambourines, cymbals and trumpets" (1 Chronicles 13:8). Seems like a no-brainer, doesn't it? The worship was wholehearted; their worship leader was a man after God's heart; they were worshiping before God.

It may seem strange to us, but God was not at all happy with the worship that day. He was so upset, in fact, that He even killed one of their worship leaders.

Here is what was going on. The leaders, in returning the Ark of the Covenant to its proper place, were careless about how they handled it, carrying it on an oxcart rather than on the shoulders of consecrated priests. King David's painful acknowledgment was: "It was because you, the Levites, did not bring it up the first time that the

LORD our God broke out in anger against us. We did not inquire of him about how to do it in the prescribed way" (1 Chronicles 15:13).

People come up with all kinds of ways to discount this kind of passage: "That was the Old Testament; we live under the New Testament now." Or "God was a God of judgment back then; now we are under grace." But behind our aversion to the idea of God being upset with our worship is, I believe, a desire to try to make Him into our own image. We want to domesticate Him.

I love the dialogue in C. S. Lewis' *The Lion, the Witch and the Wardrobe* in which Susan and Lucy, upon hearing about Aslan, ask Mr. Beaver if Aslan is a man.

> "Aslan a man!" said Mr. Beaver sternly. "Certainly not. I tell you he is the King of the wood and the son of the great Emperor-beyond-the Sea. Don't you know who is the King of Beasts? Aslan is a lion—*the* Lion, the great Lion."
>
> "Ooh!" said Susan. "I'd thought he was a man. Is he— quite safe? I shall feel rather nervous about meeting a lion."
>
> "That you will, dearie, and make no mistake," said Mrs. Beaver; "if there's anyone who can appear before Aslan without their knees knocking, they're either braver than most or else just silly."
>
> "Then he isn't safe?" said Lucy.
>
> "Safe?" said Mr. Beaver; "don't you hear what Mrs. Beaver tells you? Who said anything about being safe? 'Course he isn't safe. But he's good. He's the King, I tell you."[4]

So, let's give up trying to tame this God we serve. And in worship, let's adjust to His specifications rather than try to convince Him of ways to improve them.

- The worship of the true God in the right way but with a wrong attitude.

Ananias and Sapphira were putting money into the offering plate. Seems like a fine thing to do. They were not worshiping false gods, and they were not doing anything forbidden. How could God not be happy with that? But God saw something other people might have missed—He saw a gift tainted by bold dishonesty, and He could not accept their offering.

I have to confess, it is hard for me to picture the rest of the story—but God took their lives, right there in the meeting. They died. The last thing they heard was Peter's rebuke. The ushers came in, carried out their bodies and buried them. (See Acts 5:1–11.)

I am sure that if I had been there, I would have silently protested, *God, why did You do that?* Wouldn't you? I mean, wouldn't that make it just a little difficult to invite your neighbors to church?

"Come join us some Sunday. It is never boring."

"Yeah, I've heard!"

The point is: God does have certain dislikes. And it is just as important to learn these dislikes as it is to learn what He likes.

God does not like worship mixed with anger or contention (see 1 Timothy 2:8), broken relationships (see Matthew 5:23–24), a lack of concern for God's people (see Amos 6:5–6) or a lack of respect for God (see Malachi 1:6–14). He does not like it when we place human traditions above His Word (see Matthew 15:6–9), and He does not like legalism (see Galatians 5:4) or carnality (see Romans 8:8) to be found among His people or in their worship.

Pray with me: *Lord Jesus, You are our High Priest. It is under You that we take our place as priests. Please teach us the difference between acceptable and unacceptable worship, and may our offerings be always pleasing to You.*

Sacrifice and the Power to Bless

Related to the God-answers-sacrifice principle is the power-to-bless principle. It goes like this:

The power to bless the world around you is a direct result of your ministry to the Lord.

You will find this amazing principle in Deuteronomy 10:8: "At that time the LORD set apart the tribe of Levi to carry the ark of the covenant of the LORD, to stand before the LORD to minister and to pronounce blessings in his name, as they still do today." The priests were to (1) bear the Ark, (2) minister before the Lord and (3) proclaim blessings. Put simply, they were to (1) practice the presence of God, (2) worship and (3) bless. As we practice the presence of God and worship Him, we are empowered to bless the world around us. Utterly amazing.

So, what does it mean to bless? Here is a good definition: *Blessing is the impartation of benefit, usually by the spoken word.* According to Scripture, our words have the power of life and death (see Proverbs 18:21). Effective blessings can set in motion the course of a life. When Isaac mistakenly pronounced his blessing on Jacob, thinking he was Esau, it could not be reversed (see Genesis 27:1–40). Blessings can even determine the course of your city: "Through the blessing of the upright a city is exalted" (Proverbs 11:11).

Ultimately, God wants His people to bless the nations. Abraham's calling was to bless the nations, and we who walk in the faith he modeled have inherited that calling.[5] That means we are called to bless the nations, and it begins with practicing His presence and ministering before Him.

I once met a woman at a worship conference in Fairfax, Virginia, on whose heart God had placed the nation of Albania. Although she had never been there, she had read everything she could find about that country and constantly brought the people of Albania before the Lord. Her interest created an interest in me.

Years later, I realized that this woman's prayers were most likely part of what led to the end of the Communist rule in Albania. I thought of her when Albania was writing a new constitution and a Christian constitutional expert was brought in to help, and again when I saw a video of a large Christian outreach held in an Albanian stadium.

I read just this morning a fascinating account of how Rees Howells, the Welsh intercessor of the early 1900s, and his fellow intercessors at the Bible College of Wales discovered the power to bless the nations. In September 1940, when Germany's Goering made his bold attempt to gain mastery of the air in preparation for the invasion of England, this hidden band of intercessors exercised their priestly ministry on behalf of England.

First, *they practiced God's presence*. Three years before: "An awful sense of God's nearness began to pervade over the whole college. There was a solemn expectancy. . . . God was there."[6] Second, *they ministered unto the Lord*. They learned the importance of presenting themselves as living sacrifices.[7] And third, *they pronounced blessing*. "We prayed last night [September 11] that London would be defended and that the enemy would fail to break through, and God answered prayer."[8]

Howells' biographer, Norman Grubb, tells the story:

Mr. Churchill, in his *War Memoirs*, cites September 15 as "the culminating date" in that Battle of the Air. He tells

56

how he visited the Operations Room of the RAF that day and watched as the enemy squadrons poured over and ours went up to meet them, until the moment came when he asked the Air Marshal, "What other reserves have we?" "There are none," he answered, and reported afterwards how grave Mr. Churchill looked, "and well I might," added Mr. Churchill. Then another five minutes passed, and "it appeared that the enemy was going home. The shifting of the discs on the table showed a continuous eastward movement of German bombers and fighters. No new attack appeared. In another ten minutes the action was ended." There seemed no reason why the *Luftwaffe* should have turned for home, just at the moment when victory was in their grasp.

After the war, Air Chief Marshal Lord Dowding, Commander-in-Chief of Fighter Command in the Battle of Britain, made this significant comment: "Even during the battle one realized from day to day how much external support was coming in. At the end of the battle one had the sort of feeling that there had been some special Divine intervention to alter some sequence of events which would have otherwise occurred."[9]

Just like the prayer warriors of that day, you and I can also bless nations through the power-to-bless principle. And like them, our words of blessing toward those in our sphere of life will be charged as we practice God's presence and minister before Him in worship.

I want to learn to speak effective blessings, don't you? It is a priestly function. Worshipers, practice His presence, bring your sacrifices of praise before Him and declare blessings on the people in your life and the nations of the world.

I can imagine that maybe after a time of worship in the early Church, Epaphroditus stands up to read the opening words of Paul's letter to the church in Philippi: "Grace and peace to you from God our Father and the Lord Jesus Christ" (Philippians 1:2). As he reads, an impartation of actual grace and peace takes place, and the believers there likely look at each other and say the equivalent of, "Wow. What was that?" In my imagination, I can see the words of Paul's blessing launch out of Epaphroditus' mouth almost like water balloons, some filled with God's grace and others with His peace. When they hit their targets, they burst, splashing all over the people and leaving a glowing fragrance behind.

The power to bless the world around you is a direct result of your ministry to the Lord.

The Kingdom of Priests

Visualize with me a huge multitude of priests from every people group imaginable who have learned to practice God's presence, to minister to Him and to proclaim blessings. Do you see it? You are looking at what the Bible calls *the kingdom of priests.*

It was around 1984 when I first became intrigued by this phrase: *the kingdom of priests.* In Exodus 19, God used it to describe what He wanted His people to become. As a songwriter, I love it when words team up to create a "chemical reaction" and implications spin off like smoke from incense, intoxicating my imagination with wonder. This phrase created in me a kind of slow-motion epiphany. The more I thought about it, the more I was fascinated by its power. Slowly the picture of a priestly kingdom came into focus.

I already had a deep respect for the phrase, *the Kingdom of God*—the realm of God's uncontested will, the transcendent sphere in which His ways are freely chosen—or, my favorite, the culture of God.

But when I saw that the atmosphere of the Kingdom of God was one of worship, I realized that the current emphasis on worship is not just another fad, soon to be replaced by yet another. Instead, it is a mega-trend with a capital *M*, sent from God to acclimate us for heaven.

I hope this phrase grips you, too, so that when you hear it, clocks stop and something deep inside you stands at attention. Let's see if we can define it accurately. First, a simple definition: *The kingdom of priests is God's worship-filled Kingdom.*

Now, a more "juicy" definition:

> The kingdom of priests is the international, transcultural, wholehearted, Spirit-filled community of reigning worshipers in heaven and earth.

It is international. Around the throne of God (and increasingly on planet Earth), this great company of worshipers comes from every nation. Jewish worshipers (*King David, so glad to meet you. Have you written any new songs?*), Brazilian worshipers (*Have you heard the chords they play on their guitars?*), Italian worshipers (*They are fixing the food for the Great Feast*), Chinese worshipers (*Where are we going to put all of them?*) and American worshipers (*They have all the good gear*)—all will be praising God together.

Some of us get nervous when there is talk about cultural diversity, because often those who speak most about it tend to go soft on the Kingdom requirements of repentance and faith in Christ. Stick to the requirements, but it is a huge mistake to react and withdraw into monocultural anthropomorphism. That is the misconception that God has only one or two grooves that He really enjoys, which just so happen to be the same as mine.[10]

That position is not faithful to Scripture. Romans 1:20 says that God's invisible qualities are clearly known through His creation. Does God enjoy diversity? For the answer, check out the part of His creation called the animal kingdom. What was He thinking when He made the rhinoceros? I bet He laughed out loud with utter joy and satisfaction when He put the trunk on the elephant. And then, probably in the same millisecond, He designed the butterfly. If He created the butterfly and the rhinoceros, He likes diversity. Furthermore, He created the nations, making them different on purpose. He does not mind subcultures in His Kingdom.

I am a big fan of John Stott, one of the chief architects of the Lausanne Covenant of 1974. That historic document, which is my own statement of faith, became the basis of cooperation and unity among thousands of Christian organizations. Its tenth section, entitled "Evangelism and Culture," calls for "churches deeply rooted in Christ and closely related to their culture." In that same section, you will find these carefully chosen words:

> Culture must always be tested and judged by Scripture. Because men and women are God's creatures, some of their culture is rich in beauty and goodness. Because they are fallen, all of it is tainted with sin and some of it is demonic. The gospel does not presuppose the superiority of any culture to another, but evaluates all cultures according to its own criteria of truth and righteousness, and insists on moral absolutes in every culture. Missions have all too frequently exported with the gospel an alien culture and churches have sometimes been in bondage to culture rather than to Scripture. Christ's evangelists must humbly seek to empty themselves of all but their personal authenticity in order to become the servants of others, and churches must seek to transform and enrich culture, all for the glory of God.[11]

The kingdom of priests is transcultural. That is, it is bigger and greater than our smaller subcultures. Like a prism, it takes the pure light of God and displays it in multifaceted splendor. It is an exquisite collection of worshipers diverse in expression but strikingly similar in spirit. They are all wholehearted in their humility, wonder, reverence, joy and gratitude.

But what is the part of the definition that describes these worshipers as reigning? It is all part of the Kingdom's description found in the lyrics of one of heaven's most popular songs: "You have made them to be a kingdom and priests to serve our God, and they will reign on the earth" (Revelation 5:10; see also Revelation 20:6; 22:5). These are worshipers who rule and rulers who worship. Worshiping is their passion; implementing God's will is their privilege. (More on this in the sixth conviction, chapter 13.)

Worship is a lot like a hyperlink between heaven and earth. You start worshiping, and the next thing you know, you have clicked over to another domain, and "the things of earth . . . grow strangely dim in the light of His glory and grace."[12]

There is an interplay between heaven's worship and earth's. Sometimes theirs inspires ours; other times, ours inspires theirs. Certainly, we should be in awe of the pristine purity of their unstained songs, but they are equally awed by the unique flavor of the songs of the redeemed. The relationship is like that of two great antiphonal choirs: They sing their part, and we respond; we sing ours, and they respond; and sometimes we sing together. This kingdom of priests is headquartered in heaven, but headquarters is most interested in its earthly franchises.

You are meant to be a citizen in this kingdom of priests. It is not some inaccessible, mystic sweet communion. It is mystic and sweet, yes; but it is not inaccessible. The doorway is even closer to your heart than this book is to your eyes. And although your participation with this great multitude does require a significant commitment, it can begin today. Start placing God in the center of your life, actively worship Him and do so wholeheartedly.

As you and your church pass Worship 101 and move on to Worship 201 (and so forth), the quantity and quality of acceptable sacrifices will increase. Heaven's culture is invading your neighborhood. The adventure, begun long ago, continues.

But you cannot bookmark the next page and go to bed just yet. You have to convince me you are ready to leave "Worship Defined." Here is your next pop quiz:

1. Define worship.
   Worship is _____
   _____.[13]

2. What is a priest?
   A priest is _____
   _____.[14]

3. What is a sacrifice?
   A sacrifice is _____
   _____.[15]

4. State the power-to-bless principle.
   The power to bless the world aound you is _____
   _____.[16]

5. For extra points, define the kingdom of priests.
   The kingdom of priests is _____
   _____.[17]

You have done well. We have covered a lot of ground. Get some rest and come back tomorrow. I want to tell you the most astounding story ever. It has heroes and villains, victories and tragedies. It takes us back to the singing stars of the ancient past, and looks forward into an epic conflict between a Lamb and a Beast. It is the Story of Worship, the adventure that is ready and waiting for you.

PART 2

STORIES

> If you would understand anything, observe its beginning and its development.
>
> Aristotle

"Look to the rock from which you were cut and to the quarry from which you were hewn; look to Abraham, your father, and to Sarah, who gave you birth. When I called him he was but one, and I blessed him and made him many."

Isaiah 51:1–2

3

BEGINNINGS

SINGING STARS AND OTHER
PRIMAL CHARACTERS

"Once upon a time . . ."

>Favorite opening line for many storytellers

"In the beginning, God . . ."

>Favorite opening line for the greatest Storyteller

Introduction

There is a movie that my son Gates and I have enjoyed called *The Master of Disguise*. This rather silly story is about a boy named Pistachio Disguisey who grows up with a propensity toward imitating other people's speech and behavior. His father, a restaurant owner in America, had kept from him the fact that he was from a centuries-long line of famous masters of disguise. When the father is kidnapped, the grandfather comes into the boy's life and tells him who he is, who his great-grandfathers were and what they had done. He then tutors him in the family's craft. Of course, the boy learns quickly, discovers his destiny and uses his newfound skills to rescue his dad.

I told you it was silly. But there is a truth in the story that is irrefutable: You will understand yourself better when you understand your history.

You were called to be a worshiper—it is in your spiritual DNA. You may already be aware of some of the built-in impulses you have toward this calling. But I am willing to bet there is an "Oh, I see" in the pages ahead that will deepen your motivation to fulfill that calling. As you learn of some of the particular events in the story that follows, you may know right away what you should say to your worship team or to your elders about the worship in your church, or at least you may know better how you should pray. It may be that you will understand that the local struggles you are facing are actually part of a much larger struggle, and that your faithfulness is more important than you thought.

Rather than just going from the facts of one event to another, I would like to take you into an imaginary theater and have you watch an enactment of the Story of Worship.[1] In this theater, which is a high-tech blend of cinema and stage, we will go from scene to scene, beginning in Genesis at the dawn of Creation and working through events until the great multitude appears and every nation, tongue and tribe sings with all creation that glorious song of tribute to the Lamb. There will be two main characters: the Storyteller, usually unseen, and the Teacher, who will carry us along, prompting the players and occasionally instructing the audience.

Better hurry. The overture is about to begin.

Act 1, Scene 1: The Singing Stars

The music winds down and the lights dim. All is dark and quiet for almost two minutes. Then, faintly, a distant sound is heard. We cannot tell if it is a single instrument or many. It might be a single voice or perhaps many voices. As the sound seems to come closer, a light shines out of the blackness and, accompanying the sound, grows in power.

In a strange way, the sound and the light seem to be woven together into a single, unified energy—not separated as we usually experience them. As the sound comes closer, we hear at times a polyphony of voices, instruments and melodies, accompanied by a kaleidoscope of colors and designs, and at times a unison, accompanied by the simple power of bright whiteness. The light's brightness and colors seem to dance with the sound's changes of voicing, pitch and volume.

Words from the Storyteller mark the opening scene: "In the beginning, God created the heavens, and in the heavens He placed many brilliant stars. The stars were instructed not just to shine, but also to sing. He gave them voices like His own, and they sang of His greatness and glory.

"And then, with the music turned up, God got busy laying the earth's foundation. There was not a trace of discord as the stars worshiped together. God was loving it—and what music it was. As the ocean depths were formed, brilliant combinations of tones and rhythms emanated from an unfettered heavenly creativity. As majestic mountains appeared, awesome sonic splashes and roars filled the skies. Clouds were created to be the sea's garments, while the angels shouted for joy. And God Himself was energized by the sounds as He worked.

"How do we know all this? Many years later, God told His friend Job all about it (see Job 38:4–11)."

The drama suspends as the Teacher comes to the stage and the theater becomes a classroom. "What's the story telling us?" he asks. "Simply this: Creation took place during worship, and worship's mark is everywhere. That's how the inclination to glorify God was built into every cubic inch of creation—every stone (see Luke 19:40), every tree (see Psalm 96:12), every hill (see Psalm 114:4), every ocean (see Psalm 93:3), every animal (see Revelation 5:13) and certainly all of humanity (see Revelation 15:4). Music was playing in the delivery room, and the baby's got it in her bones."

All creation is eagerly waiting for glory to be found among the redeemed (see Romans 8:18–21).

Scene 2: Two Brothers, Two Traditions

Here is the visual backdrop: a gentle rain in the mountain highlands. A slow-motion close-up shows two drops falling to earth just inches apart. Two different frames follow the paths of these two drops down different streams to different rivers to different oceans.[2]

The scenes change, and various characters appear and converse as prompted by the Storyteller.

We hear the Storyteller's voice: "There once were two brothers born to famous parents. Like the two raindrops that fell inches apart and yet flowed to two different oceans, these brothers became like the headwaters of two very different traditions. Their names were Cain and Abel.

"Growing up, they heard their parents talk about how wonderful it was when they first got married. The neighborhood where they had first lived sounded incredible. But apparently some bad decisions were made, and hard times followed. The boys never saw that neighborhood, but Abel asked many times about that wonderful place. On occasion, the boys overheard their parents arguing at night about whose fault it was they had had to move. Cain could never forget those heated discussions.

"As they grew older, the brothers started businesses: Cain was a farmer, and Abel, a rancher. Both became successful, but their hearts were bent in different directions. Abel was a grateful, trusting person; his older brother seemed driven, and forcefully determined to be the more successful.

"Did I mention that both Cain and Abel were quite religious? That's right, but the ways in which they expressed their devotion were not at all similar. How? Well, you'd often get the idea that Cain's worship was fueled by duty or obligation; it rather reflected his own ambition. It was as though he was trying to earn points and establish his own importance, and it seemed outward and mechanical.

"Abel's worship, on the other hand, was of a different character. It was humble and heartfelt, as though he worshiped because he really loved God, not because he was trying to prove anything to Him. Abel's worship was more inward, joyful and genuine.

"One time over dinner at their parents' house, Cain became openly critical of his brother, accusing him of spiritual pride and thinking that he was more highly favored. Their mother talked to their father later that night: 'Adam, I'm concerned about Cain's anger and jealousy toward Abel. Don't you think you should talk with him?'

"Unfortunately, nothing was done, and a few weeks later, tragedy struck. Both of the sons had just come from church. Abel was glowing; Cain was agitated. God's evident enthusiasm with Abel's worship infuriated Cain. Later, Cain told his parents, 'I don't know what got into me. I found myself staring at my brother, and I couldn't quit thinking, *Who does he think he is? Who does he think he is?*'"

The Teacher speaks: "Adam, Eve, Cain . . . Could you just hold your places there on the stage? I'd like to speak directly to the audience for a moment." The lights come back on.

"Quite a story, isn't it? It's the story of humanity's first worship experience, and for worshipers, that is quite significant.

"There is a principle of biblical interpretation called the law of first mention. When a doctrine or a theme is first mentioned in the Scriptures, the basic elements of that theme are found there in seed form.

"This is the first mention of the idea of sacrifice. In this story are the basic elements of the doctrine of worship. Let's look at some of these elements:

- *"Worship is an instinctive human response to God's reality.* Probably Cain and Abel had never been to a worship conference to learn how to worship.
- *"Worship involves sacrifice.* Both Cain and Abel offered what cost them something. Their gifts were meant to be tokens of their giving of themselves.
- *"Worship reflects life.* Cain's worship was not accepted because his life was not accepted (see Genesis 4:5–7).
- *"The ways humans worship fall into two categories: acceptable and unacceptable.*
- *"The blessing and favor that attends acceptable worship can potentially provoke antagonism in those who practice unacceptable worship.* That antagonism can become very intense.
- *"God graciously extends the opportunity to those who practice unacceptable worship to learn what is pleasing to Him* (see Genesis 4:7).

"We will see variations on these themes as we watch the drama of worship unfold. But pay special attention to the two traditions that begin in this scene: the tradition of Cain (unacceptable worship) and the tradition of Abel (acceptable worship).

"There is a verse in the New Testament that distinguishes these two offerings. It is in the book of Hebrews: 'By faith Abel offered God a better sacrifice than Cain did' (11:4).

"The essential difference between acceptable and unacceptable worship is faith, without which 'it is impossible to please God' (Hebrews 11:6). Faith receives the love of God and instinctively offers back to God grateful praise. In contrast, human effort tries to earn acceptance by performance, or works. These two traditions are clearly stated in Ephesians 2:8–9: grace through faith versus man-centered works.

"Cain's tradition covers all man-made religions, not only the 'non-Christian' kinds, but the 'Christian' kinds, as well. Abel's adherents involve those who not only choose to worship the God of the Bible, but also those who worship in a way that the God of the Bible prescribes.

"Now, let's get back to the drama. Adam, Eve, Cain. We are about to begin Scene 3."

Scene 3: The Liar

At this point, the lights go dim again, and a hideous creature can be seen crouching about ten feet away from Cain at his point of temptation in the field. This personification of evil—the Liar—stretches forward to within a foot of Cain's ear, and, with a snarling rasp, convinces Cain that he is right in his jealousy of his brother. Like a hammer driving a nail, the Liar penetrates Cain's mind and heart more and more deeply with a phrase soaked in demonic jealousy: *Who does he think he is?* When Cain's anger boils over and the murder of Abel is accomplished, the Liar laughs and whirls around with jubilant shouts and a wild dance. "I shall win! I shall win!" he cries.

The sounds fade to nothing and the dancing goes into slow motion until there is none. The Liar's horror still ema-

71

nates even though he is motionless. The audience sits in shocked silence, wondering how such evil could prevail, wondering how such jealousy and hatred found its way into this ancient tale—and where it will lead.

Now, as all eyes are focused on the statuesque, dark eminence, the backdrop of the field morphs into an other-worldly realm. The Liar's repulsiveness falls off like scales, and the mysterious character becomes stunningly beautiful. Suddenly multitudes of other beings just like him appear on the stage.

Apparently we have gone back into a time before the creature's demise. Here he is called "Morning's Son." He appears to be a prince among the other angels. Sounds of glorious worship, like waves of audible color and motion, again fill the theater.

Words become distinct this time as we hear the angels celebrate God's greatness with song: "For you, O LORD, are the Most High over all the earth; you are exalted far above all gods" (Psalm 97:9). An eagle-like creature with eyes all over his body (see Revelation 4:7–8) calls out to Michael and Gabriel, the awesome heavenly captains, signaling the need for counsel. They gather and the eagle begins: "As we were singing earlier today, Morning's Son had an unusual expression on his face. I have never seen anything like it before."

"I noticed it, too," Gabriel agreed. "He seemed to choke when we sang of God's supremacy over all the gods. Could this be that about which the Lamb warned us? Is this the poison of pride?"

Michael spoke up: "I didn't see his countenance when we were singing, but I have noticed a swagger as he ascends and descends the stairway [see Genesis 28:12]. It's almost reckless. And when he's ascending, it's . . . it's just over the top."

The eagle agreed: "I hesitate to say this, but I think he is jealous of the praise that belongs to the Master alone.

Morning's Son has always been wise, but I see it turning now to cunning. He was standing near the front of the great multitude yesterday, and instead of looking toward the throne, he turned back toward the throng and seemed to drink in the praise being offered to God. I fear a dark plan has already entered his heart. He will use his greatness to deceive others—and he is well spoken of by many."

"We should not fear," Michael concurred. "Righteousness shall prevail. But there will be a war. Even now, strategies are being laid."

The Storyteller speaks: "Not long afterward, the desire of Morning's Son to set his throne above God's led to an open revolt (see Isaiah 14:13–15). Many other angels came under his delusion. Michael remembered overhearing powerful accusations against God as Morning's Son rallied his forces. 'It has long been thought that God is God alone,' Morning's Son declared. 'But He is hiding from us the knowledge that we are the same as He, lest we rise above Him. It is time for us to ask "Who does He think He is? *Who does He think He is?*"'

"The conflict was brief. The delusion collided with an unexpected, immovable Power. Morning's Son, also known as the Liar, was stripped of his authority in heaven and cast down, his followers with him. Since then, his tactics have changed from open revolt to subtlety and intrigue, for he now knows that the only authority he can use is that which is stolen from Adam and his sons. His obsession, however, is still the same."

As the lights come up, the Teacher continues the narration.

"Other lies were hatched to explain the defeat to his followers. Morning's Son's curiosity became an intention; his intention, an addiction. Humans usually put it into words they can understand and call it a 'lust for power.' In heaven, however, it is known as the most horrendous of addictions—the lust to be worshiped.

73

"In 2 Thessalonians 2:7 (KJV), the great apostle acknowledged that there is considerable mystery regarding iniquity. To be honest, there is much we don't know about the origins of evil. Our script draws from Isaiah and Ezekiel who allegorically imply a fall of Satan from heavenly prominence because of pride and the infatuation with his own beauty. (See Isaiah 14:12–15 and Ezekiel 28.)[3]

"Admittedly the details are sketchy, but there is something we *do* know, and this is essential for the training of all true worshipers: Our antagonist is driven by an intense jealousy of God, as well as a lust to own the worship that belongs to God alone. That means, by the way, that those who are determined that God would receive all honor and praise will not be very popular with this fellow.

"As proof of this lust, consider these two key events in the record in which the Liar revealed his true colors: first, Satan's ploy when Jesus was being tempted in the wilderness, and, second, the attempted deification of the man of lawlessness.

"In the wilderness, Satan overplayed his hand when he showed Jesus all the kingdoms of the world and said, 'I will give you all their authority and splendor, for it has been given to me, and I can give it to anyone I want to. So if you worship me, it will all be yours' (Luke 4:6–7).[4]

"And before the Second Coming of Christ, a figure, who is certainly a puppet of the Liar, 'will oppose and will exalt himself over everything that is called God or is worshiped, so that he sets himself up in God's temple, proclaiming himself to be God' (2 Thessalonians 2:4).

"There it is, stated in black and white—the ultimate objective of the lord of darkness."

The story will continue, but we need to pause for a moment and let the Holy Spirit mark this in our hearts: The business of *whom* we worship and *how* we worship is serious stuff. Whom are we believing when we think that it does not matter if we worship God or not? With whom are we

74

siding if we think that apathy in worship is acceptable as long as our beliefs are proper?

In war, wise generals know well the mind and motive of their enemy.

Now Scene 4 begins. The words of the heading below move across the stage in midair from right to left like a holographic ticker tape.

Scene 4: The First Priest

The lights dim, and the Storyteller begins.

"There was an ancient battle in which five tribal kings rose up against Kedorlaomer, the king of Elam, and his allies." (See Genesis 14.)

Battle scenes fill the backdrop of the theater.

"Kedorlaomer's forces prevailed, thanks in part to tar pits in the battlefields of Siddim, which became a snare to their enemies. And so it seemed that the victory belonged to Kedorlaomer that day, except for one little glitch. His armies had taken captive a young man in Sodom named Lot, who happened to be the nephew of Abram the Hebrew, a man who talked with God. Taking Lot captive was a big mistake.

"Within hours of Abram hearing of Lot's capture, an army of 318 trained men born in Abram's household was in pursuit of Kedorlaomer, who thought the fighting was over."

Three-dimensional visuals on stage show a surprise attack, a determined chase, the defeat of Kedorlaomer's armies and the rescue of Abram's nephew, his family and possessions. The audience cheers out loud as the action scenes wind down, the music swells, and Abram and Lot are reunited.

"You may be wondering how this story fits in with the Story of Worship. Well, it provides the background for one of the most incredible events in all the history of worship: The father of worship (you will understand this term shortly) meets the first and greatest (and most mysterious) of all priests.

"If you were a devoted jazz musician and could go back in time to meet the first of all jazz musicians, you would tremble at such a meeting. If you were an architect and could go back in time to meet the father of architecture, you would remember every detail.

"You know, of course, that you are a priest and part of a priestly nation. And now you are about to encounter the progenitor of all priests. (You were, in a manner of speaking, actually there in the loins of Abraham.[5]) If we knew the actual calendar date of this meeting, it would surely become an annual holiday for worshipers. This meeting should be commemorated in song.

"Maybe it happened like this: Lot was gushing with gratitude for his uncle's bravery. 'Uncle Abram, you're the man!'

"'Oh, no, Lot,' Abram replied. 'You would have done the same thing.'

"'No, Uncle Abram, you're the greatest man on the face of the earth. You took on the King of Elam and won.'

"Abram carefully redirected the praise. 'I'm very ordinary stuff, Lot. The One who helped us today, the One who stirred my courage against Kedorlaomer, He is truly great.' And then, as if he were turning to a third person in the conversation, Abram looked upward, raised his hands and said with genuine honor, 'Lord, You are truly our refuge and strength. Without You we are as empty pots, but in Your might we can conquer armies. Our thanks, together with the spoils of this rescue, belong to You, O God.' Abram paused as if he were listening for an answer.

"His eyes slowly descended to the horizon, and there, about two hundred feet away, a stranger came into view. Walking slowly toward Abram, the stranger had a natural dignity, like a king. Though he wore regal attire, it was his countenance that Abram's eyes were drawn to.

"Though his wealth and stature had brought him into the company of more than a few of the earth's great men, Abram was not generally impressed with dignitaries. Lot knew this of his uncle and was therefore surprised to see Abram bow in silence before this stranger as he drew near.

"'You are Abram, and I have overheard your praise,' the man said. 'It rises from your lips as a pleasing offering because your life is also pleasing. Your God takes great delight in you.'

"'Who are you, my lord, and of whose house?'

"'I am Melchizedek, a priest of God and the king of priests. My kingdom is called Salem. I have no beginning of days, or father as you know fathers, but the One I serve counts me as more than a son.' (See Hebrews 7:1–3.)

"'What is a priest, and where is Salem?'

"'A priest attends to sacrifices, as you shall know. As to Salem, it crosses the boundaries of nations. You have been its citizen ever since you left your father's household in Haran.'

"'Then surely you are my king,' said Abram, 'and all that I have is yours.'

"'And surely I receive what you give,' Melchizedek responded, 'for so it is with all of Salem's inhabitants. They live as sacrifices, even as the One I serve. And of His way, I am eager for you to know, for you were formed in your mother's womb after His image, and your future days shall be a mirror of His own sacrifice.'

"With this, the king of priests took the hand of Abram, who was still bowing, lifted him up and invited him to sit on a rock nearby as he prepared a simple meal of bread and wine. After he blessed the meal, Melchizedek told Abram more of his Master and how His love for what He made was always expressed in giving: 'Creation, which is His handiwork, is marked by His generosity. Lesser gods are not like Him; they only want to receive from men. It is my joy to inspire sacrifices to Him. I, along with God's Wind, instructed Abel in making his offering. Together we helped Noah know to build an altar, to make a place for sacrifices.'" (See Genesis 8:20.)

As the scene moves away from Melchizedek and Abel to Melchizedek and Noah, an aroma fills the theater.[6] The Storyteller's voice is heard again, and it sounds as if there must be a tear in his eye. "Abram heard other stories that day . . . and believe me, there have never been stories like the ones told that day.

"Abram heard the story of a future nation, created in a furnace of affliction for the purpose of praise—and the story of a worshiping king whose name would be David, the writer of many songs, including a tribute to Melchizedek's priesthood (see Psalm 110:4). And the story of a beautiful Temple made of stones, which would one day be overshadowed by the splendor of a Temple made of stones that breathe . . . and of a great multitude from every tongue and tribe. Abram could not take it all in.

"But of all the stories, Melchizedek especially wanted Abram to know of the great sacrifice, which had taken place before creation. 'And that was the rehearsal of what will happen again hundreds of years from now,' Melchizedek told him. 'A Lamb was slain from the creation of the world' (see Revelation 13:8). Melchizedek had been there and would be there again when it happened in time.

"The bread and wine were almost gone when the king looked at them and said, 'These, like the Lamb's body and blood, are tokens of the great sacrifice itself, and of the King of love who gives.'

"A rush of joy swept over Abram, and these words sprang to his lips: 'May I ever be as he is.'

"'Surely you shall,' he heard in reply. He thought he saw a brief expression of pain on his tutor's brow.

"Then Melchizedek, putting his hands on Abram's shoulders, looked deep into his eyes and said, 'Blessed are you, Abram. Blessed by God Most High, the Creator of heaven and earth. And blessed is He who delivered your enemies into your hand.'"

We watch as Abram directs his servants to bring a tenth of all the spoils and lay it down as tribute before the King of Salem. The characters fade, and the music rises.

The audience, which had almost forgotten where it was, breaks into spontaneous applause—partly for the incredible performance of Melchizedek and Abram, and partly because their identification with Abram had become so real, they had felt Melchizedek was blessing them, too.

The applause fades, and the Teacher walks to the center of the stage.

"Thank you, Abram . . . Melchizedek. Very well done." He turns to the audience. "In our final scene in this act, Abram will become a father, and then the father of worship.

"But concerning this meeting between Melchizedek and Abram, should it be commemorated on the worshiper's calendar? And if so, why?"

The audience was especially thoughtful as it considered the question. "It was the earth's first communion," one audience member called out. "Like America's Fourth of July, it was the birthday of the kingdom of priests," another cried.

"Yes!" the Teacher exclaimed. "And our first king was a priest. That's the important thing to remember about Melchizedek: This priest was, and is, a king. Throughout most of Old Testament history, priests could not be kings, and kings could not be priests, but it was not so from the beginning. Christ Jesus, our Priest and King, is not of the order of Levi, but of Melchizedek (see Hebrews 5:8–10). And the international community that the New Covenant has created, and will eventually create, is called a royal priesthood. It will be populated by worshiping kings and reigning worshipers.

"God is still looking for such worshipers—like the one He found in Abram."

Scene 5: The Test

A sky of brilliant stars fills the theater, and their songs begin again. The stars follow the conductor in a great decrescendo as they hear Him say, "No singing for a while," and then whispers, "but you can still smile." The stars begin a lovely, random twinkling.

The angle changes, and an old man can be seen looking at these stars. A voice booms forth: "Your children and their children shall be as many as the stars you see."

An anguished look on his face turns to peaceful wonder, and he whispers, "It's beyond me, Lord, but I believe You."

God whispers to Himself, "I count him righteous."

Abram is deeply moved. He recalls the words of Melchizedek about sacrifice, and he sacrifices various animals and birds. Abram lays their lifeless bodies out in an orderly fashion, but then he seems to be waiting for something. He becomes sleepy as he waits, but then is startled by the hissing of vultures. With shouts and an angry flailing of his arms, he drives them away: "This doesn't belong to you. This is not yours."

As they depart, the vultures seem to retort with a rasp, "Who does he think he is? *Who does he think he is?*"

A burning torch not held by hands floats between the sacrifices, and parts of a conversation can be overheard: "A nation of slaves . . . four hundred years . . . the gift of land . . . much land, between two great rivers."

Now we are taken to a scene of a sweaty but happy Egyptian girl who has just given birth to a son . . . an older woman looks on with contempt . . . an angel tells the girl her son will be both very fruitful and very contentious . . . a troubled old man grieves. It is Abram. He is angry at himself, saying, "What have I done?"

The Storyteller resumes.

"Thirteen years later, Abram, now called Abraham, heard the same voice he had heard before say, 'Through Sarah.' Abram fell on his face and laughed uncontrollably. Then an emphatic response came: 'Next year.'

"A year later Abraham turned one hundred and held the son that was born of Sarah. For months, their home was filled with laughter. Guests would hear Sarah say, 'I'm nursing in my nineties!' and a new round of laughter would ignite. Abram and Sarah named their special son Isaac, meaning 'he laughs.'

"There are no words to describe how deeply Abraham loved his son.[7] Every time Abraham looked at Isaac, he was reminded of the goodness and faithfulness of God. There had been many times in the past when Abraham himself wondered about the ridiculous promises he had come to believe—that he would have more descendants than the stars, would be the father of nations and bring blessings to all the peoples on earth, would be given hundreds of square miles of real estate. All those years of being childless, he heard the chuckles when he introduced himself as 'Abraham, Father of Multitudes.' More than once he probably said to God, 'Do I have to keep using that name?'

"But when Isaac was finally born, Abraham knew that the future was bright. These were days of deep joy and satisfaction for him and Sarah. The dream was coming true. Certainly Isaac would become the father of many, and God's promises would surely be fulfilled.

"One day in Abraham's meditation, a strange picture came to mind. It was a picture of the momentary pain he thought he had seen on Melchizedek's brow so many years ago. Abraham tried to make sense of it. *It was just when he*

81

told me that I would truly be like the One whom Melchizedek served. As his thoughts relived that unforgettable meeting, he remembered the mystery of the great sacrifice that had happened before creation—and would happen again.

"What would have been a sacrifice for the One who created heaven and earth? It would have to have been something greater than what He had created. But what could that be? Just at that moment Abraham, in his mind's eye, saw the face of Isaac. He knew that the greatest sacrifice he could ever give would be Isaac, for there was nothing he treasured more.

"In that moment, he heard the voice speak again: 'There was a Father who gave His only Son before you. The Lamb was the Father's Son.' Abraham burst into tears, knowing at once the full extent of his God's generosity and also what was required of him. 'If a man loves his life, he will lose it,' the voice continued, 'but if he loves Me more than his own life, more than his greatest treasure, he can never lose it. What is given to Me will always be secure, even in the life to come.'

"The next day, the instruction was specific. 'Abraham.'

"'Here I am.'

"'Take your son, your only son, Isaac, whom you love, and go to the region of Moriah. Sacrifice him there as a burnt offering on one of the mountains I will tell you about' (Genesis 22:2).

"Having been prepared, Abraham obeyed without hesitation. *In principle,* he thought, *it is no different from the victory over Kedorlaomer. Because the victory was the Lord's doing, the spoils already belonged to Him. Because Isaac was so evidently the son of God's promises, he, likewise, was already the Lord's.* And Abraham had a strange sense that God could even raise the dead (see Hebrews 11:19). His own body had been as good as dead, but it had been resurrected.

"Abraham and Isaac traveled with their servants for three days until the mountain came into view. Then Abraham asked the servants to stay with the donkey, and he and

Isaac went up to the mountain. 'We will worship and then we will come back to you' (Genesis 22:5).

"You have probably heard what happened there. Abraham built an altar, laid the wood on it, bound his son and was about to slay him, when suddenly the angel of the Lord cried out, 'Abraham. Abraham. Do not harm the boy. Now I know that you fear God, for you have not withheld your only son.'

"God provided a ram for the sacrifice; it was caught in a thicket nearby. Abraham had passed the test with flying colors. Previous promises were reconfirmed, and God tacked on another promise—that Abraham's descendants would take possession of the cities of their enemies." The Storyteller, sounding almost like the Teacher, concludes: "Worshipers, when you face tests, remember your cities."

The spotlight on Abraham dims, and another is brought up revealing the Teacher sitting on a stool on the stage.

"Quite a drama. And quite a lesson. Let's look into it.

"This story is another great example of the law of first mention. Here is the first mention of the word *worship* in the Scriptures, *shachah* (*shaw-khaw*) in Hebrew. If you ever begin to think there's nothing special about you, just say the word *shachah* out loud and remind yourself, *It was my ancestor Abraham who came up with that one.*

"And while we are on the subject of you and Abraham, remember what you have heard before in this book. This is not just about some great historical figure—this is about your own roots. It is not just Abraham's story—it is yours, as well. We are learning about *your* family tree. In that famous fourth chapter of Romans, Abraham is declared *your* father. Yes, he's the biological father of the Arab nations, and, yes, he's the genetic parent of the nation of Israel. But for those who follow in the steps of his faith—whether Arab or Israelite or something else altogether—he is a father. 'He is the father of all who believe' (Romans 4:11).

"This Abraham is not only the father of faith, as is well known. He is also the father of worship. Abraham's willing offering of what he loved best is the preeminent example of worship. Being strengthened in his faith, he 'gave glory to God' (Romans 4:20). His faith expressed itself in worship, and yours will, too.

"There are five important themes in this first mention of worship, and they are woven into almost everything the Bible says about worship:

- "Faith precedes true worship and is expressed in worship.
- "Worship involves giving back to God what was first given by God.
- "Worship acknowledges God's supremacy over all that He has made.
- "God tests worshipers.
- "God rewards worshipers.

"Worship that is not rooted in faith is simply a self-centered attempt to gain standing with God based on what we ourselves can come up with on our own. Abraham's offering of Isaac was the response of obedience within the context of a relationship of trust. We love Him because He first loved us. Faith is simply acknowledging God's love, and worship is faith's natural response.[8]

"Once we know that everything we have comes from God, then it should not be so hard to give back to Him all that we have. As Paul taught, 'all things' are *from* Him, and *through* Him, before they are *to* Him (see Romans 11:36). That is the verse just before he urges us to become living sacrifices.

"Acknowledging God as the source of all things is also to recognize that He is over all things. And here is where all of us will be regularly tested. He wants us to love and enjoy what He generously gives—our relationships, our possessions, our work. But when anything becomes more valuable to us than the One who gave it, we have crossed a very dangerous line. And God in His mercy contends with us at that line. Jesus did not just ask Peter if he loved Him; He probed more deeply, 'Do you truly love me more than these?' (John 21:15).

"Abraham passed the worship test. Consider one who failed—Eli. Eli was the priest who mentored Samuel, but whose own sons were wicked, even though they were in the ministry. God dealt with Eli about his failure to discipline his sons, but Eli never followed through. Then God sent a prophet who put Eli on the spot: 'Why do you honor your sons more than me?' the Lord asked through the prophet (1 Samuel 2:29). The issue then, as it is today, is simply, Who's first? The prophet went on to predict the violent destruction of Eli's priestly line and the rise of another family of righteous priests (see verses 30–36).[9]

"The story behind the rise and fall of the influence of individuals, families, churches, organizations, movements and even nations may be, and often is, how they responded in their worship test. Were they like Abraham or Eli? Think about examples you know that illustrate this persistent issue.

"Our 'Isaac' may not be *someone* we love. It may be our things or an ambition that we treasure above God. When He was calling His disciples, Jesus dealt with these three areas: competing relationships, possessions and plans (see Luke 14:26, 33 and 27, respectively). The habit of regularly giving thanks for what God gives is one of the most valuable disciplines of life, for it regularly confirms that God the Giver is supreme over the gifts He gives—and that we accept His terms. If we receive the good things God has created with thanksgiving, those things find their rightful place in our lives (see 1 Timothy 4:4).

"Before we leave Mount Moriah, let's look at a fascinating subplot involving this first mention of worship. According to the chronicler, this place of Abraham's sacrifice—Mount Moriah—is the very place where King David built an altar and offered another sacrifice, a sacrifice that turned back a plague (see 2 Chronicles 3:1). It was here, at the threshing floor of Araunah, that he said, 'I will not sacrifice to the LORD my God burnt offerings that cost me nothing' (see 2 Samuel 24:18–25).

"But there's more. It was at this very place where Solomon built a glorious Temple, and when he dedicated it, the Lord said that it was a place for sacrifices (see 2 Chronicles 7:12). And it will be at this very place where the man of lawlessness will make a final attempt to be the object of worship. God saw all of this ahead of time as He led Abraham and Isaac to that particular place of worship so many years ago.

"I do hope the Story of Worship is meaningful to you so far, and I hope you will tell it to others when you have a chance. Remember to tell them about the singing stars, about Cain and Abel, and about the Liar and his lust to be worshiped. Be sure to introduce them to Melchizedek, and especially to Abraham. And when you tell them the story, tell them that God is looking for worshipers like Abel, like Noah and like Abraham. Then ask them the question I am about to ask you: 'Has He found a true worshiper in you?'

"Let's take a brief break and then find our seats again. Act 2 will begin in about five minutes."

4

EARLY LANDMARKS

A NATION IS BORN—
A PLAN IS DELAYED

"Now if you obey me fully and keep my covenant, then out of all nations you will be my treasured possession. Although the whole earth is mine, you will be for me a kingdom of priests and a holy nation."

Exodus 19:5–6

The lights slowly dim, and the audience members hurry to take their seats. Conversations die down, and the overture resumes. As the rich orchestral tapestry fills the room, our eyes follow a brief visual synopsis of the story so far . . . the singing stars, Cain and Abel, the Liar, Melchizedek and Abraham. Then the holographic ticker tape again announces the first scene of Act 2.

Act 2, Scene 1: The Exodus

As the end of the message disappears to the left, the stage is dark and empty. Then a new three-dimensional scene, complete with live actors, is quickly pulled into view. What springs before the audience is a scene of two men, weathered and worn, dressed as commoners, standing before a great king in the royal courts of Egypt.

One of them speaks: "The God of our fathers—His name is *Yahweh*—has spoken to my brother"—he motions to the one standing next to him—"in the wilderness concerning these people who are your slaves. The message is that you, Pharaoh, should let them go so that they can make sacrifices to Him in the desert."

The pharaoh glances toward his counselors, who seem amused by the request. "I don't know this God of whom you speak, so why should I obey Him? Who does He think He is that He commands the king of Egypt? No, I will not let these people go make sacrifices in the desert."

After the request, hardships increase for the slaves. They are accused of being lazy and of using their religion to get out of work. Their Egyptian masters double their load and become even more cruel and oppressive. As the audience views scenes of ruthless managers harshly beating the Israelite slaves and heartlessly mocking their cries for mercy, the Storyteller adds his words to the pictures:

"All of these slaves are descended from the twelve sons of Jacob, the son of Isaac, the son whom Abraham loved and Sarah nursed in her nineties.

"Those twelve sons came down to Egypt during a drought in Canaan. At first they were friends of Egypt, but as they grew in number, the Egyptians became fearful of them and enslaved them. It has been four centuries since the days when Abraham first heard the promise of a great multitude of descendants, but now his twelve great-grandsons have become as many as several million men, women and children.[1]

"One of those twelve sons of Jacob was Levi. The two brothers in the opening scene of Act 2 were Moses and Aaron, descendants of one of Levi's sons. Forty years before, Moses had left Egypt, and his family had lost touch with him. They were surprised to hear that he had come back to Egypt, and even more surprised to hear that God had sent him to lead them out of slavery and into their own land.

"Some of the Hebrews were still fond of the stories of how God had spoken to Abraham, Isaac and Jacob. And as their hardships grew, the stories were the only thing that kept them going. Because of this, they tended to believe what Moses was saying.

"Others had become so discouraged that they gave up on the hope that the stories held and resented any talk about them. Instead, these folks said, 'Forget about a land of milk and honey; get used to the bricks and mortar.'

"The meeting that Moses and Aaron had with Pharaoh that day was the first of many. Most people who know the story of the Exodus remember the miracles and the plagues that God used to display His power and verify His message. And miracles and plagues there were. But do we truly understand the message that the miracles were to verify?"

The theater becomes like a classroom again, and the Teacher comes on stage to explain. As large, bold text appears on a massive screen behind him, the Teacher leads the audience in reading each of the passages and references out loud. The repetition has its effect.

"This is what the LORD says: Let my people go, so that they may worship me."

Exodus 8:1

"This is what the LORD says: Let my people go, so that they may worship me."

Exodus 8:20

"This is what the L ORD, the God of the Hebrews, says: 'Let my people go, so that they may worship me.'"

Exodus 9:1

"This is what the L ORD, the God of the Hebrews, says: Let my people go, so that they may worship me."

Exodus 9:13

"This is what the L ORD, the God of the Hebrews, says: . . . 'Let my people go, so that they may worship me.'"

Exodus 10:3

Pharaoh's officials said to him . . . "Let the people go, so that they may worship the L ORD their God."

Exodus 10:7

And finally . . .

During the night Pharaoh summoned Moses and Aaron and said, "Up! Leave my people, you and the Israelites! Go, worship the L ORD as you have requested."

Exodus 12:31

The Teacher then asks: "What was the message that God used to deliver those several million Israelites from captivity?"

The audience is emphatic: "Let My people go, so that they may worship Me."

The Teacher continues: "Some of you may be familiar with the word *teleological*, a philosophical term referring to the design or purpose of something. The statements above are teleological. They make plain that the purpose of the Israelites' deliverance from Egypt was not just freedom from bondage; it was worship.

"The story of the Exodus is a beautiful Old Testament picture of the New Testament reality of salvation. We see this suggested in 1 Corinthians 10:1–4, in which Paul compared Israel's being 'baptized into Moses'—being under the cloud and passing through the Red Sea—with our baptism into Christ by Spirit and by water. Moses, the deliverer, is symbolic of Christ, our Savior. Egypt is a picture of the world's system, and Pharaoh, of the world's prince (see Ephesians 2:2). The blood on the doorposts that protected Israelite families against the angel of death is a foreshadowing of the blood of Christ, which delivers us from the judgment of sin. Our salvation, so beautifully illustrated in this story, is a deliverance out of one kingdom, a dark kingdom of slavery, into another kingdom, the bright kingdom of liberty. It is a perfect biblical analogy illustrating the relationship between the Old and New Covenants: The New is in the Old concealed; the Old is in the New revealed.

"But now, because of the words we just read on the screen behind me, the great teleological '*so that*' of the Exodus becomes inescapable: 'Let My people go, *so that* they may worship Me.'

"This means that you are not just saved to escape your addictions or your troubles. Thank God for that, but you are also saved so that you can become a worshiper. God is looking for worshipers. If somehow a person becomes a Christian but not a wholehearted worshiper, something is terribly wrong. If the majority of the people in our churches are passive worshipers, we should be concerned."

The screen displays a new giant heading: *The Apostle Peter's Teleological "So That."*

The Teacher leads us to boldly declare Peter's words: "You are a chosen people, a royal priesthood, a holy nation, a people belonging to God, [so] that you may declare the praises of him who called you out of darkness into his wonderful light" (1 Peter 2:9).

"A chosen people, a royal priesthood, a holy nation, a special people—that's *who* we are. To declare God's praises—that's *why* we are who we are."

The heading changes: *The Apostle Paul's Teleological "So That."*

We read together: "[I have] the priestly duty of proclaiming the gospel of God, so that the Gentiles might become an offering acceptable to God" (Romans 15:16).

"Paul's gospel, like Moses' gospel, was designed to create worshipers."

Another heading: *The Apostle John's Teleological "So That."*

We heartily read: "To him who loves us and has freed us from our sins by his blood, and has made us to be a kingdom and priests to serve his God and Father—to him be glory and power for ever and ever! Amen" (Revelation 1:5–6).

"John's teleology of salvation[2] is the same: Worship is the goal of the Gospel.

"It strikes me that in John's doxology, he celebrates three truths: First, God loves us; second, God frees us; and third, God makes us into priests. It strikes me, too, that more people know that He loves them,[3] but a smaller number knows He has the power to free them, and an even smaller number knows that He wants them to be part of a priestly kingdom ministering before Him.[4] Christ's costly sacrifice should create wholehearted worshipers."

Stage and video, actors and effects work together and continue to illustrate the drama. Arguments between the Hebrew elders and Moses . . . eerie plagues of frogs, gnats, locusts and hail . . . the hastily eaten first Passover meal . . . Pharaoh holding the corpse of his firstborn son . . . messengers spreading the news that it is time to go . . . streets filled with excited evacuees . . . the pillar of fire . . . the parting of the Red Sea . . . the last Israelite climbing up on the other side of the bank . . . the confusion of the Egyptian army as their chariot wheels fly off . . . and the walls of water burying the entire army.

Scene 2: The "Almost Ordination"

The Storyteller speaks from the side of the stage: "When the Israelites saw what God had done for them, fear overcame them, and they placed their trust in Him and in His servant Moses (see Exodus 14:31). They were ashamed that just hours before, when it looked as if the Egyptian army was about to recapture them, they had scolded Moses: 'We knew this wasn't going to work. We would have been better off as slaves in Egypt than to die out here in the desert' (see verse 12).

"Now feeling good about the turn of events, Moses quickly wrote a song for the occasion. He thought that 'They Sank Like Lead in the Mighty Waters' would have been a good title, but it was actually remembered as 'The Song of Moses.' The fact that it was called '*The* Song of Moses' means that he probably did not write a lot of songs. But this one had such a catchy tune that they still sing it in heaven to this day (see Revelation 15:3). It works especially well in the context of surviving plagues (see verse 1). We'll all probably be singing it one day.

"Needless to say, the celebration that day out there on the eastern shore was . . . well, it was *ripsnorting*.[5] Moses' sister, Miriam, and her girlfriends got out the tambourines and sang and danced till they could sing and dance no more."

The Storyteller pauses to nod to the actors and technical director, and then the stage explodes with dancing as the theater is filled with bold music and shouts of exuberant praise, about "three notches short of wild." Less than 45 seconds later, the audience can contain itself no longer, and it jumps to its feet and joins the jubilee with clapping and shouting. The cumulative effect of the music, shouting and clapping is a huge roar, a bit like the sound of many rushing waters.

The five-minute burst finally subsides, and the audience catches its breath and sits down. The Storyteller continues:

"As much as Moses enjoyed the celebration, he seemed to be thinking of something else. Seeing these former slaves dancing brought to mind something God had said to him when he first heard Him speak at Horeb: 'This will be the sign to you that it is I who have sent you: When you have brought the people out of Egypt, you will worship God on this mountain' (Exodus 3:12).

"Moses immediately knew where he was supposed to take the people: to the southeast region of the Sinai Peninsula, the land of the burning bush. He could not wait to see the gathering there that God had foretold. As they traveled, week after week, it was all he could think about. Finally, three months to the day after leaving Egypt, this mobile nation came to the place of one of the greatest moments of opportunity, and one of the greatest tragedies, in the entire biblical record.

"What happened there that made it so important? Here's the story. After the people set up camp, Moses went hiking up the mountain.[6] He knew this place well.

"It wasn't long before he heard God speak: 'Moses, I want you to say this to the people: "I, the Lord, brought you out of Egypt on eagles' wings so that you could be with Me. Now I want to tell you why. If you will obey Me fully, you will become My treasured possession among all the nations. You will become a kingdom of priests and a holy nation"' (see Exodus 19:4–6).

"There it was. God had said it. He revealed the intended destiny of these former slaves—and ours, as well. His plan, contingent upon their obedience, was for them to become a priestly nation on behalf of the other nations of the world.

"As priests, they would enjoy a privileged place in God's presence for worship and intercession. As kings, they would

94

be given authority to judiciously and generously extend God's benevolent purposes by declaring blessing over the other nations.

"Moses came down from the mountain and told Israel's leaders what God had said. Together they called on the people to wash their clothes and consecrate themselves. The people began to make themselves ready, for they had learned what would happen: In three days, they would be set apart as a priestly nation. They responded: 'We will do everything the LORD has said' (Exodus 19:8).

"Unfortunately, the awaited day seemed to bring bad news: 'On the morning of the third day there was thunder and lightning, with a thick cloud over the mountain' (Exodus 19:16). *Guess we'd better cancel the gathering*, the people might have thought.

"God revealed His awesome presence that day, but the people were not ready for it. First, a thick, ominous darkness surrounded the mountain."

The theater goes completely dark so that audience members can barely see the persons sitting next to them.

"Then thunder and lightning began to explode like bombs throughout the morning blackness as the whole mountain trembled violently."

A powerful subtone rattles through the huge speakers.

"The people trembled as they were led from the camp to the foot of the mountain. Little children clung tightly to their parents.

"Then, as they cautiously approached, God descended to the mountain in a blaze of fire. Smoke billowed up from it like smoke from a furnace."

Fortunately, the technical director had produced many large rock concerts and knew just how to create these effects on stage.

"If the thunder, lightning, earthquake, smoke and fire were not enough to stir up the people, God had one final effect: a supernatural trumpet sound. It started in the background of the thunder and lightning and grew louder and louder until it drowned out the sound of the thunder itself. In the record, we are told it was 'very loud' (Exodus 19:16)."

("Very loud" in the context of thunder, lightning and trembling mountains is probably pretty loud. I am guessing that one of the angels, maybe Gabriel, was the talent behind the sound.)

The sound in the theater is at first ragged and eerie, but the decibels of the sound soon rise to the point of being uncomfortable. Several people near the back of the audience get up and walk out. When the sound finally relents, the entire audience is relieved.

The Storyteller continues: "The sound was the signal for the people to go up to where God was (see Exodus 19:13). But did the people accept the invitation? Sadly, no. There were several million 'no-shows' that day at Mount Sinai. As the record states, 'The people remained at a distance, while Moses approached the thick darkness where God was' (Exodus 20:21).

"Instead of moving into the privileged place in God's presence as priests, they tried to make a deal with Moses to be their mediator:[7] 'Speak to us yourself and we will listen. But do not have God speak to us or we will die' (Exodus 20:19). Israel was to have been ordained as a kingdom of priests, but the ordination was called off. There was only one priest that day who drew near, when there could have been many. In God's search for worshipers, Exodus 19 was a major setback. He would have to wait centuries for the royal priesthood to come into view again."

The Teacher enters and repeats what the people had said: "Speak to us yourself and we will listen. But do not have God speak to us or we will die." He then continues: "If you realize what was forfeited that day, you surely understand this to be one of the greatest tragedies in the Bible. Do you remember the definition of a priest? 'In precise terminology of the law, a priest (*kohen*) is one who may draw near to the divine presence.'[8] God wanted every Israelite—young and old, male and female, rich and poor—to become one of those. That did not mean there would be no farmers or herdsmen, teachers or judges. It meant that the farmers, herdsmen, teachers and judges would have been *priestly* farmers, herdsmen, teachers and judges, fulfilling the New Covenant community's commission: Whatever you do, do it all for the glory of God (see 1 Corinthians 10:31). Everyone would have been involved in the natural functions of sustaining community life, but their national specialty would have been worship, prayer and blessing the nations.

"Imagine a nation that absolutely loves soccer. Children start playing it as soon as they can walk. Education consists of reading, writing, arithmetic—and soccer. When families sit at the table, they eat, but dinner is just an excuse to talk about yesterday's soccer game. People work, but only so they can buy food, clothing and soccer tickets. You get the idea.

"The kingdom of priests would have this kind of passion—not for soccer, but for God's presence. There would not have been a special priestly class of people required to offer the sacrifices. All the citizens of this realm would take turns offering the morning or evening sacrifices or standing before the Lord in the tabernacle. And each one would look forward to his turn, with the same degree of anticipation as the soccer enthusiasts had toward the next game. Why the enthusiasm? Because being priests was what they were good at—and because of the history-changing events that would happen as a result. People are motivated when they feel that they are making a difference.

"It was to have been a fulfillment of what God said to the father of worship and the founder of this nation: 'All the peoples on earth will be blessed through you.' As we have learned, there is a connection between worship and the power to bless.

97

"What God had in His heart for Israel at Sinai is what Isaiah would prophesy many years later:[9]

In the last days the mountain of the LORD's temple will be established as chief among the mountains; it will be raised above the hills, and all nations will stream to it. Many peoples will come and say, 'Come, let us go up to the mountain of the LORD, to the house of the God of Jacob. He will teach us his ways, so that we may walk in his paths.' The law will go out from Zion, the word of the LORD from Jerusalem. He will judge between the nations and will settle disputes for many peoples.

Isaiah 2:2–4

"How important was this ordination to God? Not only was it to have been the fulfillment of Abraham's calling, it was also to have been a recovery of the dominion that Adam had given away. The original plan was that mankind would submit to God, and the earth would submit to mankind for its care and development. When Adam submitted to Satan instead, the earth came under his influence, as well.

"Had Israel drawn near that day, instead of standing at a distance, they could have become a core group of humanity with whom the Lord would have again walked 'in the cool of the day.' And through that fellowship, His blessings could have been extended to the nations.

"This is not just Israel's story—this is your story, as well. Your church there in Albuquerque or New Haven or wherever is facing the same issues the Israelites faced at Sinai: What do we do with our calling as royal priests? What do we do with the presence of God, scary as it is? Are we seizing the opportunity to become a house of living stones, acceptable sacrifices to God, or are we standing at a distance, content to pay someone else to hear from God and be priests for us?

"Why *did* Israel stand at a distance? Answering that question may help us understand the temptation to do the same today. When Moses appealed to the people, he provided this answer: 'Do not be afraid. God has come to test you' (Exodus 20:20). They were *afraid*.

"Remember what Granddaddy Abraham taught us: God tests worshipers. We want to know, like Lucy, if 'Aslan is safe.' And the story of the almost ordination is teaching us, as Mr. Beaver taught her, ''Course he isn't safe. But he's good.'[10] If the presence of God splashes down in front of you in dramatic fashion as it did in Exodus 19, the question will still be, 'Do you know that God is good and that you can trust Him?'

"Settling that question in your heart may be more important than you think. God may have similar challenges for you ahead. I strongly suspect that the closer God's people get to the throne of God, the more likely it is that we will encounter similar phenomena.

"The demonstration of His glory at Sinai was not out of character for Him. Revelation 4 confirms that around His throne are 'flashes of lightning, rumblings and peals of thunder' (verse 5). Fire from the heavenly altar, when hurled to earth, comes with 'peals of thunder, rumblings, flashes of lightning and an earthquake' (Revelation 8:5). Ezekiel agreed. He, too, wrote about the fire and the lightning of God's throne (see Ezekiel 1:1–28). Psalm 97 rejoices in the thick darkness and the earthshaking, fire-consuming, mountain-melting glory that all the people will one day see (see verses 2–6). But behind it all, God is good and you can trust Him. He said, 'Whoever comes to me I will never drive away' (John 6:37).

"There are times when God is not in the thunder and lightning, but rather in the still, small voice (see 1 Kings 19:8–12, KJV).[11] But when you have heard Him in the still, small voice, do not think for a minute that will be the only way He will ever speak. When we speak of the presence of God, we need to distinguish between the 'pleasant presence' and the 'awesome presence' of God. When the *pleasant presence* of God comes, we get goose bumps; when His *awesome presence* shows up, we wonder if we are going to die. Why do you think it is that when God, or even an angel, appeared to someone in Scripture, the first thing they would usually have to say was 'Do not fear'? That suggests that there are dimensions of God's presence beyond what most of us experience today.

"How would you have done at Sinai? Or maybe I should ask how you will do when Sinai comes to your neighborhood. Will you fear or trust? The contrast is clear in Hebrews 10: We'll either 'draw near' (verse 22), or we will 'shrink back' (see verse 38). Do not let someone else's failure cause you to withdraw. Do not let spiritual disappointment or dismay keep you from drawing near to Him wholeheartedly.

"God ordains moments of opportunity. The story of the almost ordination was one of those moments. It had a tragic outcome. When a similar moment comes to you or to your church, be courageous and draw near, no matter what. And if you have already lived through one of those moments and stood at a distance, now that you see how high the stakes are, begin drawing near again today. Do not be afraid; be like Moses, who 'approached the thick darkness where God was' (Exodus 20:21)."

Scene 3: Plan B

The screen and the music pick up the story as the voice of the Storyteller begins again.

"Life went on after Sinai. Moses was inspired to write a constitution and a legal system for the new nation. A tabernacle was created to become a physical place where God's presence would abide, a shadow of what God had desired. The furnishings for the tabernacle were exquisite: the Ark, the table, the altar, the lampstand.

"And then in Exodus 28, God gave His people their hearts' desire. He appointed the Levites to be intermediaries of His presence for the people. Rather than being a kingdom of priests, Israel became a kingdom that had priests. Not quite a priestly nation among the nations, Israel had a priestly tribe among the tribes. Though not a priesthood of the order of Melchizedek, the Levites did become a priesthood, and Aaron was selected as the first high priest."

The audience watches as a stately procession and consecration fills the stage. Aaron is impressive with his jeweled breastplate, his linen turban and his colorful robe and ephod. The faces of the Israelites beam with admiration.

"To distinguish them from 'ordinary people,' Aaron's sons and descendants would wear special clothing, too. They alone would offer the sacrifices. The people would make provisions for them to represent them before God."

The Teacher, without even a mild segue, interrupts the short scene. "Can we talk?" he asks. "What's happening here? I think the word is *acquiescence*. God is acquiescing—'tacitly accepting or complying'—to the wrong choices that were made, even as the people who made them are smiling and acting as if there is nothing wrong.

"It's like the gracious father writing a check to his impatient, rebellious son for his share of the family estate, and the son pretending that everything is fine: *We have a special kind of relationship. I knew he would understand. He is an amazing father.* The dad, who is a gentleman, knows it's not what's best, but seeing the determination of his son, he *acquiesces.* But ask the dad in confidence how he really feels, and you will get a different answer. Ask the Lord how He feels about what happened at Mount Sinai. If He will talk, you will realize that He, like this father, was deeply hurt, and yet He still hopes that one day we will understand.

"For centuries, we have smiled at how convenient it is to have intermediaries who perform the priestly duties for us. But now we are learning about God's acquiescence—and

101

His pain. He is eager, more than we know, for all of us to understand His original intent.

"There's a lot we can learn from the Levites, for many of their priestly ways are patterned after Melchizedek's greater priesthood. But do remember this: The priesthood of the Levites was actually 'Plan B.' The consecration of the Levitical priesthood represented two major changes from 'Plan A': First, there was a removal of priestly duties from ordinary people, and second, there was a division of the priestly and kingly functions in the leadership of God's people.

"On the first point of change, it is interesting to note that in early Hebrew worship, the fathers were the worship leaders, and the households were the primary places of worship. It was decentralized. From the beginning, the Passover was a family feast led by fathers, which was to be observed in homes, as was the weekly Sabbath (see Exodus 12:20 and Leviticus 23:3, respectively).

"On the second point of change, before Exodus 28, it was normal for leaders to offer sacrifices.[12] Afterward, however, only the 'official' priests were allowed to offer sacrifices. Kings were not to be priests, and priests were not to be kings.

"So, the good news at the close of this act is that the people of Israel have been delivered from their Egyptian slavery and have become a nation marked for worship. But the bad news is that they have forfeited the amazing opportunity to become a kingdom of priests, and a lesser priesthood was established. But as we shall see in Act 3 of the Story of Worship, your story will continue."

The tone of the music is plaintive and subdued as the lights come up and the curtain closes on Act 2.

5

LATER DEVELOPMENTS

GREAT HEIGHTS
AND GREATER DEPTHS

Then the fire of the LORD fell and burned up the sacrifice.

1 Kings 18:38

Let him who thinks he stands take heed lest he fall.

1 Corinthians 10:12, NKJV

Lights flicker in the lobby. We hear the orchestra's invitation to rejoin the story, and return to our seats with an anticipation of what will unfold in Act 3.

Act 3, Scene 1: David and Solomon

The holographic ticker tape signals the new act, and the music carries us heavenward. On the screen, an angel appears to be searching for something, flying about fifty feet above various groups of people. Then our view becomes his as we look down on what he sees: A lifeless sepia tone colors everyone, with the exception of an occasional person here and there who appears bright and colorful. Other scenes follow the details of the Storyteller's account.

"Although the experience at Sinai was a setback, God continued to look for worshipers who would worship Him in spirit and in truth. Eventually, Israel pressed God to give them a king such as the other nations had. Again, God acquiesced. He gave them their desire. The first king, Saul, was a disappointment. The second one, however, became a legend as a king and as a worshiper.

"Before he ever became king, David loved to worship God. As he tended to his father's sheep, he would play his lyre and sing about the goodness and greatness of God. He wrote songs that would be sung by worshipers for centuries.

"David was not only a musician, but he was also a fearless fighter. He became famous for killing a lion and a bear with only his hands, and later, for standing up to the giant Goliath, whom he slew with a sling and a stone. Sent out as a warrior for Saul, David became increasingly famous for the victories he won. Songs of David's conquests were sung in the streets of Israel.

"David's heart for worship and his love for God's presence governed everything he did. One of his first acts as king was to bring the Ark of the Covenant, a symbol of the presence of God, back to Jerusalem."

This scene is enacted on stage with great celebration.

"On this occasion, David danced in the streets with such abandon that his wife, Saul's daughter, was embarrassed."

After a vigorous dance scene with incredible music, we see the same dark character we met in the story of Cain and

Abel standing by Saul's daughter, encouraging her disdain of David's celebration.

"But David was undaunted and would not be shamed. 'Watch me,' he said. 'I'll become even more undignified than this!' (see 2 Samuel 6:20–23).

"David restored the patterns of daily worship prescribed by Moses in the Law (see Exodus 29:38–43). He hired priestly musicians from among the Levites to accompany the daily offerings and prayers (see 1 Chronicles 16:4–6, 37–42). The Ark, and the sound of trumpets, cymbals, lyres and singing that surrounded it, became the center of national life, symbolic of the fact that Israel was becoming a worshiping nation. Making God's praise glorious was the rule of the day."

The angel's view of sepia-colored groups of people returns on the screen, except that now, most of the people are bright and colorful. The perspective zooms out so that we see a map of a bright and colorful Israel surrounded by sepia-colored nations in the area.

"Although he was not from the tribe of Levi, David acted a lot like a priest: He wore a linen ephod, and he personally offered sacrifices (see 2 Samuel 6:14; 1 Chronicles 16:2; and 2 Samuel 24:25, respectively). His kingship reflected the priestly kingship of Melchizedek, and in that, he was a prototype of the royal priesthood that God was anticipating.

"What David began, his son Solomon continued and amplified. David had wanted to build a Temple for the Ark, but God made it clear that David's son was the one who was to do that. Before he died, David said, 'I have taken great pains to provide for the temple of the LORD a hundred thousand talents of gold, [and] a million talents of silver' (1 Chronicles 22:14). In today's currency, that contribution would be valued at over $57 billion. David had a great passion for God's glory.

"David's son Solomon did build a glorious Temple, a Temple dedicated as a place for sacrifices (see 2 Chronicles

7:12). As you recall, this Temple was built on Mount Moriah (see 2 Chronicles 3:1), the very same place where Abraham proved he was willing to offer his beloved son Isaac. Those who walked through the Temple were breathless with awe. The great stones, the woodwork, the engravings, the overlay of gold on beams, doorposts and walls, the precious stones throughout—it was all massive in scope, intricate in detail and rich in splendor.

"But there was something else about the Temple that is often overlooked. Here's the Teacher to explain."

The Teacher appears on the stage and begins to speak: "The appearance of Solomon's Temple was impressive in every way, but what happened inside of the Temple was even more impressive. In the Temple was a place called the Most Holy Place. There, before the mercy seat, the high priest would annually appear with animal blood to atone for the sins of the nation, foreshadowing the once-for-all sacrifice of Christ for our sins (see Hebrews 9:12–14). In the Temple, forgiveness was won and reconciliation offered. That is certainly more significant than the physical beauty of the Temple.

"The Temple was also a place of God's presence. Solomon knew, of course, that no earthly building could contain God. He even acknowledged that fact when the Temple was dedicated: 'The heavens, even the highest heavens, cannot contain you. How much less this temple I have built!' (2 Chronicles 6:18). But even though the Temple did not have exclusive rights to the presence of God, there were times when the presence of God was so strong there that the priests could not continue to minister (see 2 Chronicles 5:13–14). That is amazing.

"But there's something else that happened in the Temple that is just as amazing, something that's not as well-known as what we have just described. It was this: In the Temple— in this place of sacrifice, in this place of His presence—God put His name. In this holy place of worship, God allowed the worshipers the use of His authority.

"Solomon made this clear from the outset of building the Temple. He said, 'I am about to build a temple for the Name of the LORD my God' (2 Chronicles 2:4). Nine times in one chapter alone, Solomon referred to the edifice he was dedicating as 'a temple for the Name of the LORD' (see 2 Chronicles 6:5, 7–10, 20, 33–34 and 38).

"According to the seven points of Solomon's prophetic prayer of dedication, the Temple would be a place of: settling injustices (see verses 22–23); restoration from defeat (see verses 24–25); ending drought (see verses 26–27); ending natural disasters, including famines and plagues (see verses 28–31); blessing nations (see verses 32–33); securing victory in war (see verses 34–35); and releasing the oppressed from captivity (see verses 36–39).

"Think about it. For those who feared Him, walked in His ways and offered acceptable sacrifices, God gave the authority to end a drought, turn back a plague, determine the outcome of wars and bless nations.

"If there were a people today who knew how to end a drought or a famine, or settle injustices, don't you think there would be plenty to keep them busy? The world expects government or science to change these things, but often these expectations are unreasonable, beyond what science or government can change.

"What does this have to do with God's search for worshipers? Everything. This overlooked truth about Solomon's Temple, that it was to have been a place of steering history to conform to God's will, means that worshipers who are becoming a Temple greater than Solomon's shall have an authority to accelerate God's Kingdom rule. (See 1 Corinthians 3:16–17; Ephesians 2:21–22; 1 Peter 2:5; and Revelation 21:3 for starters.)

"To better understand this part of the story, put it in the context of the story of Melchizedek, the first priest, and

107

the international multitude of priests at the end. Looking back, Melchizedek, the Mysterious Encourager of all who offer sacrifices, was (and still is) a priest *and* a king. Looking ahead, in one of the final scenes of Melchizedek's priesthood, which you'll hear about several times in this book, heaven celebrates the fact that the redeemed from every nation have become a priestly kingdom. (See Revelation 5:9–10.) The chorus of the song declares, 'And they will reign on the earth.' These priests, like their progenitor, have become kings."

It is part of Solomon's story, and just as much a part of yours.

How do priests reign? The same way the King of all kings reigns—through intercession. "He always lives to intercede" (Hebrews 7:25). There is more on this incredible privilege in chapter 13.

The Storyteller returns to the stage: "The festival to dedicate the Temple went on for two weeks."

The audience now sees on the screen the faces of thousands of Middle Eastern men who had traveled to Jerusalem from all across Israel and other neighboring nations to witness this historic celebration. Tears of joy and gladness of heart mingle as the celebration finally ends and the people begin to travel back to their homes.

"Solomon went home that night with a deep sense of satisfaction, for he 'succeeded in carrying out all he had in mind to do in the temple of the LORD' (2 Chronicles 7:11). As he was about to go to bed, the Lord appeared to him for the second time. The first time God had appeared to him before he started building the Temple and invited him to ask for anything he wanted (see 2 Chronicles 1:7–12). But this time God came to Solomon with an affirmation and a warning.

'I have heard your prayer and have chosen this place for myself as a temple for sacrifices. When I shut up the heavens so that there is no rain, or command locusts to devour the

108

land or send a plague among my people, if my people, who are called by my name, will humble themselves and pray and seek my face and turn from their wicked ways, then will I hear from heaven and will forgive their sin and will heal their land. Now my eyes will be open and my ears attentive to the prayers offered in this place. I have chosen and consecrated this temple so that my Name may be there forever.'

2 Chronicles 7:12–16

"And then, like terms in a contract that nobody thinks will ever be needed, a warning was added:

'But if you turn away and forsake the decrees and commands I have given you and go off to serve other gods and worship them, then I will uproot Israel from my land, which I have given them, and will reject this temple I have consecrated for my Name. I will make it a byword and an object of ridicule among all peoples. And though this temple is now so imposing, all who pass by will be appalled and say, "Why has the LORD done such a thing to this land and to this temple?" People will answer, "Because they have forsaken the LORD, the God of their fathers, who brought them out of Egypt, and have embraced other gods, worshiping and serving them—that is why he brought all this disaster on them."'

2 Chronicles 7:19–22

"Many good things happened in the years that followed the Temple's dedication. Solomon increased the number of priests serving in the Temple, and there were priests ministering before the Lord 24 hours a day for years. The wisdom and wealth of Solomon was known not only in Israel, but also among the nations: 'The whole world sought audience with Solomon to hear the wisdom God had put in his heart' (1 Kings 10:24).

"This great king became a counselor to kings. He ruled over all the kings from the Euphrates River to Egypt, most of the land promised to Abraham so many years ago.

109

"Solomon continued in his father's steps in the matter of songwriting, too: 'His songs numbered a thousand and five' (1 Kings 4:32). Solomon wrote books that became part of our Bible. There were many things to commend this wise son of David. But there was one matter in which he failed his father miserably, as well as those he led. And because of that, his life ended in darkness and idolatry."

The screen shows a regal old man looking out over his lavish surroundings with a bewildered and vacant expression.

"We find this account of Solomon's latter years in the record:

> As Solomon grew old, his wives turned his heart after other gods, and his heart was not fully devoted to the LORD his God, as the heart of David his father had been. He followed Ashtoreth the goddess of the Sidonians, and Molech the detestable god of the Ammonites. So Solomon did evil in the eyes of the LORD; he did not follow the LORD completely, as David his father had done.
>
> On a hill east of Jerusalem, Solomon built a high place for Chemosh the detestable god of Moab, and for Molech the detestable god of the Ammonites. He did the same for all his foreign wives, who burned incense and offered sacrifices to their gods.
>
> The LORD became angry with Solomon because his heart had turned away from the LORD, the God of Israel, who had appeared to him twice. Although he had forbidden Solomon to follow other gods, Solomon did not keep the LORD's command. So the LORD said to Solomon, 'Since this is your attitude and you have not kept my covenant and my decrees, which I commanded you, I will most certainly tear the kingdom away from you and give it to one of your subordinates.'
>
> 1 Kings 11:4–11

"I would love to hear the wise king's counsel now that he has gained eternity's perspective. Perhaps it would go something like this."

A humble old man comes to the stage and begins to speak: "Hello, my name is Solomon, and I am a recovering idolater. . . . The first thing I would say comes from my good friend Paul, 'If you think you are standing firm, be careful that you don't fall!' (1 Corinthians 10:12). I had forgotten God's warning. I did not see it coming. The presence of God had been so real to me in the early years of my kingdom, I would have never thought I would ever turn away from the living God and serve other gods. He had given me all that I had, and I knew it. But it crept up on me so subtly—I began to value the ones I loved over God Himself. I became careless of the boundaries God had set in my relationships, and slowly my mind became callous toward God's leading (see 1 Kings 11:2).

"In talking with Aaron at one of our Idolaters Anonymous meetings, I came to see how vulnerable humans are to the temptation to worship other gods. He told me his story: 'One day you're the high priest of God's chosen people; the next day you're creating a golden calf.'

"My advice to other worshipers, after my fall, is this: Don't underestimate the temptation to create God-substitutes. And no matter how far you think you have come, know that you are prone to wander. Watch your heart carefully; pull the weeds early before they take over your garden. Especially pay attention to any unbridled appetites."

The old man walks from the stage in silence. Someone in the audience leans over to the one next to him and says, "What a privilege to hear from such a great worshiper, and what a great lesson to hear! I hope we never forget."

Scene 2: Zadok

After some moments of silence, a picture of an ancient ceremony appears on the screen, and a younger version of the old man who has just instructed us comes into view.

111

King Solomon and other officials are surrounding a middle-aged priest while these words appear beneath the scene: "In the early months of Solomon's reign, the king deposed Abiathar the priest and appointed Zadok in his place."

The Storyteller explains: "In God's search for worshipers, there is something very important that happened in the reign of Solomon that we cannot overlook. It is part of your story. The last of Eli's descendants was removed from Israel's priesthood, and a new line of Levites became prominent, according to a prophetic word that was spoken in the days before Israel ever had a king (see 1 Samuel 2:21–35).

"You may remember the mention of Eli from the story of Abraham's test. When Eli honored his wicked sons[1] more than God, an unnamed prophet made the diagnosis and the penalty clear. Because Eli had wandered from God-centeredness, his family would be removed from the priesthood. This prophet also spoke of a new line of priests: 'I will raise up for myself a faithful priest, who will do according to what is in my heart and mind. I will firmly establish his house, and he will minister before my anointed one always' (1 Samuel 2:35).

"A contemporary of David's, Zadok had been a brave young warrior and helped to establish David's rule soon after David was anointed king. Zadok was one of the consecrated priests who brought the Ark back to Jerusalem. During David's rule, the office of high priest was shared between Zadok and another priest by the name of Abiathar, who was the last priestly descendant of the house of Eli. Zadok was in charge of the worship at Gibeon where the tabernacle was; Abiathar was in charge of the worship at Jerusalem, where the Ark was.

"From all appearances, Zadok and Abiathar seemed to have the same heart toward God. It was not until a crisis took place that we see what God had seen all along: They had fundamentally different motivations.

"Just before the death of King David, one of David's sons, Adonijah, 'put himself forward and said, "I will be king"' (1 Kings 1:5). He convinced Abiathar and some other leaders to support him, but 'Zadok the priest . . . did not join Adonijah' (verse 8). Nor did David. When David heard about Adonijah's attempt to usurp the throne, he called Zadok the priest and Nathan the prophet to make it clear that Solomon would be the next king. It was Zadok who poured the oil on Solomon's head, anointing him as king.

"The story of Zadok goes back four hundred years to an incident that took place when Israel was still in the wilderness. Israel had camped on the east side of the Jordan across from Jericho, a place from which they would later launch their attack on Canaan. The king of Moab, filled with dread because of the Israelites, hired a religious expert by the name of Balaam to advise him."

At this point, the story unfolds on the stage as the audience listens in on a meeting between a shady prophet and his dark lord, whom we know to be the Liar.

With a hissing voice, the Liar counsels Moab's counselor: "You can't beat them militarily; you haven't been able to proclaim curses against them. You must pollute their worship, for that's the secret of their strength."

Balaam asks, "But how can we do that? Moses' Law does not allow them to worship other gods."

The dark majesty smirks. "Ensnare them by their appetites; then they will worship what feeds their desires."

The scene changes; Balaam is now persuading the king of Moab. "Have your men offer their wives and daughters freely to the Israelite men. Then have them invite the Israelites to join you in worshiping Baal."[2]

When the evil plan was accomplished, the Liar's hideous laughter and grotesque dancing fills the stage. He exults before his lieutenants, "It worked; we have seduced a nation. We'll use this strategy again and again."

The Storyteller continues: "God's anger burned against His people because of their idolatry. He had made the rules clear, over and over: 'You shall have no other gods before Me.' Many were sentenced to death for their sin. But as God was making known His judgment through Moses, the sin continued right in view of the judge.

"A valiant priest named Phinehas, the son of Eleazar, was moved by a passion for God's honor and courageously carried out God's judgment against the offenders. When he did, God turned His anger away from His people. He also promised to Phinehas that he and his descendants would have a lasting priesthood.

"Phinehas had a grandson whose grandson's grandson had a grandson who became the grandfather of Zadok (see 1 Chronicles 6:4–8). It was this Zadok who would fulfill the prophecy that God would raise up a faithful priest whose house would replace the house of Eli and become the leading family of priests (see 1 Samuel 2:35 and 1 Kings 2:35).

"Fast-forward 850 years after Phinehas—450 years after Zadok—and you'll find the promise still being fulfilled. Described by Ezekiel, it was Zadok's heirs who alone would be allowed to come before the Lord to minister before Him. Why? Because of God's faithful promises to two faithful members of the same family, Phinehas and Zadok."

The Teacher walks onto the stage as he explains: "Just as God had to create a division between the people and the priests at Sinai, He now had to create a division among the priests. Historically, Zadok played a role in the midst of the Levitical years similar to the role that Luther played in the midst of the church age. By his faithfulness to God, which was in direct contrast to religious waywardness, Zadok became a priestly reformer. Among priests, his name stands as a landmark between Mount Sinai and the New Testament.

"Zadok, his ancestors and his descendants[3]—maybe you are one—are examples of a deep-seated motivation to please

114

God and be faithful to Him in worship. When you think of Zadok, think of the phrase 'ministry to the Lord.' And what is ministry to the Lord? It is *drawing near to God for God's sake and not our own.*

"Most of us think of ministry as an activity aimed exclusively at other people. But those who are becoming worshipers understand what Zadok did. They know that our first ministry is not to the lost or to the household of faith, but to the Lord. That does not mean that we minister only to God and not to others; it means that we minister *first* to God, then to others. Zadok stands in contrast with those who only ministered to the people: 'They [the other priests] may . . . stand before the people and serve them. . . . They are not to come near to serve me as priests. . . . But the priests, who are . . . descendants of Zadok . . . they alone are to come near my table to minister before me' (Ezekiel 44:11, 13, 15–16). The other priests were in the ministry, but they were exiled from God's presence, an awful penalty.

"Keep in mind, too, that the exclusion of the others was not God's plan. It was the consequence of bowing to other gods, an outworking of wrong priorities (see Ezekiel 44:10). When Zadok's fellow priest, Abiathar, approved of the self-promoting spirit of Adonijah, he, like Eli before him, honored a different spirit above God.[4] Zadok, like Phinehas before him, set God's honor over all. The story of Zadok and Abiathar is a story of contrasts: a passion for God's honor versus self-promotion. God is looking for worshipers like Zadok."

Scene 3: The Power of Sacrifice

The Teacher begins to address the audience as a professor would address his class.

"Under Solomon, Zadok became the leading priest, and self-promoting ministry was dealt a blow. That was good.

However, after Solomon, the priesthood suffered some terribly bad news. Because of Solomon's idolatry, Israel became a divided nation—Judah and Benjamin in the south and the other ten tribes in the north (see 1 Kings 11:9–13). The northern kingdom became known as Israel, and the southern kingdom became known as Judah.

"What happened to the priesthood in Israel was an utter shame. Have you ever seen one of those ads where you can send in your name and address along with $25 and get back a 'real' Ph.D. diploma from Easy Street University? That's a lot like what happened to the qualifications to become a priest in Israel.

"Jeroboam, who rebelled against Solomon's foolish son, Rehoboam, knew that unless an alternate religious system was set up, the northern tribes would be drawn back to Judah and the Temple (see 1 Kings 12). So he 'appointed priests from all sorts of people, even though they were not Levites' (1 Kings 12:31).These counterfeit priests led the people in counterfeit festivals to worship counterfeit gods—two golden calves that Jeroboam created and placed at Bethel and Dan. (What is it about golden calves?) This effort to create a substitute religious system became known in Scripture as the despicable 'sins of Jeroboam.'[5] Those who participated then, and through the generations until now, follow a tradition that began with Cain.

"The first king after Jeroboam to commit 'the sins of Jeroboam' was the infamous King Ahab, who married the equally infamous Canaanite woman named Jezebel. And that brings us to Mount Carmel and the story of the history-changing power of an acceptable sacrifice. Let's watch."

The screen shows a great plain before a mountain with a great crowd gathered—thousands and thousands from all over Israel. The Storyteller's voice begins to narrate.

"This is the story of Ahab, Jezebel, the prophets of Baal and Elijah. You have heard similar stories before: It is the story of idolatry, judgment and remedy.

116

"Asa is finishing up his reign over Judah, and Asa's son Jehoshaphat is about to replace him. Ahab is the king over Israel. Israel's worship of Baal has brought on a severe drought. Ahab and Jezebel are trying to eradicate all vestiges of an earlier religion by killing the Lord's prophets (see 1 Kings 18:1–40). They had searched extensively for Elijah, believing he was the reason for their troubles, but he seemed to have a supernatural way of eluding their grasp.

"Instead of running away in fear, Elijah unexpectedly showed up before Ahab with a challenge, a challenge that could potentially undermine Ahab's dream of restoring the tradition of Cain. Boldly throwing down the gauntlet, Elijah announced what we will call 'The Great Worship Contest.'

"'Gather all Israel to Mt. Carmel.' This would be like a nationally televised contest in our day—the Super Bowl, for instance. 'Oh, and make sure that the 850 prophets of Baal and Asherah are there—the ones that Jezebel is so chummy with. We're going to find out who the real God is. Here are the ground rules: Your prophets can worship their gods in any way they want, for as long as they want. Then I'll worship my God. We'll know the true God to be the One who answers our sacrifice by fire.' Ahab and Baal's prophets accepted the challenge. Ahab gathered together the people of Israel and the 850 prophets of Baal and Asherah as instructed."

The view pans across the thousands gathered at Mt. Carmel, toward a rough-hewn prophet, Elijah, the Tishbite. His words to Israel were stinging, but bore authority: "How long will you be double-minded? If the Lord is your God, follow Him; but if Baal is God, follow him." Apparently, Elijah was not comfortable with Israel's pluralism.

The people, who collectively would be the contest's judge, agree to the terms. "What you say is good."

The prophets of Baal went first. From morning until noon, they incanted, "O Baal, answer us." But there was no

117

response; no one answered. So they became more intense. They shouted louder. They even slashed themselves with spears until their blood flowed. (They must have known that the answer would have something to do with sacrifice.) They continued their frantic prophesying into the evening. But still, "there was no response, no one answered, no one paid attention" (1 Kings 18:29). The only excitement for the fans took place when Elijah taunted Baal's prophets: "Maybe your god is traveling, or maybe he's taking a nap. You have to shout louder or you won't wake him up."

As the sun was going down, I am sure the commentators were bleary-eyed, thinking they were in for a long night, rather like television commentators around midnight after a close election. The contest had already gone on for nine hours, and it was still the first half.

Finally Elijah took charge. The team of 850 prophets left the field disappointed. They knew they could not win, but maybe they could tie. They looked on as Elijah repaired the altar, arranged the wood, cut the bull into pieces and laid it on the wood. Then, putting himself at a disadvantage, he ordered water to be poured all over the sacrifice and the altar *three times*.

After praying a simple prayer, Elijah backed up, making room for God to answer. After a brief wait, a startled shout rose from the commentators: "Look!" Tens of thousands of faces stared up into the sky. Coming toward the altar like a meteor, a great ball of fire lit up the evening. Its heat consumed the sacrifice, the wood and even the stones of the altar. As he had with both Abraham and Moses (see Genesis 15:17 and Leviticus 9:24), God answered Elijah's sacrifice with fire. When the people saw it, they fell on their faces and cried out, "The LORD—he is God! The LORD—he is God!" (1 Kings 18:39). Their votes had been registered.

The false prophets were slain. Elijah shouted out to Ahab, "And now you'll get your rain." Ahab had nothing to say as he rode off in the pouring rain, preparing an explanation

118

for Jezebel. A nation had turned back to God by the power of an acceptable sacrifice.

Scene 4: The Prophet Who Saw Stars

The screens take the audience through a collage of events that the Storyteller describes.

"The effects of the great revival at Carmel were short-lived. You would think an experience like that would leave a lasting impression. But although Jehu, Ahab's successor, put away the worship of Baal, Israel continued to worship golden calves at Bethel and Dan (see 2 Kings 10:28).

"And so it was. The northern kingdom experienced a succession of kings, some better, some worse. But they could never shake the effects of the sins of Jeroboam, who had institutionalized the tradition of Cain (see 2 Kings 17:22–23). Beginning with Jehu, the northern kingdom began to decline (see 2 Kings 10:32), until finally, in the eighth century B.C., Israel fell to the ruthless empire of Assyria. Their nobles were deported to what is modern-day Iran, and peoples from various foreign countries were brought in by the king of Assyria to repopulate Israel, now called Samaria (see 2 Kings 17:24).

"Interestingly, the new inhabitants of Samaria soon real-ized that something was wrong—lions were killing people in all of their towns. Because they began to perceive this as judgment from God, they convinced the king of Assyria to bring back one of the priests who had been deported to teach them how to worship the Lord. He taught them what he could, but this odd cultural amalgamation called Samaria just couldn't let go of its own various gods." (Many years later, a descendant from these folks *did* find out the proper way to worship when she met the Lion of the tribe of Judah at a Samaritan well. But then, you already know that story.)

119

"The southern kingdom fared little better. There were some notable kings who revived proper worship. Among them was Hezekiah, who purified the Temple and revived the priestly ministry. Because of this worship revival, Judah was miraculously protected from the same vicious Assyrian invasion that conquered Israel.[6] And there was Josiah, the consummate iconoclast,[7] who dug up the bones of faithless priests and burned them on their altars, briefly returning Judah to God-centeredness.

"But even Josiah's sons couldn't remember the lessons their father had learned, and Judah became a vassal state, first to Egypt, then to Babylon.[8] Eventually Judah, under King Zedekiah,[9] gave up all restraint against evil: 'All the leaders of the priests and the people became more and more unfaithful, following all the detestable practices of the nations and defiling the temple of the LORD, which he had consecrated in Jerusalem' (2 Chronicles 36:14).

"Again and again, God, because of His great love for His people and for His dwelling place, tried to get through to the leaders of Judah through the voice of prophets. But again and again, these leaders mocked His messengers and despised their words (see 2 Chronicles 36:15–16).

"After a horrible two-year siege of Jerusalem, Babylon's King Nebuchadnezzar broke through the wall, destroyed all the houses and burned every important building in the city, including the once glorious Temple of Solomon. King Zedekiah was taken prisoner and was forced to watch as his sons were slaughtered along with the other officials of Judah. That was the last thing he saw before his own eyes were gouged out.

"I'm sure God cried when He had to turn away and give Jerusalem over to her enemies. But He was clear that it was a worship failure that had caused Him to take such drastic measures. God had stated almost four hundred years earlier that even outsiders would know the reason: 'Because they have forsaken the LORD, the God of their fathers, who brought them out of Egypt, and have embraced other gods, worshiping and serving them—that is why he brought all this disaster on them.' (These were God's words to Solomon in 2 Chronicles 7:22.)

"A priest from Anathoth named Jeremiah watched the entire miserable story unfold. He began prophesying during Josiah's revival and wrote songs commemorating Josiah's greatness that were sung for generations (see 2 Chronicles 35:25).

"Known as the weeping prophet, Jeremiah must have felt God's own heartbreak."

A spotlight in the theater reveals a dramatic enactment of Jeremiah's deep emotions: "O my anguish, my anguish! I writhe in pain. O the agony of my heart! Disaster follows disaster, and the whole land lies in ruins!" (see Jeremiah 4:19–20).

The Storyteller resumes his narrative: "Jeremiah is featured in this story of God's search for worshipers because in the darkest hour, Jeremiah looked up and saw that God's plan ultimately would not be thwarted. Jeremiah well knew how the northern ten tribes had fallen prey to idolatry. He had watched as they had been deported from their land by a ruthless enemy. In effect, he had witnessed the disappearance of the majority of a nation which was to have been a kingdom of priests in behalf of the nations. And now Judah, the only hope left, was following in Israel's footsteps. When he tried to warn Judah's leaders of the pending consequences of ignoring God's ways, he was arrested and put into prison. How would it end? He had already prophesied that Israel would be taken captive by Babylon. But what then? Would that be the end of the story?

"Thank God for Jeremiah's 33rd chapter. You may know it for the little personal nugget of promise in the third verse: 'Call to me and I will answer you and tell you great and unsearchable things you do not know.' But there's more to that little nugget than a personal promise. In it lies the

121

promise of a future restoration of Israel, and even more, of a multitude of kings and priests that cannot be counted.

"Yes, there would be devastation—the streets of Jerusalem would be filled with the dead bodies of many Jewish men, and houses and palaces would be destroyed. But in that very place of devastation, there would be heard again the sounds of joy and gladness, the sound of those who would bring the sacrifice of praise into the house of the Lord. (See Jeremiah 33:11.)

"Jeremiah was so confident in the redemptive purpose behind God's present judgments that he even invested in real estate in Israel. He was in prison; Judah's wickedness was greater than that of the nations who did not know God; Babylon's army was surrounding Jerusalem; and Jeremiah, contrarian that he was, invested in the stock market. He knew that the land's value would return."

The actor portraying Jeremiah returns to the stage and begins speaking to the audience from the perspective of eternity: "You may wonder how I could have had such confidence about the future in a time of such overwhelming disrepair. Here's what I hung my hope on: I had heard God speak. I heard words describing what my friend Abraham had seen in Genesis 15, a "sky-full" of descendants: 'I will make the descendants of David my servant and the Levites who minister before me as countless as the stars of the sky and as measureless as the sand on the seashore' (Jeremiah 33:22).

"Recently I was talking with our sharing group. I love these guys. Abraham told me that though he had seen the "sky-full" of descendants, he had not seen as clearly as I that they were to be kings and priests. Then I told the apostle John that I had not seen as clearly as he had that the multitude was international. He deflected the compliment with words from his friend Paul, who was sitting close by: 'We were all prophesying "in part," weren't we?' Then Paul said, 'But it's all clear now, isn't it?' At that we all spoke the same words spontaneously, 'Face to face,' and burst into laughter."

Jeremiah starts to tear up when he tells of how they finished their meeting that night singing the song "Eternity's Joy." Lost in thought, he starts singing. Somehow the audience also knows the tune and sings with him without accompaniment:

> "You are worthy to take the scroll and to open its seals, because you were slain, and with your blood you purchased men for God from every tribe and language and people and nation. You have made them to be a kingdom and priests to serve our God, and they will reign on the earth."
>
> Revelation 5:9–10

The stillness that follows is like a sea of glass, and a sense of eternity fills the theater. Then as the reverie slowly fades, Jeremiah segues with finesse from the profound to the personal: "Before I leave, could I make a request? The next time you think of the words, 'Call to me and I will answer you and tell you great and unsearchable things you do not know,' look up and see if you do not see a sky full of worshipers. It will give *you* hope in *your* darkest hour."

Applause seems the most natural response as the audience delights in the actor's performance and agrees to Jeremiah's request.

Scene 5: The Captivity

The Storyteller's resonant voice continues: "After the storm of Nebuchadnezzar's conquest of Jerusalem, Jewish survivors were taken away to Babylon, and the clock began to tick. Seventy years had been set as the time of captivity, but God's plans were not on hold. In what others might call

123

'downtime,' He had a fascinating plan in place to increase the number of His worshipers.

"A young nobleman named Daniel was among those who survived. Along with others, he was trained in the language and literature of the Babylonians. Although some of his countrymen were bitter toward the Babylonians, Daniel had taken the counsel of Jeremiah, to recognize God's hand in Judah's captivity, and to make the best of it (see Jeremiah 29:4–7).

"Those who trained him took pleasure in Daniel's aptitude and excellent spirit (see Daniel 5:12). He became a counselor to Nebuchadnezzar who, because of God's dealings and Daniel's influence, ended up becoming a worshiper of God himself.[10] Nebuchadnezzar's son, Belshazzar, also promoted Daniel even though Daniel prophesied the destruction of Belshazzar's rule.

"When the Medes and Persians conquered Babylon, Daniel became one of three top administrators—and he was about to be promoted over the whole kingdom. It was then that our ancient foe, the Liar, launched a behind-the-scenes campaign. Apparently infuriated that the tradition of Abel was gaining influence in the seat of power of the world's greatest empire, the Liar began whispering in the ears of the other administrators, using his favorite weapons of jealousy and accusation. Through demonic strategizing, he found the flaw he would exploit, a flaw that he knew often existed where men enjoy great power—the desire for greater power . . . absolute power.

"Darius, the new king, listening to the Liar's argument from the mouth of the other administrators, took the bait: 'You are not only great, Darius; you are the greatest. For the unity of the empire, should it not become law that anyone that asserts anything greater than you should be punished by death?' He had not learned yet the wisdom that Nebuchadnezzar paid a high price to gain—that the truly great leaders know the boundaries of their greatness.

124

"Daniel knew that his temporal position—and his very life—were a small price to pay in order to be true to eternity's God. He had the same spirit as Martin Luther, who centuries later would pen the words, 'Let goods and kindred go, this mortal life also; the body they may kill; God's truth abideth still. His kingdom is forever.' Daniel's identity was not in his leadership, but in the One whom he followed. He continued his worship intercession in Babylon: 'Three times a day he got down on his knees and prayed, giving thanks to his God, just as he had done before' (Daniel 6:10). His life was his sacrifice—not just his words. And God answered his sacrifice by temporarily transforming the ferocious lions that were supposed to kill him into house pets.

"The same miracle didn't work for the Liar's accomplices, though. When the jealous administrators were thrown into the same den, they breathed their last when the lions' ferocity returned. And Darius himself learned the wisdom of the truly great. He became, in his own way, a worship evangelist commanding 'peoples, nations and men of every language' to 'fear and reverence the God of Daniel. For he is the living God and he endures forever; his kingdom will not be destroyed, his dominion will never end' (Daniel 6:25, 26).

"What the Liar intended to be a reinstatement of his borrowed dominion,[11] turned out to be the worldwide proclamation of God's greatness. Israel's captivity became a great moment in God's search for worshipers."

The Teacher now takes the stage.

"The story of Daniel in Babylon is an incredible tutorial for modern worshipers. When Israel was in the land, worship centered around the tabernacle or the Temple. But in Babylon, worship had to be lived out through the lives of a scattered minority. Today, surrounded by cultures that are increasingly humanistic, we can learn from Daniel about the breadth of God's purposes and how to bring God glory 'among the nations.'

"If, when you think of worship, all you see is your con-gregation, Daniel would say, 'Your God is too small.' It is time to let your father David instruct you, as he most cer-tainly did for Daniel: 'Give thanks to the LORD, call on his name; *make known among the nations* what he has done. . . . Sing to the LORD, *all the earth*. . . . Declare his glory *among the nations*, his marvelous deeds *among all peoples*. . . . Great is the LORD and most worthy of praise; he is to be feared above all gods. For all the gods *of the nations* are idols, but the LORD made the heavens. . . . Ascribe to the LORD, *O families of nations*. . . . Bring an offering and come before him. . . . Let the heavens rejoice, *let the earth be glad*; let them say *among the nations*, "The LORD reigns!"' (1 Chronicles 16:8, 23–26, 28–29, 31, emphasis added). Worship leaders, lift your vision higher. Learn from Daniel. God is interested in nations, not just congregations.

"You may have heard it said that God wants to take us out of the world and get the world out of us, so that He can send us back into the world.[12] Along the way, the people of God often forget that last part.[13] God always has the peoples of this world in view; it's why He sent His Son: 'For God so loved the world. . . .' The Temple itself was meant to be a 'house of prayer for the nations.' Being in captivity forced the issue that God is a missionary God. He puts His glory among His people to be displayed among the peoples of this world.

"For many of us, Daniel in Babylon provides a much-needed redefinition of ministry and worship. Usually when a man or woman senses 'a call to the ministry,' they are quickly routed into church work; rarely are they equipped to serve 'out there' in their world. May God hasten the day when we reconnect the Great Commission of Matthew 28:18–20 with the dominion mandate of Genesis 1:28. 'Go therefore, preach and disciple nations' is the New Testament version of 'Be fruitful, increase in number; fill the earth and subdue it.' Then, following the call to ministry will lead us into the marketplace, into government, into the arts, into teaching and into every nook and cranny of human activity. When this reconnection is made, we will rediscover what Daniel exemplified: that the call to ministry is simply a call to serve others in God's name until they bring Him glory. Daniel was involved in discipling a nation—an empire, really—through public service.

"A number of years ago, God seemed to be challenging the Church to take its praise to the streets. March for Jesus was an international movement that successfully encouraged simultaneous public parades of worship. One of the marches had an estimated twelve million participants worldwide. It was a challenge for many church people to think about worshiping God on the streets.

"But now we are being challenged in an even greater way—to be His worshipers as a city manager, or a film director, or a professor or an athlete. This is a major challenge, because much of this activity is seen as out of bounds for those who have 'a calling' on their lives. We tend to define 'church' as those officially endorsed programs and activities that take place at the facility we call the church, instead of the network of relationships that it is meant to be. We tend to view those in the marketplace as convenient sources of revenue to support the church professionals. Instead, we should see that the church is meant to equip and support the network of ministries that all of His people are meant to be.

"We should not only celebrate when the Mel Gibsons, the Bonos, and the George W. Bushes show up, but we should be encouraging *every* worshiper to become a Daniel in his sphere of influence, and to build support systems 'out there' to facilitate their success. If you are a worship pastor, and one of your best musicians feels that he can bring greater glory to God by investing himself in music outside of the church, do test his motives, but once you are satisfied, help him find the spiritual support necessary to succeed in that.

127

That's your job. This equipping ministry, not to be seen as some special para-church activity competing with the regular church for time and ministry dollars, is fundamental to the work of the regular church, not incidental."

As if he has just been tapped on the shoulder, the Teacher interrupts himself and chuckles. "I think I just moved over into preaching," he grins. "Back to Daniel.

"Daniel instructs us in two ways: in *what* he did and in *how* he did it. Although we think of Daniel as a prophet— and that he was, one of the greatest[14]—he spent most of his time in politics, in the best sense of the word. Every morning he reported for work at the 'White House' of Babylon, and every day was filled with policy-making decisions, reviewing reports, evaluating personnel and making political appointments.

"In the course of his work, he eventually faced a test of allegiance—a test of worship: 'Bow down or lose your job . . . and your life, too.' The outcome of his resolve to worship God alone inspired worship among the Gentiles. Isn't it interesting that the leaders of the world brought honor to God when the kings of God's people did not? All the while, the exiled prophets of Israel[15] were probably thinking that Daniel was backsliding by spending so much time working for Babylon's welfare.

"*What* he did was this: By becoming 'one of them,' he let his light shine before the Babylonians, who saw his good deeds and praised his Father in heaven.[16] That's part of Daniel's tutorial for today's worshipers.

"But *how* he did it is also instructive. He was uncompromising in matters of conscience, and he was unintimidated in matters of culture. He was both countercultural and cross-cultural.

"Through Jeremiah's influence, Daniel didn't buy into the anti-Babylonian harangue of Israel's empty prophets. He saw his circumstances as an opportunity to serve. He acquired the wisdom of diplomacy—he knew the difference between explicit and implicit testimony and when to employ each. For the Christian, sharing the Good News of Jesus is our explicit testimony. Indigenously identifying with the needs of others and serving them with good deeds is our implicit testimony. Knowing how the two work together is the wisdom we ambassadors need to allow us to accurately represent one kingdom to another. Jesus had this wisdom. He didn't only preach; 'he went around doing good and healing all who were under the power of the devil' (Acts 10:38).

"The Babylonian nobility and academicians knew that Daniel was different, but they also knew that he wasn't aloof. They had seen him draw the line on issues of appetite and pleasures (see Daniel 1:8). They knew that Daniel would confront even the highest in power when they went astray (see Daniel 5:22), and that he would not bow down in worship to Babylon's gods. But they also knew he deeply loved the Babylonians. He had so eagerly and thoroughly learned their language and literature (see Daniel 1:3–4, 17–20). He had interceded for and saved the lives of magicians, enchanters and sorcerers (see Daniel 2:24). Like Jesus, Daniel had built friendships with those who were very different from himself (see Matthew 11:19). He genuinely, not reluctantly, enjoyed their company. He was fascinated to talk with them.

"If the main component of our approach to the world is fear of being stained by its corruption, we are secretly believing that the gods of this age are stronger than our God, that their culture is more potent than ours. Daniel was not naïve about the corrupting potential of Babylon, but he was *more* confident that the one who was in him was greater than the one who is in the world (see 1 John 4:4). He therefore practiced the daily disciplines of maintaining fellowship with his great God. That heart of God-centeredness guided him from being an orphaned exchange student in Babylon to its prime minister.

"Worshipers, what was in Daniel is in you, too. He's your tutor, your example, your father. The nations are waiting for such worshipers."

After a pause, the audience hears the Storyteller again: "With that glimpse of the great multitude, we are just about ready for the final act, the dramatic conclusion of the Story of Worship."

6

THE CONCLUSION
OF THE MATTER

LET THE TEMPLE BE REBUILT

Now all has been heard; here is the conclusion of the matter.

Ecclesiastes 12:13

"The kingdom of the world has become the kingdom of our Lord and of his Christ, and he will reign for ever and ever."

Revelation 11:15

Since we are receiving a kingdom that cannot be shaken, let us be thankful, and so worship God acceptably.

Hebrews 12:28

Usually it is hard to gather a crowd, but not in this case. The five minutes seems too long, and the audience is ready even before the stage is. Quietness descends, and in the silence three taps of the conductor's wand can be heard before the music, and Act 4, begins.

Act 4, Scene 1: The Restoration

After the brief musical introduction, the Storyteller begins to tell the amazing story of Cyrus and the return of the Jews from Babylon. Our eyes watch a review of the rise to power of Cyrus the Great, the ruler of a Persian province called Anshan.[1] Under Cyrus, Persia conquered mighty Babylon in 539 B.C. The Persian Empire was to be the prominent world power for the next two hundred years, until its conquest by Alexander the Great in 330 B.C.

You will find all of that in the history books. But what they might not tell you there is that Isaiah prophesied Cyrus' rise to power—two hundred years before it happened, even calling him by name (see Isaiah 44:28 and 45:1).

As the audience observes scenes of Cyrus extending Persia's rule, it also watches a written text of what seems to be quotes from a reporter who lived at the time of Cyrus. When the last words appear—"Cyrus will say of Jerusalem, 'Let it be rebuilt'"—the credit and date are given: "Isaiah the prophet, circa 720 B.C." As that credit appears, suddenly the scene shifts, and Cyrus himself is seen writing some kind of official letter. Our eyes see the words, "Let Jerusalem be rebuilt," and a new date appears on the screen: 538 B.C.

The Storyteller begins to speak: "The edict that Cyrus was composing signaled the beginning of the end of Israel's captivity:

'This is what Cyrus king of Persia says: "The LORD, the God of heaven, has given me all the kingdoms of the earth and

132

he has appointed me to build a temple for him at Jerusalem in Judah. Anyone of his people among you—may the LORD his God be with him, and let him go up."'

2 Chronicles 36:23

"Once the edict was read, about forty thousand Jews in Babylon started packing to go home (see Ezra 2:64). The significance of this miraculous proclamation was so great that Jeremiah even said that God would be known thereafter as the God who delivered them out of Babylon, not as the God who delivered them out of Egypt (see Jeremiah 16:14). Just as the Israelites who left Egypt, these Israelites were sent out of Babylon with silver, gold, livestock and other gifts. And just as the Israelites who came out of Egypt, these Israelites' purpose was worship. The express purpose for their deliverance was to rebuild the Temple and restore sacrifices. King Cyrus returned the articles from Solomon's Temple to Israel's leaders, and away they went.

"The first thing the exiles did when they returned to their homeland was to make plans to rebuild the Temple. Less than a year after Cyrus' proclamation, the altar had been rebuilt and daily worship had been restored: 'On the first day of the seventh month they began to offer burnt offerings to the LORD, though the foundation of the LORD's temple had not yet been laid' (Ezra 3:6).

"Once the daily sacrifices had been restored, the builders began laying the foundations of the Temple, and the priests in their vestments accompanied the work with trumpets and cymbals and songs of praise. They were singing the songs of David with new confidence: 'He is good; his love to Israel endures forever' (Ezra 3:11). Jeremiah had been right: In the very place of terrible desolation, there *was* heard again the sounds of joy and rejoicing—the sounds of those who were bringing the sacrifice of joy into the Lord's house. Jeremiah had even prophesied the song they would

133

sing.[2] His estate probably even made some money on his earlier real-estate investment.

"But, as so often happens today, not everyone was happy with the new sounds of praise.[3] The Liar stirred up jealousy among the local residents and used intimidation, accusations and legal threats to stop the work (see Ezra 4:4–5). Tragically, it worked. As the record states: 'Thus the work on the house of God in Jerusalem came to a standstill until the second year of the reign of Darius king of Persia' (Ezra 4:24).

"The exiles who had returned with joy, laughter and renewed dreams (see Psalm 126) became discouraged and turned to taking care of themselves."

A sad song accompanies the drama as, on stage, the builders pack up their tools at the Temple site and walk away. The priests put away their trumpets and cymbals, and a hideous creature, looking on, smiles in satisfaction.

"For sixteen long, dreary years, a cloud of lethargy would hover over the returned captives . . . sixteen long years until August 29, 520 B.C., the day on which Haggai began speaking forcefully to Zerubbabel, Israel's governor, and to Joshua, the worship leader. Both of these men had lost heart through the earlier conflicts.

"Perhaps there was some praying grandmother who, as a little girl, had seen the Temple before it was destroyed by Nebuchadnezzar. She had survived the captivity, and there, in her modest backhouse, she was lifting her hands in early morning worship and prayer and reciting Scripture: 'O God, remember King David's words to his son to build the house: "Be strong and courageous, and do the work. Do not be afraid or discouraged, for the LORD God, my God, is with you. He will not fail you or forsake you until all the work for the service of the temple of the LORD is finished"' (1 Chronicles 28:20).

"Across town, a rusty old prophet by the name of Haggai was also praying and was drawn to the same passage in

1 Chronicles 28: 'Be strong and courageous, and do the work . . . for . . . God is with you.'

"'That's it!' he shouts. 'We have lost heart and become so entangled with the cares of this life that we have let the flame of God's worship go out. I need to share this with the governor and his worship leader.'

"From August to December of that year, Haggai's words inspired the leaders and the people to shake off their lethargy: 'Be strong, O Zerubbabel; be strong, O Joshua; and be strong, all you people, and work. For the LORD is with you, and his Spirit remains among you. Do not fear!' (see Haggai 2:4–5). His words also stirred the heart of a young prophet by the name of Zechariah, and together they lit a flame of passion among a disheartened people.

"The people set to work. Worship was to be restored among them. Opposition came again, but this time it was met with inspired resistance. Even when the local Persian officials threatened to shut down the construction site unless they could produce a proper building permit, rather than being intimidated, Israel's leaders confidently declared that they were servants of the God of heaven and earth—and that if the officials would check, they would find that the building project was authorized by Cyrus the Great.

"The building continued while the lawyers did their research. The matter came before the Persian emperor, Darius himself."

The audience watches as the story is shown on a split screen. On one we see the old grandmother in prayer, and on the other we see scholars studying some dusty documents in an archive in a faraway city.

"A scroll is found in Ecbatana, and it is signed by Cyrus. 'Let the Temple be rebuilt as a place to present sacrifices,' it reads. Darius gets the memo, reads it and pauses. Under his breath, he mutters, 'Very interesting,' and then dictates his own instructions to the provincial leaders in Judah:

"'Do not interfere with the building of this temple,' he wrote. 'In fact, I want you to give them whatever they need to finish the job so that their worship may be pleasing to God and their prayers for the welfare of the king and his sons will be answered.' Then, for emphasis, he decreed: 'May God, who has caused his Name to dwell there, overthrow anyone who tries to destroy this temple' (see Ezra 6:6–12).

"'So the elders of the Jews continued to build and prosper under the preaching of Haggai . . . and Zechariah' (Ezra 6:14). And on March 12, 516 B.C., just three and a half years after Haggai's revelation, the Temple was completed. Because of Israel's poverty at that time, Zerubbabel's Temple did not have the splendor of Solomon's earlier Temple, and because the Ark of the Covenant had been lost, a stone altar was placed where it should have been. But Zerubbabel's Temple, later enlarged, did stand for five centuries, and in this Temple Jesus, who was dedicated as a baby and later, as a boy, engaged the religious leaders in a fascinating discussion of God's purposes."

The Teacher eagerly walks onto the stage and begins to speak: "Several times, I wanted to interrupt the Storyteller, but I had to wait. I think you know what I am about to say: The story of rebuilding the Temple is not just their story . . . say it with me . . . it is ours. Think about the years of questioning that thoughtful people went through in Babylon: *We are in a strange land, and our kings are prisoners. Does God even care anymore? Have we so displeased Him that He has completely rejected us, once and for all? Will our future be a slow fade into oblivion?*

"Then hope drowned out all that despair when Cyrus declared the return and the rebuilding. That, too, is our story. We are set free from our bondages; it's going to be a new day. We make the exit from sin to return to God, and before we know it, the altar is restored—we have taken up the cross. We are not living for ourselves anymore, but for

God. We are praying, 'Not my will but Yours, O God.' We find ourselves with others of like heart. We dream, and we laugh. Our praise is genuine, from the heart. We are going from glory to glory. We are sure the rest of our life will be a great crescendo of increasing victories. God is showing up when we worship.

"And then, before we know it, the Liar suddenly creates turmoil from without or from within. He has several favorite tricks—scare by threats or ensnare by appetites—but usually he falls back on the simple tactic of inspiring pride and ambition (see Proverbs 18:12). The Liar gets busiest when praise is coming God's way, because he knows that worship is the atmosphere in which God's rule is extended—and that means his confinement.

"When trouble comes, God uses the occasion to test hearts. He looks for leaders, like Haggai, who know how to stand by what God says is true, rather than what they see. Victory over the Liar begins when the confidence of God's truth becomes contagious.

"Haggai saw God's truth—that the reborn nation of Israel had come to believe that taking care of themselves was more important than God's worship. He saw that they were thinking that after all of their troubles, they *deserved* some creature comfort. He identified the lie by which their minds were held captive, and his divinely empowered diagnosis demolished the stronghold (see 2 Corinthians 10:4–5). And from the day they set themselves to reprioritize and put God first, the curse was lifted, and they began to prosper (see Haggai 1:9–11; 2:15–19).

"Even the leaders saw they had become subject to wrong priorities. Haggai's confidence in God's truth spread fast. First the pastor (Zerubbabel) and the worship leader (Joshua), and then the people acknowledged that they had fallen prey to self-centeredness. When they did, progress in worship took place rapidly. That's pertinent in Pascagoula—or wherever your own church may be.

"Another point of the story is that true worship among God's people has value, even among those outside the community of faith. The Persian emperor wanted the Jews to offer acceptable sacrifices to their God for the welfare of his kingdom. Wise governments will welcome the presence of people truly connected to God, especially in times of trouble. Wise businesses, schools and communities do so, too. When darkness covers the earth and God's glory is found among us, 'nations will come to your light, and kings to the brightness of your dawn' (Isaiah 60:3).

"So, what lessons have we learned so far from this story of restored worship? Here are two:

- "When you make God's worship a priority in your life, He can take better care of you than you can of yourself.
- "True worship can affect the welfare of those around us.

"But there's something else in this story that the Storyteller didn't tell you—it is the perspective that Haggai gives us about our future. In his second message, he wrote of a time of international shaking associated with God's glory filling the Temple and abundant resources being made available for His purposes: 'The glory of this present house will be greater than the glory of the former house' (see Haggai 2:6–9).

"Because the glory of Zerubbabel's Temple never rivaled that of Solomon's, Haggai was looking through the event of the Temple's rebuilding to a greater Temple . . . a Temple in which we are living stones. Like Ezekiel and John, who both had visions of a spiritual temple,[4] Haggai and Zechariah saw into *our* part of the story.

"Listen to Haggai's apprentice, Zechariah, paint the picture of Jesus, the true Temple builder:

'Here is the man whose name is the Branch, and he will branch out from his place and build the temple of the LORD. It is he who will build the temple of the LORD, and he will be clothed with majesty and will sit and rule on his throne. And he will be a priest on his throne. And there will be harmony between the two.' . . . Those who are far away will come and help to build the temple of the LORD.

Zechariah 6:12–13, 15

"With those words a crown was set on the head of the priest in this story, Joshua, son of Jehozadak. The mysterious Melchizedek—'without beginning of days or end of life'—was very likely looking on and perhaps even prompting the words. Zechariah predicted the reuniting of the separated ministries of priests and kings that began at Sinai, saying, 'There will be a harmony between the two.'

"Those of you in the audience who have been closely following the story know that this would be no small incident: a priest being crowned a king. The Joshua who wore the crown that day was from a priestly family; he was a descendant of Aaron through Phinehas and Zadok. But he foreshadowed another Joshua[5] who was of the tribe of Judah, a priest of a higher order, an intercessory king who would be the branch that Isaiah said would come up from the stump of Jesse, David's father.[6] This priest and king would build a new Temple for God."

At this point, the Teacher's tone becomes unusually dramatic: "This One of whom we speak is the great priest who offered Himself as the great sacrifice—the Lamb of God who is Lord of lords and King of kings" (see Revelation 17:14).

As the teacher walks from the stage, a flourish of trumpets is heard. At first it seems to come from a distance and the audience cannot recognize its melody, but as it comes closer, it grows in power and clarity, and we recognize that the melodies are taken from Handel's *Messiah*. Strains of

139

"and He shall reign" from the "Hallelujah Chorus" are ingeniously woven together with strains from "Worthy Is the Lamb." As a curtain rises, we see that what we thought was a recording is actually a live choir of trumpets—four groups of thirty in each group—120 in all. On a slowly rotating stage, the four trumpet choirs, each with trumpets of different sizes, face from four directions toward the middle. The brilliant sounds swell to such intensity that our emotions are overwhelmed, and we all spontaneously rise to our feet as though we were following a visible cue.

It is hard to describe the effect of these sounds, except to say that it seems as though those trumpets clear away a space in creation where the triumph of light over darkness is total and complete. It feels as though our lives have been indelibly marked by eternity itself. And then, almost as if a parade has just passed by, the sounds begin to fade. The curtain slowly falls, and the distance seems to grow between the audience and trumpeters, until there is no more sound.

Scene 2: The Temple Builder and the Royal Priesthood

"The Lamb of God who is the Lord of lords and the King of kings," the Storyteller restates the words of the Teacher. His words bring the audience back to the awareness that it is in a theater. The people look around and then take their seats again. The screen begins to tell the story with pictures as the Storyteller uses words.

"Five hundred and fifty years passed between the building of Zerubbabel's Temple and history's introduction to the Lamb of God. During that time, the Persian Empire fell to Greece. Greece tried to 'Hellenize' the world's thinking by infusing it with Greek philosophy and art, as well as its gods. But the Greeks also had the Old Testament writings translated into the Greek language, making God's truths available to the larger world. This translation, known as the Septuagint, was widely used by Jews outside of their own land and later by the early Christians.

"Despite this positive advancement, a horrible event took place in the Temple during this time. Around 167 B.C., the Liar orchestrated another familiar display of his lust for worship. History records that Antiochus IV Epiphanes,[7] who had tried to replace all Jewish learning and practices with Greek culture, erected a statue of Zeus in the Temple, and there sacrificed a pig, a blatant mockery of the Hebrews.

"This event stirred a heroic resistance led by an old priest named Mattathais, likely a descendant of Zadok.[8] On his deathbed, he rallied his sons with the story of ancient Phinehas,[9] whom he called their father.[10] Their resistance became known as the Maccabean revolt, which temporarily won Judah's independence. Judas Maccabeus would later cleanse the Temple from the defilement of Antiochus.

"Eventually the political prominence of Greece began to fade as Rome's began to rise. In 63 B.C., Rome conquered Judea, the territory to which they gave the name 'Palestine.' In about 20 B.C., King Herod, the Roman ruler over Judea, dramatically revitalized Zerubbabel's Temple, probably more for his own vanity than as an act of kindness toward the Jews—this was the Temple that was standing in Jesus' day.

"Fifteen years later, the faithful in Judea began to sense a stirring. There were rumors of people seeing angels, of a miraculous birth in Bethlehem, of dignitaries coming from faraway places to honor the baby born in a barn. It was commonly understood that this Promised One would become king. The same Herod who had revitalized the Temple was so nervous about these rumors that he actually had all the babies in Jerusalem killed in an attempt to destroy any potential rival to his throne.

"Not much more was heard about this coming king for years. But one old priest by the name of Simeon was sure he had held the Messiah in his hands when he consecrated a little month-and-a-half-old boy at the Temple. He never quit talking about it.

"And now we come to the heart of the story, and the part that is the most difficult to tell. We come to the part about Jesus, the story's hero. He has actually been in every scene of the story so far, for He, like Melchizedek, is without beginning or end of days. But where our protagonist has been hidden and invisible until this time, He now comes into full view.

"This part of the story is difficult to tell because some parts have been told so often that hearers often think that they know the whole of it. But as John the apostle wrote, Jesus did so many things that if all of them were written down, 'I suppose that even the whole world would not have room for the books that would be written' (John 21:25).

"Who is this Jesus? He was the baby born to a virgin, whose birth announcement was delivered by angels. He was the miracle worker, who caused blind Bartimaeus to see again, who raised Jairus' daughter from the dead, who ordered a legion of demons to come out of the man who had wandered among the tombs.

"We know Him as the one who forgave the woman caught in adultery, as the preacher of the Sermon on the Mount, as He who took time with misfits, who enjoyed the company of children and who confronted religious hypocrisy.

"As a storyteller, I know Him as the greatest of storytellers. He is known as one who spent time with twelve ordinary men and transformed them into powerful leaders who shook the kingdom of darkness. We know Him as the one who was unjustly convicted of crimes and sentenced to death. We know that He was tortured by scourging and then was nailed to a cross, where He died. Maybe we know that He was buried in a rich man's tomb, heavily guarded by Roman soldiers. We have heard it told many times, I am sure, that while in the grave, His body was quickened by the Holy Spirit, He rose from the dead, and angels rolled back the grave's massive stone door.

"I hope we all know Him as the one who is daily transforming our lives and preparing us for an eternity with Him.

"But do we know Him as the builder of a Temple more glorious than Solomon's, and as the gatherer of priests more numerous than the stars? If the answer is *no*, we will be hindered in becoming what He had in mind when He gave His life for ours. If we don't know Him as the recruiter of worshipers, we will not understand the part He wants us to play in the Story of Worship.

"So who *else* is this Jesus?

"As the Teacher told us, the prophet Zechariah said that the Messiah would be a priest-king who would build a Temple. Here is the Teacher again to help us understand."

The Teacher again takes the stage and begins to explain: "When Jesus died, the most magnificent building project ever conceived was begun: the building of a Temple made with living stones that would span nations and centuries. Can you imagine?

"Consider the explanation of this amazing endeavor from one of Jesus' disciples: 'You also, like living stones, are being built into a spiritual house to be a holy priesthood, offering spiritual sacrifices acceptable to God through Jesus Christ' (1 Peter 2:5).

"And listen to the greatest theologian of the first-century Church describe the progress: 'In him the whole building is joined together and rises to become a holy temple in the Lord. And in him you too are being built together to become a dwelling in which God lives by his Spirit' (Ephesians 2:21–22).

"And: 'God's temple is sacred, and you are that temple' (1 Corinthians 3:17).

"The writer of Hebrews confirms to us what Zechariah foretold, that our Messiah is a builder of a spiritual house: 'Jesus has been found worthy of greater honor than Moses, just as the builder of a house has greater honor than the house itself. . . . And we are his house, if we hold on to our courage' (Hebrews 3:3, 6).

"In Jesus' own words, we can see His excitement as a builder when He identified the foundation where this Temple would be built: 'On this rock I will build my church, and the gates of Hades [hell] will not overcome it' (Matthew 16:18).

"From Peter we learn that the Temple is a connection of living stones who are priests offering sacrifices. From Paul we learn that the Temple is a dwelling place of God's Spirit. From the writer of Hebrews and from Jesus Himself, we learn that Jesus is the builder.

"But the cost of such a project is massive. Remember the billions involved in building Solomon's Temple? The greater Temple is even more expensive to build. The building material—that's us—had to be purchased from another kingdom whose king, like Pharaoh, was quite unwilling to let us go. This purchase is what redemption is all about: 'You are worthy . . . because you were slain, and with your blood you purchased men for God from every tribe and language and people and nation. You have made them to be a kingdom and priests to serve our God, and they will reign on the earth' (Revelation 5:9–10).

"In this song of heaven, two major truths can pass us by if we are not observant:

- "The blood from the Lamb's slaughter was the extravagant price required to purchase the multitude, and

144

- The purpose of the purchase was that the multitude would become reigning worshipers.

"Is that purpose being fulfilled in you?

"This Jesus is a gatherer of priests and a temple builder. His great act of redemption is incomplete until we become that international throng of wholehearted worshipers.

"Do we understand how pervasive Jesus' role is in this Story of Worship? Jesus explained to the Pharisees, who so diligently studied the Old Covenant, that they had missed the real story: 'These are the Scriptures that testify about me' (John 5:39).

- "It was Jesus who created all things, listening as the morning stars sang. 'Without him nothing was made that has been made' (John 1:3; see also Colossians 1:16).
- "It was Jesus who would become the 'last Adam' (1 Corinthians 15:45), regaining Adam's lost dominion by choosing to please the Father in sacrifice rather than bowing to the Liar's invitation to worship a puny God-substitute.
- "Abel's blood cries out, but Jesus' blood cries out even more (see Hebrews 12:24).
- "The most quoted Old Testament passage in the New Testament, Psalm 110, in which the Father swore to the Son that He was a priest according to the order of Melchizedek, is all about Jesus.
- "Ultimately Abraham's calling, to father an international multitude, can only be fulfilled by the sacrifice of Christ Jesus (see Revelation 5:9–10). Abraham's offering of Isaac foreshadows the Father's offering of His beloved Son.
- "Moses' message defining Israel's teleological design—'Let My people go, so that they may worship

145

Me'—foreshadows our High Priest's message—'the Father is seeking worshipers.'

- "Mount Sinai is overshadowed by the greater Mount Zion, from which Jesus mediates the New Covenant.[11]

- "Jesus, who builds a nation[12] around His passion to glorify His Father, is called the Son of David, who also built a nation around God's worship. As mentioned, the extravagant price David paid for the building materials to construct a glorious Temple is trumped by the even more extravagant price that Jesus paid for the building materials to make an even more glorious Temple.

- "Jesus' sacrifice, like Elijah's, crushed the powers of darkness (see Colossians 2:15).

- "It was Jesus who would fulfill Zechariah's prophecy of a temple builder and would repair the breach between the ministry of priests and kings.

- "The end of the story is that in everything Jesus will have the supremacy (see Colossians 1:18), that all things in heaven and on earth will be brought under His headship (see Ephesians 1:10), and that He will be exalted to the highest place (see Philippians 2:9).

"Jesus' earthly ministry began with His introduction by John the Baptizer as the Lamb of God, a name that indicated His ultimate sacrifice. It would end with His giving His life as a ransom for a wayward universe, which housed a wayward mankind. But the joy that was set before Him was that a multitude of people from every tongue and tribe would lead a bought-back universe[13] in unending tribute to God. And so it was worth the suffering.

"The Storyteller is about to tell us the story's magnificent ending. But before he does, let me tell you a bit more about the Temple and its progress.

146

"First, let's understand the *nature* of this Temple.

"Remember what God was after in wanting Israel to become a kingdom of priests? If they had accepted God's offer at Sinai, they would have become a nation of priests on behalf of the nations. The cloud of God's glory, attended by ubiquitous prayer and worship, would have hovered over their households, workplaces and national life, and the blessings on their endeavors and the power to bless others would have given them a leadership role among the nations. God was looking for a core of humanity through which He could extend His rule in the world.

"When that didn't happen, God's presence became more localized. It was associated with a tabernacle and later with a Temple and the special priestly class that attended those holy places. The Temple that Jesus is building today is an undoing of that localization. The Samaritan woman asked *where* people should worship: 'Our fathers worshiped on this mountain, but you Jews claim that the place where we must worship is in Jerusalem' (John 4:20).

"Her question was *where*; Jesus answered *how*. His answer was and is a challenge to a centuries-old mind-set: 'neither on this mountain nor in Jerusalem, but in spirit and truth.' This new Temple is not a place; it is a network of relationships that emanates from a spiritual reality—Spirit and truth—which is God Himself.

"The relational nature of this Temple can be seen in how the New Testament writers so easily interchanged descriptions of it with other analogies that were relational in nature. Paul, for instance, in his letter to the Ephesians, speaks of the building as a household (see Ephesians 2:19–21), and two chapters later, as a body (see Ephesians 4:4, 16). Peter also mingles the building image of the people of God with the household image.[14]

"So the House of God is found today in many prisons, as it was when Paul and Silas worshiped and prayed in a Philippian jail. It is found in homes in China where believers gather in secret and sometimes have to whisper their praises to God. So it was found in Roman households in Paul's day (see Romans 16:5). You can find the Temple today in the marketplace where men and women gather for early morning prayer and fellowship and, later in the day, do their work as service to God—even as Daniel did in Babylon. And, of course, you find the Temple in the priests' weekly gathering for worship.

"The Temple that Jesus is building is a network of relationships made to reveal His glory. As living stones finding relationships with other living stones, we 'are being built into a spiritual house to be a holy priesthood, offering spiritual sacrifices acceptable to God' (1 Peter 2:5). That is the nature of this Temple that Jesus is building and of the priesthood He is gathering.

"Now let's turn to the *importance* of this Temple.

"Just as Solomon's Temple was a place for sacrifices and a place to bless the nations, this spiritual house, though not primarily a place, has the same function. We are built together so that God's worship will be acceptable and so that others around us will be blessed. When the priestly ministry ceased at various times in Israel's history, the power to bless came to a screeching halt. And so it has been and still is today: When the Temple's ministry to the Lord is in disrepair, we lose our salt and become 'good for nothing' (Matthew 5:13, KJV).[15] When the light goes out in the Temple, the world grows really dark. We are meant to be the world's light (see Matthew 5:14).

"We're talking here about becoming a people who remain in the presence of God. God wants us to be built together so that His glory can be made known: 'You . . . are being built together to become a dwelling in which God lives by his Spirit' (Ephesians 2:22). When the Queen of Sheba saw the worship in Solomon's Temple, she became breathless (see 1 Kings 10:5). So it will be in the greater Temple: As we make God's worship and His presence our priority, we will find a supernatural magnetism working to attract people from all walks of life. As we make our boast in the Lord, 'the humble shall hear of it and be glad' (Psalm 34:2, NKJV), and as God's glory appears over us, kings will be drawn to the brightness of the light (see Isaiah 60:2–3). God says that the gifts they bring with them 'will be accepted as offerings on my altar, and I will adorn my glorious temple' (verse 7).

"The priestly ministry of this Temple, then, becomes the central activity of the people of God, and the secret of blessing those around us. This Temple becomes the sphere of God's authority to extend His will. Now that powers and authorities have been legally disarmed (see Colossians 2:15), what is needed is an executive body that will carry out the established legislative will. And that's why Zechariah prophesied that the Messiah would build a Temple: to be a place where His name would abide. That's pretty important.

"Next let's understand the *process* of building the Temple.

"Just as the Temple spans national boundaries, it also spans generational boundaries. Like the building of some of Europe's great cathedrals, the work of one generation builds on what has gone on before it. Building the Duomo in Milan took centuries.[16] In the Middle Ages, it was not uncommon for a mason to spend his entire life continuing to build the same structure that his family had worked on two or three hundred years earlier.

"So the workers on this Temple take up where the previous generations leave off. And along the way, as in Israel's history, there have been times of renewed vision and energetic activity and other times when the work has languished and fallen into disrepair.

"The process of building the Temple is moving toward the final completion and its dedication. Its master builder, like Solomon, is eager to see the job finished so that His glory can be revealed. We should share His eagerness.

"Permit me to offer a brief outline and perspective of the Church's history of worship: the early years and then the three eras that followed. It is a story in itself, a story of truth building on truth."

The Early Years

"The early Church was officially inaugurated on the Day of Pentecost. And like the intended inauguration of the kingdom of priests at Sinai, Pentecost was attended with a dramatic display of signs and wonders. I am sure Melchizedek was avidly watching and listening as the Spirit of God came down on those 120 believers and transformed them into worshipers. He probably danced a little 'Melchizedekian jig' when he saw their praise displayed among the nations. There were God-fearing Jews 'from every nation under heaven' who heard these 120 royal priests 'declaring the wonders of God' in the many languages of the visiting nations (see Acts 1:15; 2:5, 11).

"The separation between the office of king and the office of priest, which had existed since the 'almost ordination,' was finally ended. This new priesthood, which is sustained by 'the power of an indestructible life' (Hebrews 7:16), brought with it a change of the law governing the behavior of its new society. Furthermore, a new sanctuary was revealed, 'the true tabernacle,' of which all others were mere shadows and copies. All of this—a new priesthood, a new law and a new sanctuary—is explained in the seventh and eighth chapters of the book of Hebrews.[17]

"Because the early Church met mostly in homes, the worship was probably simpler than what we know today. The songs were probably the kind that you could sing with little or no accompaniment. When they celebrated the Lord's Supper, it was probably not like the formal religious ceremony we know today, but more an extension of their joyful fellowship, taking place in the context of shared meals (see Acts 2:46), like the first one.[18]

"Because most of the apostolic leaders of the early Church were there on the Day of Pentecost and had experienced His awesome presence, I would imagine the early churches were taught to expect His presence in association with worship. It also seems that dynamic corporate prayer was a bigger part of their worship than in our more institutional approach to worship (see Acts 4:23–31; 12:5).

The Table, the Pulpit and the Throne

"After the early years, the development of worship seems to follow a script suggested in Paul's Ephesian letter—a script that implies three eras of worship, each with a slightly different emphasis.

"In Ephesians 5:25–27, Paul used the mystery of Christ's love for the Church as a model for Christian husbands. The obvious application is for husbands to be more Christlike. But think about this, too, as an insight into the awesome love that Christ has for the Church, and how it is being progressively revealed.

> Husbands, love your wives, just as Christ loved the church and gave himself up for her to make her holy, cleansing her by the washing with water through the word, and to present her to himself as a radiant church, without stain or wrinkle or any other blemish, but holy and blameless.
>
> Ephesians 5:25–27

"First Jesus gave Himself for His Bride. Then He cleansed her by 'the washing of the water through the word,' until finally she will be presented to Him as a glorious Bride 'without stain or wrinkle or any other blemish.' Since we know that the 'no-wrinkles, no-stains' part of this analogy

151

has a future fulfillment, it would not be a stretch to interpret this revelation of God's love as a historical progression.

"It started with His giving Himself for us. In the first era of Christian worship, the table is central, focusing on Christ's sacrifice for us. Imagine that you are interviewing Christians in this era on their way to worship: 'Excuse me. I'm involved in a religious research project. Could you tell me what is the main thing you are going to do in your worship service?' Most of the answers would go something like this: 'We are going to celebrate the Eucharist, the body and blood of our Lord.' There were other elements, of course, but the central activity was a celebration of His sacrifice. This is not just a historical model of worship; some traditions still hold the table as central.

"The Protestant Reformation brought a very significant change in the development of Christian liturgy. At least in most Protestant churches, the pulpit has replaced the table as the central activity. Of course, the table is still a very important part of worship, but if you did your interview with these worshipers, the majority would say something like, 'The main thing we are going to do is listen to God's Word.'

"This is stage two of Christ's Bride's experience of His love. We know of His sacrifice and we celebrate it regularly, but now we are experiencing the washing of His Word, and that has become central in our worship. This is not to imply in any way that the table is no longer important. The washing of the Word vitally depends on an understanding of the awesome price He paid for us to enjoy fellowship with Him.

"But now there is in view a third stage of knowing God's love for His Church. In this third liturgical era, the focus is on how God's love inspires our sacrifices. The Lamb receives His reward, the glory and honor and power from those for whom He died. Finally a radiant Bride is presenting herself to her magnificent Bridegroom. The central symbol here is not the table or the pulpit, but an invisible throne.

"The word in Ephesians 5 that describes how the Bride *presents* herself is the same Greek word Paul used in Romans 12 when he urged us to become worshipers who *offer* ourselves as living sacrifices.

"In the first two eras of Church history, we were the beneficiaries—He gave Himself for *us*; he washed *us*. In this third era, He is the beneficiary—He receives. In the first two eras, we came to church to 'get'; now we're coming to give. Now the rule of the day is, 'No one is to appear before me empty-handed' (Exodus 34:20).

"The songs in heaven, never forgetting His sacrifice, celebrate the glory and honor He receives: 'Worthy is the Lamb, who was slain, to receive' (Revelation 5:12). 'To him who sits on the throne and to the Lamb be praise and honor and glory and power, for ever and ever!' (Revelation 5:13). As the second Reformation brings in the third era of worship, heaven's throne becomes the invisible center. 'Never forget the benefits,' the psalmist wrote (see Psalm 103:2), but if you are just in it for the benefits, there's still some growing up to do. Live as a sacrifice for Him.

"Interview these folks and you will find that they love preaching and teaching, and they love to celebrate the Lord's Supper, but the main event that takes place when they gather is God's worship. They might say something like, 'When we gather, we gather to worship, to minister to Him.'

"This threefold progression found in Ephesians 5 is corroborated by the apostle John's tribute to Jesus in the opening chapter of the last book in the Bible: 'To him who loves us and has freed us from our sins by his blood, and has made us to be a kingdom and priests to serve his God and Father—to him be glory and power for ever and ever! Amen' (Revelation 1:5–6).

153

"What begins with knowing His sacrificial love, leads to cleansing, and produces those who present themselves to Him as a kingdom of priests.[19]

"This third model, in which we minister before the Lord's throne, is found in our past as well as in our future. David appointed priests 'to minister before the ark of the LORD, to make petition, to give thanks, and to praise the LORD' (1 Chronicles 16:4). And in Revelation 5:10, we see that this priestly ministry before the throne is our destiny as part of the great multitude.

"This brings us up to the final scene, and concludes my part in this Story of Worship. But before I go, I must say that I have enjoyed being your instructor. I hope that you have learned, and will continue to learn, so well that you will not just remain students of these things, but will become teachers, as well. In that I would be most satisfied. Good evening, and the Lord bless you."

The audience stands and claps in gratitude to the Lord. The lights dim as the applause is joined with a sound we have heard before. As the applause fades, the sound continues and rises. It is the sound we heard in the opening scene of creation, the sound that is intertwined with lights . . . sometimes a multicolored polyphony of voices, instruments and melodies, sometimes a brilliant white unison.

Our eyes and ears are filled with the wonder again, and then the sound slowly fades. We take our seats.

Scene 3: The Sound of Many Rushing Waters

We hear the Storyteller's voice again.

"Do you remember the singing stars, how their voices filled the heavens as God created the earth? Their sound wrapped every mountain and plain, every river and ocean. Even the animals knew that sound."

The screen shows various scenes of animals. In a gentle meadowland, we see the ears of rabbits twitching. In the western plains, we see a herd of wild horses running, the sound of their hoofs resonating with a dramatic flourish of percussion. We hear a slow-moving sound as we watch whales swimming together in what seems to be a celebration of sorts. Their sound is a fascinating blend of the upper range of a bass violin and the lower range of a French horn. We see a child on a seashore listening with delight to the sound coming from a seashell. From the ocean the sound of seagulls takes us to a forest filled with the sounds of many other birds. As night falls, we hear the delightful singing of crickets and croaking of frogs. The visuals continue to follow the Storyteller's narration.

"When Adam and Eve bit into the apple, it was as if somewhere, a cosmic mute button was switched, and even though the glory of God continued to shine through, it has been a restricted glory. Creation has been frustrated for eons, wanting to sing the song sown into its every molecule, but, like a dream in which you want to speak but can't, a subsonic groan has been expressed instead (see Romans 8:18–22)."

The audience feels a rumbling sound it cannot hear.

"The great sacrifice awakened a great hope in creation's breast. On the cross the last Adam paid the first Adam's debt, and a promise of liberation ran through the foundations of great mountains and seas. When the Messiah's body went limp and His breath was gone, 'the earth shook and the rocks split. The tombs broke open and the bodies of many holy people who had died were raised to life' (Matthew 27:51–52).

"When the innocent blood fell from His slaying, hope radiated through the ground to the ends of the earth, washing away a horror that had existed since the ground first tasted blood so long ago—the innocent blood of Abel. A rumor spread throughout the realm of which humans know very little that evil tyrants had been disarmed and led in a humiliating procession behind a triumphant Lamb (see Colossians 2:15). It would only be a matter of time now.

"Since then creation has been eagerly watching and waiting. In this realm, most of which is mistakenly referred to by humans as inanimate, the Lamb is known as the 'firstborn' (Colossians 1:15). His was the first resurrection of many; His glorification, the foretaste of a renewed heaven and earth. His sacrifice bought back all that was made, guaranteeing the eventual overthrow of the imposter's destructive rule. It was the long-sought promise that one day creation's Creator would be recognized as supreme over all—over heaven, over earth, over things visible and things invisible, over all thrones and powers and rulers and authorities (see Colossians 1:16).

"The domain of skies and seas, whose language is so different than our own, rejoiced as a core of humanity was separated from the dark domain and became the Church of the firstborn (see Hebrews 12:22–23). When these called-out ones were given authority over the imposter, the rivers clapped their hands, the mountains sang for joy and the seas roared, for they knew that God's judgment would be executed (see Psalm 98:7–9). In their lore, a story is told of a time when a great company of worshipers will devote themselves to serve the Firstborn and make His praise glorious, and that this glorious praise would unlock a great universal anthem throughout all of creation. The mute button would finally be switched off and their full voice would return.

"In the Church's early years, the skies and mountains rejoiced when they heard the simple, unrestricted praise of the Redeemed. The world was being turned upside down. (See Acts 17:6, KJV.) But then the groans returned when the company lost their place in the Great Adventure and took up lesser stories.

"Their early fervor fell as a seed into the ground. Repeating the pattern of the building of Zerubbabel's Temple, the foundation of the greater Temple was completed with great joy. But the Liar stirred up a vicious outrage and persecution,[20] and then 'the work on the house of God . . . came to a standstill' (Ezra 4:24).

"Melchizedek entered into council with his Master."

The stage is smoky. Two characters are vaguely seen but clearly heard.

"It seems strikingly similar to Sinai. They are forfeiting again the opportunity to be Your priestly people."

"I do share Your sadness, Melchizedek, but there are some differences. Before there was no oath—those at Sinai were never included in your order. These have been, and the mark runs deep. The Lamb's offering is complete, and a better covenant is intact.[21] The outcome is sure, even if we have to wait until the third millennium. We are patient. Along the way you will inspire revivals and awakenings. The promise will not be lost—the adventure will continue. Oh, and I should mention that, unlike Sinai, the promise has been sown among the nations. In the darkness its power is working, like yeast through dough.[22] The calamity the Liar has created will work in our favor. The Lamb's enemies will become His footstool."[23]

The Storyteller continues: "Long centuries passed from the stir that was felt at the great sacrifice. The Liar's darkness confused many. Empty stories were thought to be great. Halfheartedness became acceptable. The priestly ministry was taken back by the few. A meager glory was passed off as normal.

"There were dark years, but even then there were those who did not allow the light in the Temple to be snuffed out. Near the middle of the second millennium, a Reformation made some progress in reasserting Melchizedek's priestly agenda. Whereas once singing was reserved for the ordained choirs, songs broke forth again among ordinary people. Gates of praise were mounted on the walls of salvation (see Isaiah 60:18). Mountains and hills took note.

157

"But it wouldn't be until centuries later that an activated priesthood would begin to function in full force. The power of God's Word would resurrect (see Ezekiel 37:1–14) and regather a scattered Israel from among the nations (see Ezekiel 37:21–22); the temple builder, with tape measure in hand (see Ezekiel 40:3) would complete the Temple,[24] God's glory would fill it (see Ezekiel 43:1–5), His throne would be reestablished (see Ezekiel 43:7), the sons of Zadok would take their place, ministry to the Lord would become the central activity of the people of God (see Ezekiel 44:15–16) and the mountains and hills would rejoice.

"When God comes into this completed Temple, Ezekiel wrote that His voice would sound 'like the roar of rushing waters' (Ezekiel 43:2). This is the sound that the skies and seas know well. This sound, which was heard in Creation, was also heard when God was bringing forth his new creation[25] on Pentecost: 'Suddenly a sound like the blowing of a violent wind came from heaven' (Acts 2:2)."

The theater in which we are sitting has hundreds of smaller speakers covering the ceiling and walls. Through those speakers and through the larger ones concealed in the front and back, we hear a fearsome sound, the sound of a violent storm. On the screen we see footage showing roofs flying off houses, trees bending over and breaking, waves crashing over piers. The caption explains: "Hurricane Ivan, September 12, 2004, Grand Cayman Island." The caption pauses, then continues: "Suddenly a sound like the blowing of a violent wind came from heaven (Acts 2:2)."

The first sound fades, and a picture of a distant waterfall appears. As the waterfall comes closer, its roar grows in intensity. Now the caption makes plain that it is "Horseshoe Falls, Niagara Falls, Ontario, Canada." The camera takes us right up to water as it breaks over the edge, following it down as it crashes on the rocks below. Then the caption quotes: "And I heard a sound from heaven like the roar of rushing waters and like a loud peal of thunder (Revelation 14:2)."

As before when we heard the trumpet sound at Sinai, the volume of this sound grows to the point of discomfort. We are relieved when the volume subsides and the splashing waters transform into a scene of clouds—great, dark clouds.

Then without warning, we hear an explosion inside the theater and see a brilliant flash of light. It seems as if we are literally inside a thunderstorm. The sonic power of this is even greater than that of the sound of Niagara Falls, only bearable because it is brief. Other crashes of thunder and bolts of lightning resound in the theater but with less force.

Next we see a single harpist playing a large harp, and we hear the most pleasant sound imaginable. The harp sounds as if it is singing with deep, resonant emotions. Another harp joins in. As we watch, ten more harpists join the two . . . then fifty . . . then hundreds. As the caption explains, "The Great Eternal Festival of Harps, Location: Unknown," layers of delicious, enchanting sounds fill the auditorium. Then the holographic caption quotes from John's Revelation again: "The sound I heard was like that of harpists playing their harps (Revelation 14:2)." In the last few moments, our own emotions have raced from wanting to run and hide to wanting to linger forever.

Finally, four frames simultaneously show Hurricane Ivan, Niagara, the thunderstorm and the harpists. Their sounds are blended in what we know to be a toned-down reduction of their reality, although it is still an invigorating experience.

The Storyteller waits for both the sounds and the emotions of the audience to settle, and then begins to explain: "'Like the roar of rushing waters.' John heard it in the Spirit, but Luke heard it in Jerusalem. It is going on around the throne of God, but the rocks and hills long for it to be heard on 'this terrestrial ball'[26] in time and space . . . in your neighborhood.

"Ezekiel said that sound is the sound of God coming into His Temple (see Ezekiel 43:2). And wherever God's glory shows up, there you will find the instinctive human response—singing. As John listened to the sound around the throne, he heard the singing of a new song—voices of praise in the roar (see Revelation 14:3).

"There are many stories told of times along the way when God's glory came down. These are the stories of revivals and awakenings. Usually, in these special moments of history, a forgotten truth is recovered, and almost always, new songs and heartfelt singing attend as God's presence appears.

"The Reformation was very song-intensive. Samuel Taylor Coleridge said this of Martin Luther, the great reformer: 'Luther did as much for the Reformation by his hymns as by his translation of the Bible. In Germany the hymns are known by heart by every peasant; they advise, they argue from the hymns, and every soul in the church praises God like a Christian.'[27]

"Two hundred years later, the same effects took place in New England during the Great Awakening. Referring to the revival influence on Philadelphia of George Whitefield and Jonathan Edwards, Benjamin Franklin said this: 'It was wonderful to see the change soon made in the manners of our inhabitants. From being thoughtless or indifferent about religion, it seemed as if all the world were growing religious, so that one could not walk through the town in an evening without hearing the psalms sung in different families of every street.'[28]

"At this same time, the Wesleyan movement, which itself was born through contact with the singing and faith of the Moravian movement, brought new truth and new songs into the hearts of many. Nearly 6,500 hymns sprang up through Charles Wesley alone.

"In the last half of the twentieth century, various revival movements produced a renewed interest in Scripture songs and choruses. In the last fifteen years of the second millennium, there was a broad proliferation and popularization of new, heartfelt songs that affected Christians worldwide. The water level of God's presence was rising. The gatherer of priests and the Temple builder was seeing great success. The Good News, the message intended to produce worshipers, penetrated cultures and nations that had been previously closed. A new courage and savvy was found among its messengers.

"But as you might expect, with every step of progress that took place among the worshipers, the Liar was always close at hand, contesting the progress with accusations, exaggerations, confusions and misunderstandings. Persecutions and martyrdom also increased as the kingdom of darkness fought back.[29]

"Despite the efforts of the Liar, nothing could hold back the glorification of the Lamb. The throne-room sound that had summoned the nations on Pentecost invaded the earth in the third millennium after the great sacrifice. Some of what I am about to tell you has already begun.

"Believers become worshipers. A great outpouring of praise and prayer covers the nations, creating an atmosphere in which God's rule can be implemented. The great prophecy from Isaiah 61 is fulfilled. The priestly anointing (see Isaiah 61:1–6), which was on Jesus (see Luke 4:18–19), also comes upon His people, and righteousness and praise spring up before all the nations (see Isaiah 61:11). These praisers begin to be called 'priests' again and are known for their ministry to God (see Isaiah 61:6).

"The hopes and dreams of Melchizedek, Abraham, Moses, David, Jeremiah and all the others in this great story are finally fulfilled. What was officially a royal priesthood from the first century is finally becoming an activated priesthood. The Church gathers to give and not just to receive.

"The context of these changes is a massive historic convulsion affecting governments, economies and cultures. Remember Haggai? He had predicted that a great shaking would accompany God's glory filling a completed Temple—a shaking that would affect the heavens and the earth (see Haggai 2:6–7). Such will be the case.

"This story is told in detail in John's Revelation. But many who don't know the great epic (which you now know) think the story is about the terrors of the dark kingdom. Quite the contrary, it is about the glories of God's Kingdom, the coronation of its great King and the installation of those who rule with Him. Its plagues and judgments are about the rectifying of all history, the bringing of 'all things in heaven and on earth together under one head, even Christ' (Ephesians 1:10). As stated in the opening sentence of the Revelation, it is about the unveiling of Jesus Christ (see Revelation 1:1).[30]

"Living stones, once scattered and disconnected, join together to become a dwelling place for God's Spirit. Worship and prayer from the earth fill the courts of heaven and stimulate a release of God's power on the earth (see Revelation 8:3–5). A trumpet sounds (see Revelation 11:15) . . . a Temple in heaven is opened (see Revelation 11:19) . . . and a war in heaven begins (see Revelation 12:7). Angels fight against the Liar and finally dislodge him from the unseen realm he had occupied and cast him to the earth. The heavens rejoice, but the final conflict on earth is only just beginning.

'Now have come the salvation and the power and the kingdom of our God, and the authority of his Christ. For the accuser of our brothers, who accuses them before our God day and night, has been hurled down. . . . Therefore rejoice, you heavens and you who dwell in them! But woe to the earth and the sea, because the devil has gone down to you! He is filled with fury, because he knows that his time is short.'

Revelation 12:10, 12

"Blinded by his own lies, the Liar thinks that this will finally be his time. Filled with fury, he anoints a character who astonishes the world with his power and authority. All of the Liar's pent-up jealousies and blasphemies pour through the mouth of his puppet. The true worshipers endure the greatest of all ignominies: For three and a half years, this beast rails against God on a worldwide stage, slandering His name and His dwelling place (see Revelation 13:6). The beast is given authority over 'every tribe, people, language and nation' (verse 7).

"For those of us who know the Story of Worship, this sounds amazingly similar to the incidents that got Daniel thrown into the lions' den, and his friends Shadrach, Meshach and Abednego, thrown into the fiery furnace. Listen to the account from Daniel 3:

'This is what you are commanded to do, O peoples, nations and men of every language: As soon as you hear the sound of the horn, flute, zither, lyre, harp, pipes and all kinds of music, you must fall down and worship the image of gold that King Nebuchadnezzar has set up. Whoever does not fall down and worship will immediately be thrown into a blazing furnace.'

Daniel 3:4–6

"In the end-time version of his attempt to rule the world, the Liar tries to claim the very location where Abraham had offered Isaac and where Solomon had built a Temple: 'He will oppose and will exalt himself over everything that is called God or is worshiped, so that he sets himself up in God's temple, proclaiming himself to be God' (2 Thessalonians 2:4). An image is set up, and 'all who re-

163

fused to worship the image' are sentenced to death (see Revelation 13:14–15). A desperate world becomes intoxicated with the sound of this counterfeit call to worship,[31] and 'all the inhabitants of the earth worship the beast' (see verse 12)—all, that is, except for the true worshipers who worship only the Lamb.

"Forced worship of an intolerant god . . . and the world buys it? Who would have thought that only decades before, human culture had been so adamantly committed to relativism, pluralism and radical human autonomy? The pendulum swings. Now it becomes evident that those delusions were only the seducing fantasies meant to erase humanity's memory of its Creator. Their crafty perpetrator never believed those fantasies himself. They were simply a devious means to accomplish his determined ends: to become history's new absolute, and to forbid any and every attempted autonomy.

"But now we come to the part of the story I love the most: The Liar does not have the last word.

"Just as it seemed that the international scam would succeed, laughter was heard in heaven. As the Liar led a choir of kings in a responsive reading entitled, 'Who Does He Think He Is?' and as 'rulers gathered together against the LORD and against his Anointed One,' saying, 'let us break their chains' and 'throw off their fetters'—'the One enthroned in heaven' laughed" (see Psalm 2:2–4).

Throughout the theater, we hear the powerful, victorious laughter of a single voice. Joy overtakes us all, and our laughter joins His. We are washed by a deep peace and confidence.

"Reminiscent of David's installing Solomon after Adonijah tried to install himself, God the Father makes it clear: 'I have installed my King on Zion' (Psalm 2:6). 'You are my Son,' He said. 'Ask of me, and I will make the nations your inheritance' (Psalm 2:7–8).

"The Son must have asked, for an angel was sent out of the roar of heaven's worship (see Revelation 14:2–3) to proclaim this message to every nation: 'Fear God and give him glory, because the hour of his judgment has come. Worship him who made the heavens, the earth, the sea and the springs of water' (Revelation 14:7). The next thing we know is that the earth is harvested (see Revelation 14:16), and those who were victorious over the Beast are singing about all the nations worshiping and bringing glory to the King of the ages (see Revelation 15:2–4).

"'The temple was filled with smoke from the glory of God' (Revelation 15:8). Plagues, like the plagues in the ancient land of Egypt, were poured out."

On the screens the audience sees various scenes of chaos in city streets . . . looks of horror and despair on faces of the once great . . . picture after picture of devastation.

"Babylon, the ancient system of man-centered culture, collapses. Its domination over government, business, education and art is finally ended. 'The music of harpists and musicians, flute players and trumpeters, will never be heard in you again' (Revelation 18:22)."

On the stage, a curtain rises, and a multitude appears, all shouting aloud. The sound of the shouting gets louder and louder until it becomes a roar. Music joins the roar. Violins race up and down scales and arpeggios; trumpets spit out percussive-sounding blasts.

Like a sea captain shouting to his crew in the midst of a fierce storm, the Storyteller cups his hands over his mouth and shouts to the audience over the roar. We can barely understand what he is saying, but as he points to the words on the screen, we understand: "Read these verses with me!" he is shouting.

After this I heard what sounded like the roar of a great multitude in heaven shouting: "Hallelujah! Salvation and glory and power belong to our God, for true and just are his judgments. . . ." Then I heard what sounded like a great multitude, like the roar of rushing waters and like loud peals of thunder, shouting: "Hallelujah! For our Lord God Almighty reigns. Let us rejoice and be glad and give him glory! For the wedding of the Lamb has come, and his bride has made herself ready."

Revelation 19:1–2, 6–7

We have to shout the words to even hear ourselves: "Let us rejoice and be glad and give Him glory!" After we finish reading together, we all begin our own spontaneous, unscripted shouts: "Hallelujah! Glory and power to You, O God! We rejoice. We are glad. You are awesome."

For quite some time, the roar mixed with music continues. Colorful patterns of light blend with the sound. Superimposed over the multitude are scenes of nature in worship—skies and mountains, forests and fields, rivers and oceans—they seem almost alive as indescribable sounds come from their movement. The sound we hear now is like the sound we heard at the time of Creation, except it is even fuller. We do not want it to stop—and it really never does.

The roar slowly becomes a distinct, hymn-like song. Its melody is intuitive, and we in the audience are able to sing with what sounds like a massive choir. The lyrics are the words we just shouted:

> Hallelujah!
> For our Lord God Almighty reigns.
> Let us rejoice and be glad and give him glory!
> For the wedding of the Lamb has come,
> and his bride has made herself ready.

As we continue to sing together, the screen shows a brilliant light that becomes a horseman on a white horse, coming out of heaven. The rider's eyes are like blazing fire as He leads heaven's armies against the rebel armies. We see written on His robe the name "KING OF KINGS AND LORD OF LORDS." The cavalry He leads are all riding white horses, too. They are dressed, not in the armor you would expect of great warriors, but in fine linens, white and clean—the type of robes priests would wear. The Beast and his company are quickly captured and thrown into a burning lake of fire.

Still no sound is heard but the sound of singing—our own voices with the voices of an invisible choir.

A great throne appears; judgments are rendered and rewards bountifully bestowed. The old heaven and the old earth fade, and within swirls of light, we see new mountains and rivers, new clouds and skies. Glory fills the new creation.

The sound of the choir fades, and our own voices fade, too. A curtain hides the screen and the stage. After some silence, the Storyteller appears and walks in front of the curtain to speak the final words of the story:

"So the tale, which began with a heavenly sound, ends with the same glorious sound. Though there were attempts to silence the sound, and times when the sound was hardly heard at all, God's unrelenting search for worshipers proved successful. The great sacrifice won the great reward: a great multitude—more than the stars in the sky or the grains of sand on the seashore—from every tongue and tribe and people and nation worshiping the Creator and the rightful ruler of all. And so ends the drama we call 'Worship Lost, Worship Found.'"

A thoughtful silence holds the audience for several moments as we weigh the story's implied challenge: How will our own lives fit in with the story?

A musical finale begins as the curtains rise again. The characters parade before us. We applaud as we see Cain and Abel, Melchizedek, Abraham, Sarah and Isaac, Pharaoh, Moses, Aaron and Miriam. Look—there's David, Solomon and Zadok, King Ahab and Elijah, Jeremiah, Daniel and Nebuchadnezzar. Oh, and Zerubbabel and Joshua, Haggai and Zechariah. We see many others, but when the Teacher and the Storyteller take center stage, the applause erupts to a new level, only to be overshadowed by an even greater roar of praise when the rider and His white horse stride across the stage.

When the curtain finally falls for the last time, a sea of bright faces pours out of the theater, through the lobby and out into the streets.

PART 3

CONVICTIONS

I will put my laws in their minds and write them on their hearts. I will be their God, and they will be my people.

Hebrews 8:10

7

THE TWELVE
CONVICTIONS OF TRUE
WORSHIPERS

They said to the woman, "We no longer believe just because
of what you said; now we have heard for ourselves, and we
know that this man really is the Savior of the world."

John 4:42

I hope you will never forget the Story of Worship and its
central message—that God is looking for worshipers. And
please remember that it is not just their story—it is your
story, too.

Now we want to consider the question: What would
it look like if you and I truly became the wholehearted
worshipers that God is seeking? How would our lives be
different?

Let's review our definition of worship: *Worship is the act
and attitude of wholeheartedly giving yourself to God—spirit,
soul, mind and body*. Remember the *what* and *how* of worship?

171

Self-giving is the *what* of worship; wholeheartedness is the *how*. And wholehearted self-giving is expressed through certain acts and attitudes.

When believers take the first steps in becoming worshipers, they usually think it is just about adopting a few new changes—maybe a fresher musical style or a more honest manner of communication: "Let's allow people to lift their hands in worship and, hey, the transformation will be complete." It does not take long to realize that becoming true worshipers is a bigger process than anticipated.

I was involved in the early years of Integrity Music, and we released our first recording of worship songs in July 1985. Every two months, through a subscription program, we would send out another collection of songs that were being sung throughout the body of Christ. We were amazed at the impact these recordings had on churches of all kinds. The growth of praise and worship as a segment of Christian music became an industry phenomenon.

In response, churches began to inquire about how to bring this new sound of worship into their congregations. Before working for Integrity, I had been the music director of the congregation out of which the company was formed, and I loved to teach. So I developed a weekend seminar entitled "Becoming a Kingdom of Priests."

For a number of years, Don Moen and I traveled to churches all over the country and shared what we knew about how to become a worshiping church. Later, Randy Rothwell joined me, and we found ourselves taking the training to other nations, as well. We were delighted to find the same enthusiasm for renewed worship that we saw in America present in other nations like Russia, Malaysia, Latvia and Singapore.

Early on, the emphasis was on the *how-tos* of worship: *how to* use a guitar to lead worship, *how to* create a flow in worship using segues between songs, *how to* build effective rhythm sections and vocal ensembles. But increasingly we found that there was a hunger to know the *whys* of worship, as well: why worship is so important, what our motivations should be, how a new worship experience in church should affect our daily lives.

Over the years, the issue of helping believers become worshipers has become the focus of my teaching and ministry. What I am discovering is that God is after an overhaul, not just a tune-up. As you have probably heard from many sources, worship is not just something you do on Sundays—it is a lifestyle. Becoming a true worshiper is a pervasive change of habits and values; it is a root-level reorientation.

The Worship Ethic

To describe the goal of this reorientation, I want to use the phrase "worship ethic." Like the "work ethic," the "worship ethic" is a set of deeply held convictions that governs a person's thinking and behavior. Similar to a "work ethic," which values diligence and hard work along with the related virtues of thrift, self-discipline, responsibility and respect for property, the "worship ethic" is a hierarchy of values, too—values that God intends to sow into the soil of our hearts.

In this section, we are going to dissect this worship ethic by identifying within it "the Twelve Convictions of True Worshipers." First, however, let's look at the nature of convictions and how we acquire them. To have a conviction is to be convinced of a truth, to know that you know something. There are some things I think I believe, some things I believe, some things I know and a few things that I know that I know. Those few things are my convictions.

Years ago, I accidentally erased our ministry's hard drive, including a database of thousands of names. Did I have a backup copy? I am embarrassed to say that I did not. As I

173

realized what had happened, and as I frantically and un-successfully tried to find someone to help me retrieve the data, a conviction formed in me about backing up data. Before the disaster, I could have told you that backing up data was important, but afterward, I *knew that I knew* that I should back up data. Guess what? I now back up important data every day; it has become part of my life.

The formula I have come to is this: *belief + experience = conviction.* When I think of how a belief becomes a conviction, I sometimes think of how range cattle are branded. A branding iron is heated in a fire and then pushed against the hide of a cow—*ouch!*—and for the rest of its days, that cow is marked. When God writes His laws on our hearts, it involves a similar process. Sometimes convictions are formed through the testimony of others, and sometimes through personal revelation, but usually through personal trauma or the heat of testing and trials. Whatever the method, a conviction is formed when we subjectively encounter God's objective truth.

The apostle John put it like this: "We proclaim to you what we have seen and heard" (1 John 1:3). He spoke out of personal experience. When the Samaritan woman went back to her town to tell them about her encounter with Jesus, a level of faith was created in them. But when He came to their town, and they heard Him themselves, their belief became a conviction. They told the woman, "We no longer believe just because of what you said; now we have heard for ourselves, and we know that this man really is the Savior of the world" (John 4:42).

I would rather have a few convictions than many beliefs. It is what we are truly convinced of that affects our behavior and makes a difference in the lives of others. Our testimony is essentially the confession of our convictions.

In becoming a worshiper, or a worshiping church, expect a process. You may learn the information quickly, but truly acquiring the twelve convictions will take some time.

I am impressed with how Alcoholics Anonymous uses its Twelve Steps to help in the recovery from alcoholism. Its members are encouraged to constantly "work the program" by attending meetings and going through the steps with their sponsors. Those twelve fundamentals are constantly spoken of and applied, and the approach has been effective in helping millions overcome destructive addictions and form new habits.

I hope the following twelve convictions will serve the same function of defining fundamentals and will give would-be worshipers targets for their faith. Let the next twelve short chapters become regular meditations and heart disciplines for you. Let these twelve themes become part of your conversation with those whose lives surround you.

Please do not look at these twelve convictions as one more list of unattainable goals. Instead, bring to God your desire to be a true worshiper and ask Him to help you develop a worshiper's mind and heart. Then let the convictions be like a road map, showing you the ground to cover. In the context of your group and your set of relationships, let the Holy Spirit develop these convictions in you, from the inside out.

As you do, the worship ethic will become rooted and begin to flourish in your life and your church . . . and God will be finding in you the Abels and Davids and Daniels He is looking for in this very special generation.

8

CONVICTION #1

WORSHIP AND GOD'S LOVE

Worship is a response to God's great love.

How deep the Father's love for us,
  how vast beyond all measure,
That he should give his only Son
  to make a wretch his treasure.
How great the pain of searing loss,
  the Father turns his face away
As wounds which mar the Chosen One
  bring many sons to glory.

Stuart Townend

In view of God's mercy . . . offer your bodies as living
sacrifices.

Romans 12:1

The first conviction has to do with knowing—really knowing—how much God loves you.

Learning worship does not start with learning techniques. It begins with trusting God's kindness toward you. When Paul urged us to present ourselves to God as living sacrifices, he began with the phrase "in view of God's mercy." In other words: Knowing God's great love for us, let's worship. If we do not personally know God's love, our worship will be forced and mechanical.

Remember Cain and Abel? Both worshiped—both brought their sacrifices—but one was acceptable and the other was not. My guess is that Cain approached worship thinking, *What can I do for God to win his favor?* Abel simply received God's love and expressed gratitude. Those are the two primary paths people usually take. The one is called *works*, the other *grace*.

"For it is by grace you have been saved, through faith—and this not from yourselves, it is the gift of God—not by works, so that no one can boast" (Ephesians 2:8–9). The *works* way tries to earn a standing with God by what we do for Him; the *grace* way simply accepts by faith His love for us as a gift, and our worship then becomes a natural response to that love. The acts and attitudes of worship are simply the by-products of knowing His love, not the means of trying to gain it.

We love God—and we worship Him—because He first loved us (see 1 John 4:19). That love wins our trust and gratitude, and dispels all our fears. Remember the problem at Sinai? Because of their fear, they did not draw near to worship. "There is no fear in love. But perfect love drives out fear" (1 John 4:18).

Ask yourself this question: "Has God's love won my heart?" If you think you have to earn His love with your performance or achievement, listen to this: "God demonstrates his own love for us in this: While we were still sinners, Christ died for us" (Romans 5:8). His love for us

177

is not based on our goodness, but on His own. You cannot earn it; you can only receive it.

Maybe you have trusted in someone and gotten hurt, or you think that God has let you down in some way, and there's a wall between you and Him. That may be why you feel that you are just going through the motions when you worship.

Many of us are like cats. Aloof and independent, cats are suspicious when someone approaches them. But once convinced of gentleness and goodwill, they will sit in your lap and purr. Let God's love win your trust. He is not a heartless, impersonal taskmaster whose only goal is to keep you in line. He is the One who knows you better than you know yourself, and who has the key that can unlock the prison doors that keep you from the glorious freedom He has in mind for you. His is that rare love that sacrifices His personal gain for your well-being. That's what His death on the cross was all about. By that selfless act, God has shouted out, "I love you, Bill. I love you, Jennifer. I love you, _____." (Fill in your own name.)

As we realize His love, our trust flourishes. Our fears of being let down—and all other fears, as well—evaporate. And like the purring of a contented cat, our worship effortlessly springs out of heartfelt gratitude. Our hearts have been won by His incredible love.

Conviction #1: *Worship is a response to God's great love.*

Lord Jesus, we know that Your love can totally conquer all our doubts and fears, and we invite You to do just that. Form in us an unshakable conviction of Your amazing love. We give up trying to achieve a standing with You and instead, by faith, receive as a gift the love You so freely give. May our worship spring out of knowing Your love. Thank You. Amen.

178

9

CONVICTION #2

WORSHIP IN SPIRIT AND TRUTH

Acceptable worship springs out of life in the Spirit and love for truth and reality.

Jesus declared, ". . . God is spirit, and his worshipers must worship in spirit and in truth."

John 4:21, 24

It is interesting to me to hear the different terms used to describe renewed worship. For a while, it seemed as if the term that would stick was *praise and worship,* but that now seems to be fading. Some call it *contemporary worship,* but that's not quite accurate because this term implies that only contemporary songs may be sung—and when is a song no longer contemporary? When it is more than five years old . . . ten . . . twenty?

179

Some churches use the term *blended worship*, indicating that their worship includes the old as well as the new. That term seems to imply that the change simply adds in a percentage of newer songs to the standard fare of traditional songs. The term is okay, but it would seem that renewed worship has a deeper purpose than just slightly expanding our song repertoire.

I have heard people use the term *postmodern worship*, but that seems to take too much explanation to have staying power among ordinary folks. More recently I heard *post-contemporary worship*, but that will only be good until the style changes a little more, and then there would have to be *post-postcontemporary worship*.

So, what do we call it? You might be disappointed, but I do not have a suggestion. I do think, however, that what God would like to get out of the movement is a greater number of worshipers who, regardless of their particular Christian subculture, appreciate the importance of *spirit* and *truth*. Those two words hold the essence of renewed worship. They are the two main criteria of worship that is pleasing to God.

"God is spirit, and his worshipers must worship in spirit and in truth" (John 4:24, emphasis added). Notice the word *must* in this passage. Jesus did not say, "I would strongly suggest that you worship in spirit and truth, but it is really up to you and how you feel about it." Spirit and truth are biblical essentials. Together they are the inescapable imperative of worship. If you want to be a true worshiper, spirit and truth are required; they are not optional.

So, what does it mean to worship in spirit and truth?

Worship in Spirit

First, let's consider the word *spirit*.[1] The Scripture says that "the spirit of man is the candle of the LORD" (Proverbs

180

20:27, KJV). That picture gives us a good starting point. Our innermost being is like a candle's wick. As we fellowship with God, our human spirit is set aflame with God's Spirit.

With that picture in mind, consider three characteristics of worship in spirit:

- Worship in spirit centers on Jesus Christ.

Jesus said this of the Holy Spirit: "He will bring glory to me" (John 16:14). If we allow ourselves to be filled with the Spirit, we will become saturated with the Holy Spirit's desire to glorify Jesus. Emphasizing the centrality of Christ in worship will become increasingly important as other forms of spirituality and worship rise in popularity.

- Worship in spirit is born out of dependency on God and stands in contrast with confidence in the flesh.

Confidence in our own strength or wisdom apart from God is called the "flesh," and it is our biggest hindrance to life in the Spirit. We have been made to rely on God. Without a vital relationship with Him, we simply will not accomplish what we were designed to do. We are like an electric appliance, a coffeemaker for instance, that has to be plugged in to work. Fulfilling our calling requires that we be continually connected to Him in abiding fellowship.

Paul said that the true believers are those "who worship by the Spirit of God, who glory in Christ Jesus, and who put no confidence in the flesh" (Philippians 3:3). The contrast between the Spirit and the flesh is huge. One is about life empowered by God's energy; the other is about life powered by human effort. One is about following godly desires; the other is about following self-centered desires. In Romans 8, we learn that those who are controlled by the sinful nature cannot please God (see verses 5–8).

Unfortunately, we often use the term *flesh* to refer to a narrow set of sins and ignore how often we actually put our confidence in something other than God. When Paul spoke of the "flesh," he included his potential confidence in his own education and religious pedigree (see Philippians 3:4–6). If our confidence is in our musical talent, or our knowledge, or our appearance, or our religious heritage apart from God, we are in the flesh, and our worship, like Cain's, will be unacceptable.

Worship in spirit is stirred by God's Spirit, not mere human enthusiasm. Religion that is exercised by manipulation, intimidation or domination is carnal, rather than spiritual.

- Worship in spirit is always somewhat unpredictable.

Describing the way of the Spirit, Jesus said, "The wind blows wherever it pleases. You hear its sound, but you cannot tell where it comes from or where it is going" (John 3:8). Just as it is impossible to control the wind, it is impossible for us to manage the Spirit.

God is orderly, and He encourages us to make plans (see Proverbs 16:1, 3, 9), but He always reserves the right to override our own plans. When it comes to worshiping in spirit, we must learn that the Spirit is like the wind. He has a mind of His own, and it is wise to learn to cooperate with Him.

Worship in Truth

What does it mean to worship in truth?

The New Testament word for truth, *aletheia*, has two dimensions: one has to do with content, the other with manner:

- Worship in truth means that the content is biblically accurate.

Obviously, a song or an expression of worship that celebrates other gods would not meet Jesus' criteria. And though we may quickly think that all the worship in mainstream Christian churches will be solidly aligned to God's truth, we would be wrong to do so.

According to the research of George Barna,

- Ten percent of those who say they are evangelicals agree with the statement: "The Bible, the Koran and the Book of Mormon are all different expressions of the same spiritual truths."
- Forty percent of those who say they are Protestants believe that protection from eternal condemnation for one's sins is earned rather than received as a free gift from God.
- Fifty-two percent of those who say they are evangelicals agree with the statement, "When people are born, they are neither good nor evil—they make a choice as they mature."[2]

That is why those who lead our worship must not just be talented artists, but also careful students of God's Word.[3]

- Worship in truth means that it has spiritual reality.

The second dimension of truth, spiritual reality, is just as challenging as the first. According to W. E. Vine, the New Testament word for *truth* refers to "the reality lying at the basis of an appearance; the manifested, veritable essence of a matter."[4]

This means that external expression without internal reality is unacceptable worship. How many times do we simply go through the motions without realizing that what we are doing does not really qualify as true worship? Jesus referred to "words-only worship" as "vain worship" (see Matthew 15:8–9).

If we take Jesus' specifications for worship seriously, we must take up the discipline of excising our conversations and our expressions of everything that is not genuine, authentic and honest. For me that is a rigorous challenge that I encounter every day. So much of our communication is riddled with empty words: "How are you doing?" "Fine. How are you?" "Fine, thanks."

To underscore the importance of spiritual reality, consider how the Scripture treats its opposite, pretense or pretending. According to 2 Corinthians 10:4–5, we are to see pretensions as enemy territory. They are strongholds behind which our enemy operates, and they should be ruthlessly torn down and demolished. In the instruction to the Ephesians regarding spiritual warfare (see Ephesians 6:10–18), the first piece of armor we are instructed to put on is the "belt of truth" (verse 14), which is spiritual reality.

Along with the challenge to become truthful is an encouraging promise. Jesus said that the Holy Spirit, "the Spirit of truth . . . will guide you into all truth" (John 16:13). It is He, who is utter Reality Himself, who will bring us into all reality.

Interestingly, the predominant culture characteristic for which today's teens are searching so desperately is *authenticity*. George Barna summarizes his research on current attitudes among teens with this: "In a nutshell Mosaics [his term for today's teens] are looking for an authentic experience with God and other people."[5] As we become the true worshipers God is seeking, we will also become the kind of authentic community for which others are searching.

Spirit *and* Truth

When we talk about spirit and truth, we cannot disconnect them and choose one or the other. From our perspective, there is a tension that exists between the two. Spirit is like the wind, dynamic and unpredictable; truth is like the rock, fixed and immutable. From God's perspective, however, spirit and truth are in complete harmony. His subjectivity and objectivity are a unified whole. The Holy Spirit is called the "Spirit of truth," and He, the Spirit, is in charge of leading us into all truth.

Personalities, as well as traditions, often tend to develop strengths on one side or the other. It is common to have "left-brained" church cultures that are intellectually rich and emotionally poor, or "right-brained" cultures that are emotionally rich and intellectually poor. Knowing what we are helps us to know what we need to work on and develop.

Conviction #2: *Acceptable worship springs out of life in the Spirit and love for truth and reality.*

> *Jesus, convince us of our deep need for Your Spirit. Give us a heart to yield to Your ways. Convict us when we put our trust in our own abilities instead of in You.*
>
> *Holy Spirit, grant us the courage to demolish any and all belief systems that are contrary to Your truth, and replace all our pretending with emotional and intellectual honesty and authenticity. Lead us into all truth so that the watching world can better see who You are. Let us worship You in spirit and in truth. Amen.*

10

CONVICTION #3

WHOLEHEARTED WORSHIP

> A true worshiper engages the totality of his being in worship.

"The most important [commandment]," answered Jesus, "is this: '. . . Love the Lord your God with all your heart and with all your soul and with all your mind and with all your strength.'"

Mark 12:29–30

The goal of spiritual formation is that "all of the essential parts of the human self are effectively organized around God, as they are restored and sustained by Him."

Dallas Willard

How would you describe the worship in your congregation last Sunday? Was it a genuine response to the knowledge of God's love? Were the people worshiping in spirit and in truth? More particularly, what proportion of those who were there participated with all their hearts, minds, emotions and bodies?

Some of you may say, "How can we possibly know how people were worshiping? Only God knows that." That's true—but what percentage would you *guess* was worshiping with all their hearts, minds and physical beings? An even more important question is, "Were you one of them?"

The fact is, the percentage is less than it should be—and less than it is going to be. This third conviction is all about exchanging a *partial* expression of who we are in worship with a *total* expression—spirit, soul, mind and body.

The Great Commandment and Worship

Quoting Deuteronomy 6:4–5, Jesus said in Mark 12:29–30 that the greatest of all commandments is to love God with all that we are. That is pretty important, wouldn't you say? In this great commandment, we find that God values a comprehensive response to His comprehensive love for us. In another passage, we find that halfheartedness is actually repulsive to Him, and that He would actually rather that we be cold than lukewarm: "I know your deeds, that you are neither cold nor hot. I wish you were either one or the other! So, because you are lukewarm—neither hot nor cold—I am about to spit you out of my mouth" (Revelation 3:15–16).

Here we find a significant difference between how God thinks and how we generally think. We tend to believe that a little bit of fervor is better than none; God does not agree. He makes it plain that halfheartedness is worse than coldheartedness.

Because worship is simply the expression of our love for God, the great commandment has much to say about how God would like us to worship. Wholehearted worship

187

reflects wholehearted devotion, and halfhearted worship reflects halfhearted devotion. God is looking for whole-hearted worshipers.[1] We should be disturbed when we allow ourselves to become halfhearted.

Understanding Ourselves

Each of us has been created as a fascinating combination of physical, spiritual, mental and emotional components. Because these components are so intricately linked, and their names are sometimes used interchangeably, it is hard to neatly dissect a human personality. Sometimes biblical lists include four parts—heart, mind, soul and strength; others, three—heart, soul and strength.

Every person is a unique combination of these elements with differing strengths and weaknesses. For instance, some people may be very articulate intellectually, but very inarticulate emotionally. Others may have high physical aptitude and yet lack intuitive skills.

Although a person's basic framework will remain pretty much the same year after year, growing in Christ requires that we progressively bring more and more of our lives under His rule. How we worship is probably a good indicator of how healthy the various components of our personalities are. For instance, if your emotions do not engage in worship, there may be a need for healing and restoration in your emotional life.

One complication to all of this is the effect of the traditions in which we grew up. When I first came to the Lord, I was exposed to teaching that implied that emotions, because they were unreliable, were fairly useless. And so it followed, the more spiritual a person was, the less emotional they should be. It took me years to realize that, in the name of spiritual discipline, I had developed a habit of suppressing my God-given emotions. I remember the liberating truth

I came to as I was meditating on Psalm 23:3—that is, God wants to *restore* my soul, not *destroy* it. He wants to show me how my emotions were meant to work.

Another sub-Christian tradition is the one that creates suspicions toward the mind. I had a close friend whom I influenced to become a Christian. He was a thorough thinker, an engineer with a degree from a top engineering school. Unfortunately, he became part of a ministry that looked down on the value of the mind. In coming under that influence, he was forced to shut down a vital part of who God had made him to be. Something valuable was lost.

Finally, there is the tradition that deems the physical side of worship as inappropriate. Those who hold to this belief would say that thoughts and feelings are fine, but do not lift your hands in worship. Movement in worship or anything that stimulates movement, according to this tradition, is not spiritual but based on "the flesh." But regarding the body, most of the "worship imperatives" in the book of Psalms require that we *do something* physically. Activities such as bowing before Him, lifting up our hands, singing and dancing are all physical movements. Worship without physical involvement is like a car that is running on three cylinders.

A Greek and Hebrew scholar, referring to Romans 12:1, has asked, "Why did God, in describing worship, say to present our 'bodies'? Why didn't He say to present our souls or spirits?" Answering his own question, he said, "For the Hebrews, the body was the container of the soul and the spirit. When you give your body, you give your soul and spirit."

If you have been unduly influenced by any of these unbiblical traditions, take a good look at the great commandment again, as well as God's plan for you as a worshiper. He wants the whole of you to serve Him—intellectually, spiritually, emotionally and physically. Of course, any expression can become self-serving. For instance, the proper exercise of emotions and emotionalism are worlds apart. And redeemed thought—thinking God's thoughts after Him—is worlds away from becoming proud in our thinking.

Evaluate your own strengths and weaknesses. In what part of the great commandment do you feel you need to be strengthened today?

Conviction #3: *A true worshiper engages the totality of his being in worship.*

> *Dear Lord, You wholeheartedly gave Yourself for us. Forgive us for our halfhearted responses to You. Convince us, by Your Spirit, that You are worthy of a better offering. Let our bodies become Your temples, let our hearts be moved with compassion like Yours, and may our minds grapple with the depth of Your thoughts to enlarge our praise.*
>
> *May our churches be filled with worshipers faithful to Your greatest commandment. We ask these things in Your name. Amen.*

11

CONVICTION #4
DIVERSITY IN WORSHIP

Practicing songs, hymns and spiritual songs
enlarges our worship.

Be filled with the Spirit. . . . Sing and make music in your
heart.

Ephesians 5:18–19

Sing psalms, hymns and spiritual songs with gratitude in
your hearts to God.

Colossians 3:16

Singing is a natural response to God's activity in our lives.
When Paul told the Ephesians to be "filled with the Spirit,"
he immediately said that they should sing and make music
in their hearts (see Ephesians 5:18–19). The history of reviv-

als verifies the connection between the Holy Spirit's activity and songs.

Twice in the New Testament, we are encouraged to sing three kinds of songs: psalms, hymns and spiritual songs (see Colossians 3:16 and Ephesians 5:19). This apostolic instruction regarding worship provides an incredible insight into how God designed us, and also His love of variety. Like all of the other convictions, this one will enlarge us and increase the quantity of pleasing worship that passes through our lives. Exactly what are these three song forms, and why is it important to God that we employ them?

What Is a Psalm?

To help us understand, I am going to substitute the term *song* for *psalm*. A psalm is a song. When used in a general sense, the word *song* refers to all kinds of sung music. In that sense, a hymn is also a song. But when used in contrast to a hymn (i.e., sing songs, hymns and spiritual songs), the word *song* takes on a more specific meaning. A song is usually shorter and more personal than a hymn.

A psalm, or a song, has a folk quality to it, in that it is more testimonial and experiential than a hymn. More closely related to the vernacular of the current culture, a song is generally simpler and often carries high emotional value. This song form would include what we call choruses.

What Is a Hymn?

In contrast to a song, a hymn has a more formal, literary character to it. Hymns are generally more content oriented and require a more thoughtful process to fully appreciate. Usually having more verses, hymns are more theological and poetic. They often deal with the character and work of

God above human experience. Because they are less tied to contemporary trends, they usually have a longer life span than songs.

What Is a Spiritual Song?

The spiritual song is even more a song-of-the-moment than a psalm or a hymn. When Paul referred to singing with his spirit, he contrasted it with singing with his mind, and said that he would do both (see 1 Corinthians 14:15). This "less rational" song form, the spiritual song, consists of improvised melodies and words, inspired by the Holy Spirit and sung around a chord or slowly moving chord progression. You'll notice bits and pieces of spiritual songs in contemporary worship when the band repeats a tag and the worshipers collectively sing random praises. It is the beginning of a spiritual song when you are praying and have the urge to hum or sing your prayers. Chants are a form of spiritual songs. Some have suggested that the Gregorian chants are the codification of early spiritual songs.

This song form has been referred to as "the song of angels" because of its mystical, otherworldly quality. Even as the Spirit is the believer's down payment of the future age (see Hebrews 6:5), the spiritual song must be a foretaste of heavenly worship itself.

Native Expressions—Not Learned Behavior

If any of these three song forms seems strange to you, remember that the same One who designed humanity itself designed all three of them. Built into you is an existent correspondence with these expressions. Rather than thinking of them as learned behavior or acquired tastes, think of them as native to you. If they seem foreign to you, it is because what God put in you from the beginning has been forgotten. When you discover them—even late in life—you will feel as if you are getting reacquainted with an old friend.

Most people understand the attraction to songs; they want to hear about the experiences of others to help them understand their own. Psalms, or songs, make up the *pop music* of worship. The attraction to hymns, to the expressions that transcend us, is also innate, although it took a while for me to recognize this. The hymns provide much of what you reach for when you experience the majesty of lofty, snowcapped mountains. They make up the *classical music* of worship.

The impulse behind spiritual songs is the same impulse children on the playground experience when they make up a song to the rhythm of the seesaw—"my dog's bigger than your dog." It is behind what makes us want to hum or whistle a random melody. It is what we feel in the shower when we think we can sing like Caruso. Spiritual songs are the *jazz* of worship. The Holy Spirit likes this jazz. It was named after Him.

All Three Together

The genius of these three song forms is that each is uniquely appropriate to express a different dimension of God's nature, and each will speak for a different kind of personality, as well as to the different facets within an individual.

God is not easy to figure out. He is our Judge, our Advocate and our Comforter; He is Father, Son and Holy Spirit; He is King, Priest and Prophet. We cannot just pick the aspects of Him that we like and ignore the rest. He is God.

There are times He rebukes, times He defends and times He inspires. There are times that He seems like your best friend, and you can say anything in the world to Him. There are other times when it seems more as if you are in a courtroom standing before a Judge. Your words are few:

194

"Yes, Your Honor. . . . No, Your Honor." There are other times when it seems you are running in a race and, like a wind, a rush of inspiration overwhelms you.

And in worship, there are times to show respect, times to speak like friends, and times to revel in God's prophetic nature. That's why we need hymns and songs and spiritual songs.

In our humanness, we often get comfortable with just one aspect and try to reduce God to our own most recent snapshot. When you have grown up with traditional worship and then discover contemporary worship, your temptation is to conclude that traditional worship is intrinsically empty. I would bet that fifteen years later, you would be looking around for a good book of hymns. It is not that any of these three is inferior, but each of them by itself is inadequate.

Once I was part of a symposium on church music with a well-known Christian musician. An older man who had been a pioneer in his own generation, he was a patriarch to many of us in the room. But he had a real issue with the new songs that some of us were involved with, and he made no bones about it: "It's all 'throwaway' music. It won't last. Don't waste your time with it."

As I thought about his basic argument—life span determines value—the picture came to mind of a redwood tree, an apple tree and a field of mountain flowers. There are redwood trees living today that were already hundreds of years old when Jesus was born. Redwoods, the world's tallest trees, are awesome. Dwarfed by a redwood, an apple tree usually only bears apples for twenty or thirty years, but there is nothing like biting into a good, juicy apple. And mountain flowers. I will always remember an experience in the Colorado Rockies. After hiking on a glacier for a day and a half, we crossed the Continental Divide and on the other side discovered the most refreshing field of wildflowers. I knew that some of those flowers would

195

not be there the next day, and that I was the only one who would ever see some of them. I felt privileged to be the one to enjoy them.

Redwoods, apple trees and mountain flowers—God took the time to make them all to express His multifaceted character. And so God created hymns, songs and spiritual songs.

A Call to Greater Flexibility

What would worship be like if the Holy Spirit Himself was the worship leader at your church? I think there would be dignified, thoughtful songs appropriate to standing before the Judge, songs that call us to attention, ancient songs that seem to be timeless. There would also be simple, familiar, emotive songs that make us feel as though we are hanging out with our best friend, as well as mysterious songs that challenge the part of us that is deeper than our rational or emotional selves. And the segues between these three dimensions of worship would be very natural.

The idea of the Holy Spirit becoming our worship leader is something to consider. But for that to happen, we will need to be prepared for a challenge. We will have to let go of some of our prejudices, and many of us will have a hard time with that process. I know I have. Left to ourselves, we almost always will choose a view of worship that is much narrower than the view the Holy Spirit would choose. He'll probably have to say to us as He did to Peter (and to me), "Do not call anything impure that God has made clean" (Acts 10:15). Peter, who had been personally trained by Jesus and was one of the primary Christian leaders of his day, still had some opinions that had to be dealt with before he was prepared to take the Gospel out of the milieu of a Jewish culture into the Gentile world. The command to employ songs, hymns and spiritual songs requires a greater cultural flexibility than most of us have had, so that we can enjoy the variety of worship expressions God has planned.

How is it working in your church? Is there an ongoing debate regarding reverence toward God versus celebration of God? Regarding structure versus spontaneity? Regarding testimonial worship versus theological worship? Regarding emphasis on the rational versus the emotional?

Here is God's answer: Be reverent and celebrative . . . structured and spontaneous . . . testimonial and theological . . . rational and emotional. Be filled with the Spirit and sing songs, hymns and spiritual songs.

Conviction #4: *Practicing songs, hymns and spiritual songs enlarges our worship.*

Lord, again we are realizing that You are bigger than we thought. Forgive us for trying to make You like us. Help us to let go of our prejudices and learn Your ways in worship. Enlarge us to be able to move between the rational, the emotional, the physical and the spiritual dimensions of worship more naturally. Let us become the kind of worshipers You are seeking. Amen.

12

CONVICTION #5

WORSHIP AND GOD'S PRESENCE

Our praise opens the gates into God's presence.

Sing yourselves into his presence.

Psalm 100:2, MESSAGE

Then Moses said to [God], "If your Presence does not go with us, do not send us up from here. How will anyone know that you are pleased with me and with your people unless you go with us? What else will distinguish me and your people from all the other people on the face of the earth?"

Exodus 33:15–16

Fundamental to the worship ethic is a deep appreciation for the presence of God. Some churches have it; some do not. May this fifth conviction become an integral part of the hierarchy of values in every one of our congregations.

The correlation between worship and the presence of God has always been important, but like justification by faith, it has been rediscovered and is now becoming part of the believing Church's basic understanding: "Enter his gates with thanksgiving and his courts with praise" (Psalm 100:4).

Here is how it works: We worship, bringing acceptable sacrifices before God, and great, invisible gates open, welcoming us into His presence. It is as if our thanksgiving and praise triggers some highly sophisticated security system, and in we go, right into the presence of the Lord.

There are many examples in Scripture of the relationship between worship and God's presence. One dramatic example is the dedication of Solomon's Temple, which, as you know, is part of the Story of Worship.

> They raised their voices in praise to the LORD and sang: "He is good; his love endures forever." Then the temple of the LORD was filled with a cloud, and the priests could not perform their service because of the cloud, for the glory of the LORD filled the temple of God.
>
> 2 Chronicles 5:13–14

When Paul and Silas sang their praises in prison, God revealed His powerful presence (see Acts 16:25–26). Worship ushers in the presence of God.

Although it is a vague memory, I think I first experienced this correlation at Camp Sumatanga, a Methodist camp in northern Alabama, when I was about ten years old. It was the last night of camp, we were sitting around the fire, and someone led us in the greatest-of-all camp songs, "Kum Bah Ya."

I have this theory that all of us have implanted somewhere in our hearts a "presence meter" that works much like a Geiger counter, except that it measures God's presence (see Romans 8:16, NKJV). Well, after singing "Kum Bah Ya," my little ten-year-old presence meter clicked on and went up to about a two or a three. I would have forgotten about that experience, but years later it clicked back on again in a bank building in Tallahassee and started buzzing at about an eight or a nine. (For more details, see the opening chapter of this book.)

Sometimes, when talking about "coming into God's presence," people have objected, saying that God is omnipresent, meaning that He is always everywhere. They might quote Psalm 139:7, "Where can I go from your Spirit? Where can I flee from your presence?," or Matthew 28:20, "Surely I am with you always, to the very end of the age." And they have a point: God *is* omnipresent.

But it is also true that He reveals Himself in special ways in particular times and places. That is called His "manifest presence." It is in that sense that Jacob said, "Surely the LORD is in this place" (Genesis 28:16), and David said, "Do not cast me from your presence or take your Holy Spirit from me" (Psalm 51:11).

The biggest reason that God is looking for worshipers is that they are the ones who welcome His presence, and more than anything, He wants to dwell with us. In the second to the last chapter of the Bible, a loud voice from heaven is heard, filled with great satisfaction: "Behold, the tabernacle of God is with men, and he will dwell with them, and they shall be his people, and God himself shall be with them, and be their God" (Revelation 21:3, KJV).

The other reason that God wants to find true worshipers who make room for His presence is that it is in His presence that His name can operate. Remember, Solomon's Temple was a place where God put His name. Jehoshaphat discovered the name—God's authority—when he prayed in God's presence as his enemies were about to attack (see 2 Chronicles 20:9). Jesus Himself said that heaven pays attention when we gather in His name and in His presence. There—in His name and in His presence—He gives us the authority to bind and to loose as we pray (see Matthew 18:18–20).

Becoming a People of the Presence

When God told Moses that he could enter the Promised Land, but that He would not go with him, Moses did not take the bait. Instead, he wisely said, "If your Presence does not go with us, do not send us up from here." He went on to say, "How will anyone know that you are pleased with me and with your people unless you go with us? What else will distinguish me and your people from all the other people on the face of the earth?" (Exodus 33:15–16).

Moses had a conviction about the presence of God. He knew three very important truths about God's presence:

- God's presence was more important to him than any blessing,
- God's presence attests to His pleasure in us, and
- God's presence is what distinguishes His people from all others.

To become a people of the presence of God, we must treasure His company, His manifest presence, as Moses did. In living to please Him, we should look for His presence in our lives. And we should be quick to search our hearts if He ever has cause to withdraw His presence from us.

When we have this fifth conviction, the most important question concerning our gatherings will be: Was God in attendance today?

Conviction #5: *Our praise opens the gates into God's presence.*

201

Dear Lord, will You form in us a conviction about Your presence? Will You give us the same heart Moses had so that we would value Your presence over every other blessing? Let us grow in discernment to more ably recognize Your presence. And thank You for teaching us to enter Your presence with our praise. Amen.

13

CONVICTION #6

WORSHIP AND PRAYER

> Entering God's presence in worship,
> we can extend His purpose in prayer.

The four living creatures and the twenty-four elders fell down before the Lamb. Each one had a harp and they were holding golden bowls full of incense, which are the prayers of the saints. And they sang a new song: "You are worthy. . . ."

Revelation 5:8–9

To Him shall endless prayer be made, and endless praises crown His head; His Name like sweet perfume shall rise with every morning sacrifice.

Isaac Watts

Are you ready for conviction number six? It is about the connection between worship and prayer. If we adopt this part of the worship ethic, the intercessors among us will become worshipers and the worshipers will become intercessors. Here's our hypothesis: God wants to form a royal priesthood to reign with Him, and we will reign this way through worship and prayer.

As It Is in Heaven

First, let's look at how important worship and prayer are in heaven. In the Revelation 5 passage quoted above, the two primary activities around the throne of God are described as worship and prayer. Each of the four living creatures and the 24 elders holds a harp and a bowl of incense. The harps signify worship; the bowls of incense, prayer. Those who are closest to the throne are creating sounds and fragrances as they express their tribute to the One who sits on the throne and to the Lamb. I think it is fascinating that the Lord, who is always interceding for us, is listening to music and smelling incense, as our prayers to Him become His prayers to the Father.

Why all the talk about heaven's worship and prayer? Because that's what we should be praying for on earth. Jesus taught us to pray, "Your will be done on earth as it is in heaven" (Matthew 6:10). When we realize how intricately heaven connects worship and prayer, we have a small glimpse of what God wants to do among us on earth.

History-Changing Ramifications

As we have already learned, *a priest is one who draws near to God, offering gifts and sacrifices, and who represents the needs of others before Him.* Priests have two primary functions: first, to enter God's presence with sacrifices, and second, to stand in His presence to intercede on behalf of the needs of others.

God has been busy gathering worshipers and interces-sors. In the last several decades, we have witnessed the parallel development of a very broad worship movement and a very determined prayer movement.

The worship movement has been learning the art of en-tering: "Enter his gates with thanksgiving and his courts with praise" (Psalm 100:4). The prayer movement has been learning the art of standing on behalf of others—"a house of prayer for all nations" (Isaiah 56:7). Good worshipers know God's presence; good intercessors know God's purposes. Put them together, and you have biblical priests.

Someone once said that we do not fully understand prayer until we understand worship; nor do we fully understand worship until we understand prayer. To help us understand the fuller view of prayer and worship, I recommend using the term *worship intercession*. Worship intercession is more than worship, and it is more than prayer. Worship interces-sors know how to take time in offering bountiful sacrifices of praise, and they know how to route the waters of God's presence out to the needs of others. Worship is the harp; intercession is the bowl. Worship intercession is the harp *and* the bowl.

In Scripture, the two emphases are not separate. The book of Psalms (Songs) is a book of prayers, as well. What we read as prayers were originally sung. Try singing the Psalms. Make up your own melodies. Sing your own prayers, too. In older editions of *Strong's Concordance*,[1] one alternative meaning for the word *prayer* in Isaiah 56:7—"a house of prayer for all nations"—is hymns. We are meant to be a singing house of prayer. Notice how many of our songs and hymns are actually prayers set to music.

The song sung by the 24 elders and the four creatures ends by stating that the kingdom of priests will reign on the earth. What does it mean to reign, and how does that happen practically?

205

Reigning means to exercise rule or authority, often by decree or pronouncement. When Jesus was in Capernaum, He commanded an evil spirit to come out of a man. The spirit obeyed His command, and the people who watched this said with amazement, "With authority and power he gives orders to evil spirits and they come out!" (Luke 4:36). That's reigning.

A few chapters later, Jesus gave authority to the 72 disciples, who, when they returned, reported that "even the demons submit to us in your name" (Luke 10:17). Not only does Jesus have the authority to reign, but He wants to share that authority with us.

Learning Worship Intercession

The problem with worshipers who have not become intercessors is that they are slow to shift gears out of worship into prayer. You have probably been there where the last song gently subsides, God's presence is thick, and the door into history-changing prayer is wide open. There is an expectant pause . . . and then someone nervously starts up a new song. Presence meters throughout the room drop from the "7" and "8" range to "1" and "2." Here is where a good intercessor could help the worshiper recognize the door and segue into prayer.

The problem with intercessors who have not become worshipers is that they fail to mix in thanksgiving with their petitions. Paul taught on this in his letter to the Philippians and in his first letter to Timothy: "Do not be anxious about anything, but in everything, by prayer and petition, with thanksgiving, present your requests to God" (Philippians 4:6); "I urge, then, first of all, that requests, prayers, intercession and thanksgiving be made for everyone" (1 Timothy 2:1).

In both cases Paul instructed that thanksgiving should be mixed with requests and petitions. There was a specific recipe for incense that God gave to Moses, which contained four ingredients (see Exodus 30:34). Thanksgiving is certainly one of the ingredients that God is looking for in the incense of our prayers—three other very important ingredients are petition (see 1 Timothy 2:1), faith (see Hebrews 11:6) and confession (see James 5:16). Without thanksgiving, anxiety rules, and we become beggars. But with thanksgiving, we are acknowledging that God's sufficiency and greatness is greater than even the most profound human need we bring before Him.

Someone once referred to prayer without thanksgiving as "worry with your eyes closed." Intercessors who are not yet worshipers are like Mordecai, who, when he learned what to pray for, "put on sackcloth and ashes, and went out into the city, wailing loudly and bitterly. But he went only as far as the king's gate, because no one clothed in sackcloth was allowed to enter it" (Esther 4:1–2). On the other hand, Esther "put on her royal robes" (Esther 5:1), went before the king and made successful intercession. Her royal robes, like our garments of praise, got her past the gates into the place where petitions were handled. And thanksgiving will do the same for us.

Conviction #6: *Entering God's presence in worship, we can extend His purpose in prayer.*

Lord Jesus, You have become our High Priest, and we know that You are always interceding for those who draw near to You. We ask that You train us in the ministry of intercession. Let us become deeply convinced of the eternal, history-changing value of worship intercession. Help us to put on the garments of praise before making our petitions. Let it be on earth as it is in heaven. Amen.

14

CONVICTION #7

WORSHIP GOD ONLY

> We must carefully guard against all forms of idolatry.

Dear children, keep yourselves from idols.

1 John 5:21

"Those who cling to worthless idols forfeit the grace that could be theirs."

Jonah 2:8

At the mention of idolatry, probably most of us think along these lines: *Other times, other places. Sure, Israel made a golden calf in the wilderness, but that was a long time ago; they did that kind of thing back then. Or, idolatry may be a problem today in some parts of the world, but not really in educated countries like our own.*

In becoming the worshipers God is seeking, we must take seriously the warning to keep ourselves from idols. Satan, as we know, will be busy at work trying to divert worship to anything other than God until he is finally thrown into the lake of burning sulfur.

And he is pretty clever. When you first consider becoming God's worshiper, he will give you every reason in the book to dissuade you: "That's fanaticism." "You'll lose all your friends." "Just don't get carried away." "Be your own person." "You don't want to worship the Christian God—remember the Crusades?" "They're all hypocrites. Why, I knew an evangelist who . . ."

But if Satan sees that you are going to become a worshiper of God no matter what, he changes his tactics. Now his trick is to introduce other gods, and then subtly, over time, to elevate one of them to the number one position. "I'm really glad to see how enthusiastic you are in worship. I think that will help you be enthusiastic in other endeavors of your life, too. Your work, you know, is really important. How else are you going to provide for your family? Use the enthusiasm you have learned in church to really get ahead. You love your children, don't you? Go for it." Three years later, Satan has crafted a workaholic who does not have time for God or his family.

If you think idolatry is not a problem among the truly devoted, remember that it was Israel's first high priest, Aaron, who oversaw the creation of the golden calf, and it was David's son Solomon who in his later years worshiped the goddess Ashtoreth and the god Molech. Aaron had personally witnessed the miracle of the Red Sea, and Solomon, who authored important parts of our Bible, had seen the glory of God fill the Temple.

What Is an Idol?

The biblical discussion of idolatry begins with the Ten Commandments. The first commandment forbids other

209

gods; the second, the worship of idols. So God forbids both the worship of other gods and the worship of the symbols or images of other gods.[1] In the Scriptures, the words *other gods* include the so-called deities of other religions like Baal or Ashtoreth, as well as other spiritual powers that operate behind the scenes. For instance, Paul defines sensuality and greed as idolatrous (see Colossians 3:5 and Ephesians 5:5). That is, they are not just bad habits, but false worship, and the powers behind them, are "gods" before which people worship.[2] In idolatry, as in true worship, there is a self-giving, a yielding, a submission to a will outside of yourself. Because it is inherently built into man to submit to something greater than himself, the question is not, "*Will* you worship?" but, "*What will* you worship?"

In our day, the names of other deities may have changed, but there is still only one Creator, and He still forbids the worship of anything that is created. Behind every God-substitute is a pathetic character, Satan, who desperately craves to be worshiped. His rule is, "Worship anything but God," and if you agree to this rule, you are actually bowing down to him.

God-substitutes come in the form of religions, philosophies, political movements, dynamic people, possessions, objects in nature, experiences and other created powers. We are often slow to recognize the religious nature of our devotion to other gods. For instance, Paul referred to a time when people would be "lovers of pleasure rather than lovers of God" (2 Timothy 3:4). Few recognize that a culture addicted to entertainment and pleasure is involved in a form of forbidden worship, but indeed that culture's love for pleasure has become a substitute for love for God.

Sometimes good things can supplant God as the ultimate Being in our lives. It could be a person you love, a purpose God has set in your heart or a strength He has given you. When kept in their place, these may be very valuable to us, but if they take over the number one spot in our hearts and become more important than God, Satan rejoices. Remember his motto: "Worship anything but God."

One example of a good thing that can become an idol is tradition. In Matthew 15:3–6, Jesus rebuked the religious teachers for allowing the traditions of men to become more important than the Word of God. He was not saying that tradition was bad in itself, but that tradition should never take the place of God Himself.

A Final Note

Being alert to the dangers of idolatry will become increasingly important as we come closer to the rise of the antichrist. Jesus said that deception would increase and that false Christs would arise and perform miraculous signs (see Mark 13:5–6, 22). The whole world will be astonished by the miracles and will worship the beast (see Revelation 13:3–4). An image will be erected, and the lives of all who will not worship it will be threatened (see Revelation 13:13–15).

Hard stuff, but true. The issue of all of history is this: *Whom will we worship?* Settle it now—worship God, and God alone.

Conviction #7: *We must carefully guard against all forms of idolatry.*

> *Who will not fear You, O Lord, and bring glory to Your name? For You alone are worthy of praise. Fix in us a heart not only to worship You, but to worship You alone. Let this conviction govern our lives and our churches. We ask this in Your name and for Your glory. Amen.*

211

15

CONVICTION #8

WORSHIP AND WARFARE

A true worshiper must become a warrior.

For our struggle is not against flesh and blood, but against the rulers, against the authorities, against the powers of this dark world and against the spiritual forces of evil in the heavenly realms.

Ephesians 6:12

May the praise of God be in their mouths and a double-edged sword in their hands . . . to bind their kings with fetters, their nobles with shackles of iron, to carry out the sentence written against them. This is the glory of all his saints. Praise the LORD.

Psalm 149:6, 8–9

It needs to be said that the Great Adventure you have joined (or are about to join) involves controversy. But that

212

is actually putting it too mildly—it will be a life-and-death struggle before it is all over. At issue is the question: Who will receive mankind's worship? As Israel in Elijah's day witnessed the showdown between the worship of Baal and the worship of God on Mount Carmel, history is moving toward its own Great Worship Contest between the worship of the Beast and the worship of the Lamb (see Revelation 13–15). It will be the final clash between the tradition of Cain and the tradition of Abel.

That may sound overly dramatic compared to the little skirmishes you are facing there in Cleveland or Philadelphia or Sacramento, but knowing the larger picture will give you perspective wherever it is that you are taking a stand.

Let's try to understand. Ever since the Great Sacrifice, a process of coronation has been underway. According to Philippians 2, the Father has already exalted Christ above every name, and at the name of Jesus every knee will bow and every tongue will confess that He is Lord (see verses 9–11). But like the gap of time between when Samuel anointed David king and when he actually took his throne,[1] there's also a gap of time between the declaration of Jesus' kingship and its actual taking effect in history. As the writer of Hebrews declared, "In putting everything under him, God left nothing that is not subject to him. Yet at present we do not see everything subject to him" (2:8).

But worshipers, who by faith see what God has done, declare Him the present king over their lives and their spheres of influence. And in those spheres, He rules. Even as you who read this book speak His name and declare His praise, His domain expands. It expands as the Church's praise moves out of halfheartedness into wholeheartedness. When the woman at the well became a worshiper and declared God's greatness to her town, the boundaries of the Kingdom grew.

The implication is that when Christ is enthroned in our praises, someone else is dethroned, someone who is called

213

"the ruler of the kingdom of the air" (Ephesians 2:2) and who thinks it all belongs to him. And now you know why there's a battle. The relationship between worship and warfare is twofold: First, worship is the issue behind the fight, and second, worship empowers warfare.

Here are some facts about our warfare:

- Our warfare is both offensive and defensive. We are instructed to demolish strongholds (see 2 Corinthians 10:4–5) and to pray that God would deliver us from the evil one (see Matthew 6:13).
- Our warfare is not like the world's. Our enemy is not other people, but unseen spiritual powers and principalities (see Ephesians 6:12).
- Our weapons include:
  - Prayer—"Pray in the Spirit on all occasions with all kinds of prayers and requests" (Ephesians 6:18).
  - Our testimony—"They [the saints] overcame him by . . . the word of their testimony" (Revelation 12:11).
  - Our knowledge of the finished work of the cross— "They [the saints] overcame him by the blood of the Lamb" (Revelation 12:11).
  - Praise—"As they [the singers] began to sing and praise, the LORD set ambushes against [Israel's enemies] and they were defeated" (2 Chronicles 20:22). "May the praise of God be in their mouths and a double-edged sword in their hands . . . to bind their kings with fetters, their nobles with shackles of iron" (Psalm 149:6, 8).
  - The Word of God—"The sword of the Spirit . . . is the word of God" (Ephesians 6:17).
- The qualification for battle is that we do "not love [our] lives so much as to shrink from death" (Revelation 12:11). That quality grows by grace with every battle.

- Our general strategy is: First, submit to God, and second, resist the devil (see James 4:7). As we submit to God, He gives us the specific strategy (see 2 Chronicles 20:3–21), and He empowers our weapons (see 2 Corinthians 10:4).

Two Realities

Our confidence in battle rests in two realities: first, that our weapons are "mighty through God" (2 Corinthians 10:4, KJV), and second, that our adversary is vulnerable to those empowered weapons.

Regarding the first reality, it is important to know that it is not by our strength that the battle is won: "Do not be afraid or discouraged because of this vast army. For the battle is not yours, but God's" (2 Chronicles 20:15); "You will not have to fight this battle. . . . Go out to face them tomorrow, and the LORD will be with you" (2 Chronicles 20:17); "As they began to sing and praise, the LORD" defeated their enemies (2 Chronicles 20:22).

I love the picture Isaiah paints of the "mighty-through-God" reality: "Every stroke the LORD lays on [our enemies] with his punishing rod will be to the music of tambourines and harps, as he fights them in battle with the blows of his arm" (Isaiah 30:32). That is what is going on in Brooklyn when the praise team finds its connection with the Holy Spirit. If we could only see what is *really* happening.

Regarding the second reality, our foe is conquerable: "They [the saints] overcame him" (Revelation 12:11). He would like us to think that he is omnipotent, omniscient and omnipresent, like God. But he is none of that. He is not God's counterpart, but the counterpart of one of the angels. Though his fury may be great, it is only because he knows his time is short (see Revelation 12:12).

215

Our confidence should be like that of David's: "Who is this King of glory? The LORD strong and mighty, the LORD mighty in battle" (Psalm 24:8). My, how He can fight. It is awesome to behold.

Remember how Zerubbabel was discouraged by the conflict, and the work on God's house came to a standstill? Do not be discouraged by what you encounter. Remember how Solomon carelessly compromised his worship, and his kingdom was divided? Be watchful; be vigilant. Remember the heroes of our faith "whose weakness was turned to strength; and who became powerful in battle" (Hebrews 11:34). We are worshipers who are at war.

Conviction #8: *A true worshiper must become a warrior.*

Lord, give us a conviction that we must courageously fight the fight. Let us see more clearly the importance of worship in our churches and in the world around us. Strengthen our feeble arms and weak knees. Help us to know what the prophet told his servant in 2 Kings 6:16, that "those who are with us are more than those who are with them." Make us to know that our weapons are truly mighty through God to the pulling down of strongholds, and that our victory is sure. For Your name's sake. Amen.

16

CONVICTION #9

WORSHIP AND SERVICE TO OTHERS

Sacrificial service to others is fundamental to a life of worship.

Do not forget to do good and to share with others, for with such sacrifices God is pleased.

Hebrews 13:16

The King will reply, ". . . Whatever you did for one of the least of these brothers of mine, you did for me."

Matthew 25:40

To communicate the power of this ninth conviction, I must tell you of my encounter with a simple woman of God whose life was an anthem of worship.

It was 1988, and I was in Calcutta with my friend Jim Gilbert, teaching Indian pastors about the importance of worship. Just down the road from the conference was the compound of the Missionaries of Charity, a Catholic Order devoted to its ministry to the poor, founded by the woman the world knew as Mother Teresa.

I was warmly greeted when I went in to see if I could arrange an interview with the woman about whom I had read so much, and I was delighted to learn that I could meet with her the following day. When I arrived, I presented her with a booklet I had written on worship and two recordings from Integrity Music, *Glorify Thy Name* and *Give Thanks*, both vintage albums from 1986.

After offering the gifts, I described what I saw going on internationally in the area of worship. "There is a world-wide revival of joy," I reported. "God is clothing His people with garments of praise." I just knew these faithful servants of God would be eager to hear.

Her eyes were kind, but unimpressed, and as she pushed back the cassettes, she told me that they did not have any cassette players in the compound. They had chosen to live without such distractions. Immediately I thought to myself, *How can you be a worshiper and not keep up with all the new songs?*

I was daunted, but I regained my equilibrium and tried again. "What kind of music do you like? What kind of instruments do you use in your worship? What songs do you sing?"

I learned that their early-morning worship times were very reverent, and prayer was more prominent than singing, mostly unaccompanied by instruments.

A chance-of-a-lifetime conversation, and I was blowing it. It was as though we were speaking different languages.

I desperately recalled the words of my friend who had invited me to India and had encouraged me to meet Mother Teresa. "Ask what worship means to her," he had said. And so I did.

Finally, her eyes brightened, and her answer went something like this: "If you really want to honor the Lord and

218

pour out your love to Him, He has told us how we can do just that." And then she quoted Jesus' words from Matthew 25: "Inasmuch as ye have done it unto one of the least of these my brethren, ye have done it unto me" (verse 40, KJV). She said that when the Missionaries of Charity minister to lepers from the streets of Calcutta, they do it as an act of worship to Jesus. She challenged me with these words: "If you really want to lavish your love on God, pour out your life on the least of the least."

"Mother Teresa," I said, "would you pray for me, that I would become a true worshiper?"

She answered, "Only if you'll pray for me first that I would be one, too." We prayed for each other.

On my flight home, somewhere between Delhi, India, and Frankfurt, Germany, I came across these words in Hebrews 13: "Through Jesus, therefore, let us continually offer to God a sacrifice of praise—the fruit of lips that confess his name" (verse 15). I knew that verse well, but not the next: "And do not forget to do good and to share with others, for with such sacrifices God is pleased" (verse 16). God was right there on the plane with me, teaching me that the sacrifices that pleased Him included *both* what we say with our lips *and* how we serve the needs of others, especially the poor.

Just as the cross of Christ is vertical and horizontal, and just as the two great commandments—to love God and neighbor—point upward and outward, so the true worship of God has two directions: spoken praise to Him and selfless service to others. One without the other is an incomplete expression of worship.

I had hoped that Mother Teresa could have spoken at a large worship conference somewhere, or that somehow she could have shared her wisdom with those of us involved with the worship movement. She died in 1997, and to my knowledge, it never happened. If it had, maybe her words would have been something like these: "You mustn't think worship only happens when you are singing; it happens also when you are serving others. Until we are vitally involved with those our Lord called 'the least of these,' we are not yet the worshipers He is seeking. Until we find joy in serving the insignificant—the children, the powerless, the prisoners, the unborn—God's pleasure in our worship will be incomplete."

So if you are part of the worship ministry in your church and it is all starting to feel a bit empty, maybe it is time to cancel the regular worship band or choir practice and find out where the "least of these" are, so that you can tell Jesus just how much you really love Him.

Conviction #9: *Sacrificial service to others is fundamental to a life of worship.*

Jesus, we would become Your true worshipers. As we hear Your call to be living sacrifices, please give us new hearts to sacrificially serve others and to do so as an offering unto You. Impart this conviction into our hearts and minds. Amen.

17

CONVICTION #10

WORSHIP AND COMMUNITY

True worshipers will be built together with other worshipers.

In him the whole building is joined together and rises to become a holy temple in the Lord. And in him you too are being built together to become a dwelling in which God lives by his Spirit.

Ephesians 2:21–22

How good and pleasant it is when brothers live together in unity!

Psalm 133:1

In the development of worship there seem to be three stages. First, we learn *the expressions of worship*, like lifting hands and singing new songs. Next, the Holy Spirit leads us to learn *the lifestyle of worship*, in which the attitudes of worship become part of our daily life. But ultimately, God wants to build worshipers together to become *a community of worshipers*, in which, like a symphony, our individual worship joins with the worship of others. As much as God loves our individual praises, He is eagerly waiting for the sound of worship that comes only from genuine community.

In order for that to happen, we must first acquire a conviction of the value and necessity of togetherness. Imagine two pictures: The first is a field of scattered stones; the second is a picture of those same stones built together into a beautiful temple. Now ask yourself, which picture better describes where you are? How far along in the process are we?

Both Peter and Paul used the phrase "built together" to describe how the Lord wants us to become a community of worshipers. Peter wrote that we are being built together to become a priesthood (see 1 Peter 2:5); Paul wrote that we are being built together to become a Temple (see Ephesians 2:21–22). The whole idea of the kingdom of priests implies a community of worshipers.

Jesus prayed that we would become unified, as one—just as He and the Father are unified. He was saying that the Father's love had to be demonstrated, not just explained: "May they be brought to complete unity to let the world know that you sent me and have loved them even as you have loved me" (John 17:23).

The way in which Jesus laid His life down for us should be replicated in His followers as they lay down their lives for their brothers. Because being a true worshiper includes living as a sacrifice, the natural way to relate to others is sacrificially. Biblical love is measured in this way: "This is how we know what love is: Jesus Christ laid down his life for us. And we ought to lay down our lives for our brothers" (1 John 3:16). We should ask ourselves two questions: First, for whom am I laying my life down? And second, who is laying his or her life down for me?[1]

How Does It Happen?

Community begins with a new mentality. Self-sufficiency and independence need to be exchanged for an eagerness to serve others and a vision of interdependence. We need to be convinced that we cannot accomplish God's purpose for our lives by ourselves. The centrality of self, which is the spirit of this age in which we live,[2] must be torn down in our thinking and replaced with the centrality of Christ.

Community develops in a context of specific, not virtual, relationships. Think about the analogy of living stones. Wherever you are in the wall, there are other living stones surrounding you, that touch your life directly. What are the names of those five to ten specific people that God has given you to walk with in transparency and trust? There will always be a secondary circle around those, but true community must form inside of that first circle. Ideally, a congregation will have both larger meetings and small groups. Both are important. Unfortunately, though, small groups are often incidental rather than fundamental to the life of the church. And equally unfortunate is the fact that small groups, because of their serial nature, rarely develop into genuine community.[3]

Community matures as we practice humility, patience and forgiveness in our circle of specific relationships. As we walk in close proximity with others, things come to light about ourselves and others. That's all part of the process of how God changes our lives. Our temptation will be to go hide in the crowd and give up on the idea of being built together. But Paul's words to the Ephesians will help us hang in there: Be humble and gentle; be patient, bearing with one another in love; make every effort to keep the unity; speak truthfully to one another in love; be kind and compassionate to one another, forgiving each other just as in Christ God forgave you (see Ephesians 4:2–3, 15, 32).

223

The same elements that produce community among individuals—humility, patience, forgiveness, truthfulness, kindness and love—will produce community among congregations, as well. As the process of being built together advances, networks will form. These networks of relationship will become increasingly visible in interchurch prayer and worship events until stadiums are regularly filled with priestly worshipers who enter God's presence in worship to extend His purpose in prayer.[4]

As we enter this third stage in the development of worship—becoming a community of worshipers—we will learn that it does not come easily. But if you take the first few steps and find that you want to turn back and just be an individual worshiper, remember that until we are built together, God's worship is incomplete.

Conviction #10: *True worshipers will be built together with other worshipers.*

Lord Jesus, we have treasured our individualism instead of Your glory. Work into our hearts a conviction that will lead to true community. Build us together with other living stones until we rise to become Your holy Temple filled with Your glory.
May Your kingdom come. Amen.

18

CONVICTION #11
WORSHIP AND SUFFERING

A true worshiper sings songs in the night.

Though the fig tree does not bud and there are no grapes on the vines, though the olive crop fails and the fields produce no food, though there are no sheep in the pen and no cattle in the stalls, yet I will rejoice in the LORD, I will be joyful in God my Savior.

Habakkuk 3:17–18

The magistrates ordered them to be stripped and beaten. After they had been severely flogged, they were thrown into prison, and the jailer . . . put them in the inner cell and fastened their feet in the stocks. About midnight Paul and Silas were praying and singing hymns to God.

Acts 16:22–25

225

American theologian, philosopher, preacher and the president of Princeton University, Jonathan Edwards (1703–1758) distinguished between two kinds of gratitude in his *Religious Affections*: "natural" gratitude and "gracious" gratitude. *Natural gratitude* involves being appreciative for good gifts: "Thank You, Lord, for a beautiful day." *Gracious gratitude*, however, gives thanks for who God is, not just for benefits received: "Thank You, Lord, that nothing can separate us from Your love." According to Chuck Colson, gracious gratitude is "relational, not conditional."[1]

Anyone can give thanks for blessings. But true worshipers have learned to give thanks in everything. It was gracious gratitude that flowed from Paul and Silas in the pain of their prison experience. Their story is a high-water mark in God's search for worshipers, the kind of story that should help form in us the eleventh conviction. I want to become a worshiper like them.

There was a time when I thought that by exercising faith, almost any unpleasant situation would turn around. When my wife's mother was sick with cancer, our fellowship mounted a vigorous prayer assault. We were certain she would be healed. After all, didn't Jesus say, "Ask and you shall receive"? We were stunned when she died. How could that have happened?

That was the beginning of a refining process that my faith is still undergoing today as I learn gracious gratitude. Several years after my mother-in-law's death, I was in Manila and heard the testimony of a leader in the Chinese church. This man had been sent to prison multiple times and spent years there for his faith. I will never forget how he told of volunteering for a job in prison that required him to wade in human excrement and sewage up to his chest. The stench was awful, but because no one else was around, it provided him with the rare occasion to sing God's praises unhindered, especially the hymn, "In the Garden."[2] Since that day, I have often cried when I hear the words of this hymn and think of his story: "And He walks with me, and He talks with me, and He tells me I am His own; and the joy we share as we tarry there none other has ever known." I want to be a worshiper like this amazing man.

Praise that is dependent upon blessing can easily turn into grumbling when the blessing is gone. It reveals that we measure what is good by a temporal standard, rather than by an eternal one.

When we suffer, we must first learn endurance: "If you suffer for doing good and you endure it, this is commendable before God" (1 Peter 2:20); "endure hardship as discipline; God is treating you as sons" (Hebrews 12:7); "if we endure, we will also reign with him" (2 Timothy 2:12).

But beyond patiently waiting out a difficulty is an even deeper response—*giving thanks* for the difficulty: "Dear friends, do not be surprised at the painful trial you are suffering, as though something strange were happening to you. But rejoice that you participate in the sufferings of Christ, so that you may be overjoyed when his glory is revealed" (1 Peter 4:12–13).

How can we rejoice in our sufferings? By realizing that through those sufferings, our identification and fellowship with Christ will increase and we will better know Him and His love for us: "I want to know Christ and the power of his resurrection and the fellowship of sharing in his sufferings" (Philippians 3:10).

I went through a severe period of financial testing during a time when I had three children in college. Early one morning, I was desperate to know why God was not answering my prayer and ending the trial. He brought to mind that my own father and mother had gone through a business failure and were also nearly bankrupt at a time when they had three children in college. The Holy Spirit led me to remember things to which I had been oblivious at the time. In that moment, I said "thank You" for the trial I was experiencing—I would not have known the depth

227

of my parents' love without it. In identifying with their sufferings, I knew them better.

Peter encouraged us to "greatly rejoice" when we experience trials. He said that they, like the refiner's fire, prove that our faith is genuine and will result in praise and glory: "And even though you do not see him now, you believe in him and are filled with an inexpressible and glorious joy, for you are receiving the goal of your faith, the salvation of your souls" (1 Peter 1:8–9).

When Stephen was stoned, he exulted in God's presence. He "looked up to heaven and saw the glory of God, and Jesus standing at the right hand of God" (Acts 7:55). Jesus is usually seated at the right hand of God, but in Stephen's case, He stood up to welcome him into His presence.

God is certainly pleased with natural gratitude, the kind that springs up in response to His blessings. But when He hears songs in the night—rejoicing in the midst of suffering—He stops what He is doing and gives it His undivided attention.

Conviction #11: *A true worshiper sings songs in the night.*

> *God, we are humbled by the kind of worship we see in Paul and Silas—and in the Chinese pastor. We ask You to let our worship be like theirs. Convince us that You are worthy of worship, no matter what the circumstances are. Help us sing songs of praise even in the darkness of night. Amen.*

19

CONVICTION #12

WORSHIP AND THE GOOD NEWS

Up-reach in worship leads to outreach to others.

He put a new song in my mouth, a hymn of praise to our God. Many will see and fear and put their trust in the LORD.

Psalm 40:3

[God gave me grace] to be a minister of Christ Jesus to the Gentiles with the priestly duty of proclaiming the gospel of God, so that the Gentiles might become an offering acceptable to God, sanctified by the Holy Spirit.

Romans 15:16

The twelfth step in Alcoholics Anonymous is to help others with their recovery as you have been helped in yours. Our twelfth conviction is similar: to let the contagion of our worship infect others.

Worship and the Gospel

There is a vital relationship between our *up-reach* to God in worship and our outreach to others. The irony is that we are most effective with *outreach* when *up-reach* becomes our passion. The rapid growth of worshiping churches verifies this, as does the testimony of Scripture.

Here is how I would describe the relationship between worship and sharing the gospel: *Worship is the goal of evangelism, and evangelism is the fruit of worship.*

Let's look at the first half of this relationship: *Worship is the goal of evangelism.*

When Jesus evangelized the woman at the well, He talked to her about what it meant to be a worshiper. Remember, this was not Jesus in the synagogue; this was Jesus "on the street," communicating with an immoral, worldly woman. This was one-on-one evangelism with the Evangelist of evangelists. The result? The woman believed and became a worshiper, spreading God's praise to everyone she knew.

Incidentally, praise can be vertical *to* God or horizontal *about* God. When we say, "God, You are so good," it is praise; when we brag on God to others—"God is so good"—it is also praise. Sometimes worshipers make too big of a distinction between vertical ("to the Lord") and horizontal ("about the Lord") expressions, almost always minimizing the horizontal. The expressions of praise in Scripture are very fluid as they move between the vertical and the horizontal. Take Psalm 104 for example: "You are very great. . . . He wraps himself in light. . . . He set the earth on its foundations. . . . You covered it with the deep" (verses 1–2, 5–6). The psalmist easily moves back and forth between the Lord as "You" and the Lord as "He." The real issue is God-centeredness, not whether it is vertical or horizontal;[1] evangelism is simply horizontal praise.

When Paul evangelized, his goal was to produce worshipers. According to Romans 15:16, when Paul preached the Gospel, it was "so that the Gentiles might become an offering acceptable to God." He evangelized in order to produce worshipers.

Worship is the goal of evangelism. It is the same truth we discovered in the Exodus: "Let My people go, so that they may worship Me." It is what we learned from Peter, that we are "called . . . out of darkness into his wonderful light" so that we can "declare [his] praises" (1 Peter 2:9). Let this become the governing principle—a true conviction—in your church planting, in your church's mission activities and in your own personal evangelism.

Now let's look at the second part of the relationship between up-reach and outreach: *Evangelism is the fruit of worship.* In other words, as our lives are filled with worship, evangelism will happen.

Almost always, it is in an atmosphere of worship that God commissions us to go and take His message to the world. It was after he experienced heaven's worship—"Holy, holy, holy"—that Isaiah was sent—"Go and tell this people" (Isaiah 6:3, 9). The Great Commission itself was given during a time of worship: "When they saw him, they worshiped him. . . . Then Jesus came to them and said, '. . . Go and make disciples of all nations'" (Matthew 28:17–19). Paul's first missionary journey was commissioned during a time of worship: "While they were worshiping the Lord . . . the Holy Spirit said, 'Set apart for me Barnabas and Saul for the work to which I have called them.' So . . . they placed their hands on them and sent them off" (Acts 13:2–3).

In the Philippian jail, what began in worship ended in evangelism: "About midnight Paul and Silas were praying and singing hymns to God. . . . He [the jailer] then . . . asked, 'Sirs, what must I do to be saved?' They replied, 'Believe in the Lord Jesus, and you will be saved'" (Acts 16:25, 30–31).

But the greatest illustration of how evangelism can spring out of worship is also the greatest New Testament example

231

of evangelism—the Day of Pentecost. One hundred twenty disciples were gathered together when a sound from heaven filled the house (see Acts 2). As we have already learned, that sound was the same sound that John described in Revelation 14—the sound of worship around the throne of God.

On the Day of Pentecost, the whole city heard the sound, and a large crowd gathered at the place where the 120 disciples were. This crowd included Jews from every nation under heaven, and they all heard the 120 "declaring the wonders of God" (Acts 2:11). Peter stood up and explained what had happened, and their little church experienced 2,500 percent growth in one day. Notice, they had not planned this outreach campaign for six months. They had simply gathered to pray, experienced the presence of God and worshiped Him—and, oh, by the way, three thousand people were saved (see verse 41).

The Essential Gospel and the Greater Gospel

The basic message of the Gospel is that Jesus, the Son of God, was born of a virgin, became a man, lived a sinless life, died a sacrificial death paying the penalty for our sins, rose from the dead and now offers the gift of salvation and eternal life to all those who believe. That basic message is what most people think of when they think of the Gospel, and this is what I would call the "Essential Gospel." I first became acquainted with the simplicity of this message through Campus Crusade's "Four Spiritual Laws." I am eternally grateful for how that little booklet caused the good news to make sense to me in the fall of 1967.

But in Scripture, the Gospel has some other dimensions that we need to discover as well—dimensions that I call the "Greater Gospel." The Greater Gospel is not different from the Essential Gospel; rather, it is a fuller understanding of the Essential Gospel.

As we mentioned, Paul made it clear in Romans 15:16 that the Gospel he preached was meant to produce worshipers. That's a dimension of the Gospel that is often overlooked, but it is confirmed in the book of Revelation, in which an angel is described as declaring the eternal Gospel internationally. Here's his message: "Fear God and give him glory. . . . Worship [God]" (Revelation 14:7). I think we could safely say that if our gospel does not include a similar call to worship, it is in contrast to the Gospel of the Scriptures.

There is one additional phrase that can help us understand the Greater Gospel and therefore acquire the much-needed worship ethic. It is the phrase, "the gospel of the glory of Christ." In 2 Corinthians 4:4, Paul wrote that "the god of this age has blinded the minds of unbelievers, so that they cannot see the light of the gospel of the glory of Christ." As he developed the thought, he pointed to the message that can lead us to an experience of "the light of the knowledge of the glory of God in the face of Christ" (see 2 Corinthians 4:4–6).

That's the good news of Jesus Christ—a message that leads us to an encounter with God's presence and glory. You could say that *the Gospel of the glory of Christ is the facts of the Gospel plus the phenomenon of His presence*. It is a demonstration, as well as an explanation. Peter's sermon on the Day of Pentecost communicated the facts of the Gospel, but it was the context of the phenomenon of His presence that made Peter's words so effective. The combination of the message and the presence of God *was* the Gospel of the glory of Christ.

The point of all of this is to give us a conviction of the importance of sharing with others how they can also experience the love of Jesus and know His presence. When that happens, they will become His worshipers, too.

Sharing the good news is simply an extension of our own gratitude. It works like this: Someone tells you about the love of Christ and you become a Christian. You are so grateful that you decide to give God everything that you are and all that you have: *Lord, here's my heart, my relationships, my resources, my future, my everything. Let my whole life be a praise unto You.*

But then, after you have totally given yourself to Him, you realize, *I have given Him all that I am, but God is worthy of an even greater offering. What more can I give?* A few days go by, and then suddenly it hits you: *My friend at work . . . he could become a worshiper, and then God would receive a greater sacrifice. And then there's my neighbors . . . I should have them over for dinner. Lord, I see how my life can bring You great glory.* You have just discovered how the desire to glorify God compels us to become messengers of His glory.

This is not a new methodology; it is a passion to glorify His name. It is a conviction.

Conviction #12: *Up-reach in worship leads to outreach to others.*

> *Lord, we are truly grateful for how You came to the earth to die in order to save us from our sins. You are worthy to receive unending praise from all that You have made. Let our lives win worship for You from all those who are around us, that they may see Your light in our lives and glorify our Father in heaven.*
>
> *Form in us the strong desire to see the multiplication of worship. In Jesus' name. Amen.*

234

PART 4

LET THE ADVENTURE BEGIN

These are the days of miracle and wonder.

Paul Simon

20

MAY ALL THE PEOPLES PRAISE YOU

May the nations be glad and sing for joy, for you rule the peoples justly and guide the nations of the earth. May the peoples praise you, O God; may all the peoples praise you. Then the land will yield its harvest, and God, our God, will bless us. God will bless us, and all the ends of the earth will fear him.

Psalm 67:4–7

This Is the Day

Regarding this Great Adventure, is there something special about these days? I think so. There is ordinary time (*chronos*) and extraordinary time (*kairos*).[1] I believe that we are living in a special *kairos* moment, experiencing the prophetic fulfillment of Isaiah 61:11: "The Sovereign Lord will make righteousness and praise spring up before all nations." And detailing the time more accurately, verse 6 of the same chapter declares, "You will be called priests of the LORD, you will be named ministers of our God." As God's praise continues to spring up internationally, the people of God will increasingly be known as priests, those who minister to the Lord.

I have a suspicion that the angel mentioned in the last chapter, the angel with the Gospel who was calling the nations to worship, has already been dispatched (see Revelation 14:6–7). Ask yourself, *Is that call to worship being heard in my town?*

Jesus said that He always did what He saw His Father doing. If we can recognize what God is doing and join in, we'll find life's highest joy, and we'll be nourished as we participate. Jesus said that doing the will of His Father was just like food to him (see John 4:34).

O God, give us eyes to see what You are doing. Let this be the day that the nations sing and are glad. May the peoples praise You; may all the peoples praise You. May the spirit that was in David be among Your people today. May his intercessory cry become ours: "Let everything that breathes worship You."

The Five Fingers of Worship

The theme of this book is that *God is looking for worshipers*. That is the drama behind the stories of Scripture and the unfolding of history. His eyes are running to and fro, throughout villages and cities, seeking hearts that are wholehearted in their devotion to Him.

I was curious one day and simply asked the Lord the question: "Where are You finding these worshipers today?" Over the next several days, the answer formed in my mind: *I am finding worshipers in many different places. Though they are diverse, and some worshipers of one kind might not recognize worshipers of another kind, they are like the five fingers on your hand. They have different tasks, but they are all connected to the palm, and in My eyes, they are one hand.*

From that inspiration flowed these five categories of worship in which I have discovered God is finding worshipers: (1) youth worship, (2) neo-liturgy, (3) user-friendly worship, (4) prophetic worship and (5) small group worship.

As we look at the contributions of each of these five sub-movements within the worship movement, let me qualify my statements. My starting point is the definition that *a worshiper is someone who really worships,* and that *worship is the act and attitude of wholeheartedly giving yourself to God— spirit, soul, mind and body.* I would not want to imply that every single person in each of these movements meets those criteria, only that God is at work in all of these emphases, developing a special quality of worship in each.

Let's look at the key characteristics of worship for each of these "Five Fingers of Worship."

Youth worship is currently a very active area of development in worship. Characteristics of youth worship include lots of new songs, guitar-based praise bands, pop/rock sounds and very experiential, emotional, testimonial and demonstrative expressions. Youth worship generates many, if not most, of the new songs for the larger worship movement.

The key word embedded in the ethos of youth worship is *radical.* Younger people have less to lose, so they are more willing to think radically. In my vocabulary, *radical* is a good word to describe worship. It implies that worship should not be stuck in old patterns and that it is capable of significant change. The changes Jesus brought to His world were radical; the changes He brings to our own lives are just as radical. Wouldn't you agree that our worship should be radical? After all, it is about us becoming living sacrifices.

Neo-liturgy is an emphasis that values what the historic church has learned about worship.[2] In neo-liturgy, ancient patterns are valued, worship is thoughtful more than emotional, symbols are appreciated, and hymns are more prominent than newer songs. At the heart of neo-liturgy is the key word *rooted*. It is important to these worshipers that their worship be connected to a continuum of history that transcends their own generation.

I have many Pentecostal and charismatic friends who have migrated to some form of neo-liturgical worship. They would say that being connected to the strengths of the historic church is an anchor for their contemporary faith, and that the Church's unity should extend beyond their own moment in history.

In *user-friendly worship*, the worship service is adapted to the visitor, *"insider terminology"* is eliminated, the use of media is prominent, references to contemporary culture are more common, and the primary purpose of public gatherings is to win the lost. If you are wondering, *Where's the worship?* remember that evangelism is worship (see Romans 15:16).

Behind user-friendly worship is a quest for *relevance*. To be relevant means to be in touch with those whom you are communicating with. To some outsiders, relevance looks like the fundamentals are being compromised, that the Gospel is being "dumbed-down" for the sake of popularity. But to talk with the practitioners of user-friendly worship, you would never get that impression. They see that what they are doing is being *incarnational*,[3] like Jesus, or like Paul who, to the Jews became like a Jew and to the Gentiles became like the Gentiles, "so that by all possible means I might save some" (see 1 Corinthians 9:20–22).

Prophetic worship, which developed out of charismatic worship, is an approach to worship that is highly spontaneous, subjective and free form. Spiritual songs are prominent over songs or hymns. Prophetic worship uses

240

the praise band, like youth worship, but improvisation is more common.

In prophetic worship, the key word is *revelation*. These worshipers believe that God is constantly speaking to us through our thoughts and impressions. Their contribution to the larger picture of worship is in their emphasis on intimacy and God's dynamic activity in worship.

Small group worship is what happens when the church gathers in homes or in smaller settings. It is corporate worship in its simplest form. Usually a single guitar is used rather than a band. The songs are easy to sing along with, and the setting allows for greater spontaneity and participation. Worship, fellowship, testimony and prayer are easily connected. Small group worship has a folksy feel, and the key word is *related*. Its adherents feel that worship is most genuine in the context of personal relationships and community.

So, in the worship of the Church today, there is *radical* worship, *rooted* worship, *relevant* worship, *revelational* worship and *related* worship. If we see our various emphases as part of the same hand, we can enjoy the fruit of what others are developing, and they can also be enriched by our contribution.

Increasingly, there has been a convergence of these elements, so that there are fewer and fewer "pure" forms of any of these. New church movements, especially the emerging church, are doing a good job of combining all five of these elements. It is very important to see the interrelationship of these submovements and to understand that none of these, on its own, provides the whole picture.

Without that perspective, a sectarian spirit ("we are the only ones who are doing it right") can lead to fragmentation. But with that perspective, we will become like those who rebuilt the wall in Nehemiah 3, in which specific family groups had responsibilities to build specific sections of the wall until it all joined together.

The big picture is that the Church is becoming a house of worship, fulfilling the centuries-old desire of God that His people become a priestly people… and that's exciting.

Now It Is Your Turn

Throughout this book, we have learned that the story is not just "theirs," but it is ours, as well. And now it is your turn—the story is knocking at your front door. Many of you have probably already accepted your part and have become worshipers in your world, as Abraham and David and Paul were in theirs. For those of you who have already enlisted, I invite you to become a worship advocate, an influencer of others and a gatherer of worshipers, for the glory of God.

But if you have not enlisted yet, I would hope that you would not want to get all the way to the end of this book without personally joining the great multitude yourself—it just would not be the same without you.

Who knows how the story could involve you or how it might unfold as you accept your role in it? You may begin leading your family in worship. Your eagerness to honor God on your job may influence a co-worker to ask what motivates you, and he would become one of us, as well. You might write a song that will be sung in your home group—or in other nations. God might move you to intercede for a situation that would transform a family or a community. You might become involved in planting a new fellowship of worshipers or in teaching a home group about what it means to be a priest. You might be the beginning of a new lineage of worshipers that would replace a lineage of whiners and complainers.

Whatever happens, I can tell you this: You were made to be a worshiper—it is in your DNA. The Adventure you would be joining ties you to a great heritage that includes Abel, Abraham, David, Solomon, Zadok, Josiah, Elijah, Jeremiah, Haggai, Zechariah, Simeon, the Samaritan woman, Peter, Paul and many others. Your name will look good on the list.

In joining the Adventure, you will respond to God's love, learn the secrets of Spirit and truth and express the whole of your being in worship; you will sing songs, hymns and spiritual songs—and become a worship intercessor who worships God alone; you will experience victories in battle and joy in serving others; you will be built together with other worshipers; you will sing songs in the night, and you will see worship multiplied.

And in joining the Adventure, you will discover your life's highest calling.

21

THE BENEDICTION

POWER TO BE
THE WORSHIPERS GOD SEEKS

"The LORD bless you and keep you; the LORD make his face
shine upon you and be gracious to you; the LORD turn his
face toward you and give you peace."

Numbers 6:24–26

In the old days, the benediction was an important part of
worship. The gathered worshipers had been called to worship; they had sung praises, confessed their sins, prayed for
others, listened to God's Word and shared in the covenant
meal. Now it was time to be sent forth with God's blessing
and empowering.

As you read these last few pages, imagine a great cathe-
dral filled with all the others who *have* come and *will* come
to these final words. Together we know that it is about time
for us to leave the sweet communion of our gathering and

go out into a world that is sometimes hostile toward what we cherish. We want a last touch, a final word of encouragement and a banner of purpose to carry with us as we leave. And rightly so, for we know that without the sustaining presence of the Holy Spirit, our renewed aspirations will quickly falter. The best intentions that may have formed in you while reading this book can quickly evaporate unless there is a blessing to transform those intentions into realities.

And so, here it is—your benediction:

> *May the Lord's blessing be upon you as you grow in your understanding and practice of worship. May His awesome power sustain you and protect you. And may the light of His face ever shine upon you and your family as you live transparently before Him. May that amazing brightness become real to you, always reminding you of His nearness. May His empowering grace be upon your endeavors, and may you always know His favor and abiding peace.*

And all the people said, "Amen."

NOTES

Chapter 1: Defining Worship

1. Dallas Willard, *Renovation of the Heart* (Colorado Springs: NavPress, 2002), 142.

2. I believe that the interactive nature of worship will eventually force a broad rethinking of the Church itself as we move increasingly from the model of being passive attendees and listeners to interactive participants and worshipers, and thus, from Church as the ministry of the few to the ministry of the many.

3. I love the scene in Numbers 23:21, in which the enemies of the people of God were unsuccessful in trying to put curses on them. They saw that "the LORD their God is with them." How did they know? "The shout of the King is among them." Their shout testified to the Lord's presence, and the attempted curses failed.

Chapter 2: The Calling of a Worshiper

1. Merrill F. Unger, ed., *Unger's Bible Dictionary* (Chicago: Moody, 1973), *kohen*.

2. Parenthetically, what we are learning here about offering acceptable sacrifices does not just have implications for our personal lives and our churches. It has incredible implications for shaping the course of nations, as well. As we, the Church, begin to understand and accept our priestly calling, I believe that we'll better understand how we are meant to serve the nations—"Christian" or "non-Christian"—in which God has placed us.

Our prophetic role toward the state—faithfully acting as its moral conscience—will be greatly helped when we passionately exercise our priestly role in its behalf—humbly serving as worshipers and intercessors, pleading for God's protection and blessing over it. Here are two biblical examples of this: (1) When God's people were captive in Babylon, God told them to seek Babylon's peace and prosperity—even to pray for it, "because if it prospers, you too will prosper" (Jeremiah 29:7); and later, (2) when Persia's King Darius was questioned about the legitimacy of the Israelites building a Temple to God in his empire, he wisely replied: "Let the temple be rebuilt . . . so that they may offer sacrifices pleasing to the God of heaven and pray for the well-being of the king and his sons" (Ezra 6:3, 10). Keep in mind that both of these situations involved empires that certainly did not share the faith or the values of God's people.

3. Contrast Revelation 5:13 with Revelation 13:8.

4. C. S. Lewis, *The Lion, the Witch and the Wardrobe* (New York: HarperCollins, 1994), 79–80.

5. Compare Galatians 3:8 with 3:14, 16.

6. Norman Grubb, *Rees Howells, Intercessor* (Fort Washington, Penn.: Christian Literature Crusade, 1980), 231–32.

7. Ibid., 233.

8. Ibid., 261.

9. Ibid., 261–62.

10. Someone should create a bumper sticker that says, "Help stamp out monocultural anthropomorphism."

11. John Stott, ed., *The Lausanne Covenant* (South Hamilton, Mass.: Lausanne Committee for World Evangelization, 1975).

12. Helen H. Lemmel, "Turn Your Eyes upon Jesus," public domain.

13. "Worship is the act and attitude of wholeheartedly giving yourself to God—spirit, soul, mind and body."

14. "A priest is a worshiper who draws near to God offering gifts and sacrifices, and who represents the needs of others."

15. "A sacrifice is a unit of worship."

16. "The power to bless the world around you is a direct result of your ministry to the Lord."

17. "The kingdom of priests is the international, transcultural, whole-hearted, Spirit-filled community of reigning worshipers in heaven and on earth."

Chapter 3: Beginnings

1. Obviously, a complete history of worship would fill many volumes. This abbreviated version is particularly concerned with understanding worship as sacrifice, and the development of the kingdom of priests.

2. This actual creek on the Continental Divide in Wyoming sends some of its water westward 1,353 miles to the Pacific Ocean; the rest of its water flows eastward 3,348 miles to the Gulf of Mexico.

3. Some scholars question whether this applies to Satan at all.

4. After He had done the will of God by going to the cross, Jesus was able to say, "All authority in heaven and on earth has been given to me" (Matthew 28:18). It is interesting that Satan tempted Jesus with a shortcut to His own destiny. Be advised of this tactic.

5. In Hebrews 7:9–10, we see this manner of speaking. Levi, a descendant of Abraham (like you), was there in the body of Abraham at this meeting.

6. Noah's sacrifice had a pleasing fragrance (see Genesis 8:21).

7. In fact, the first time the word *love* shows up in the Bible in the King James Version, it is used to describe Abraham's love for Isaac (see Genesis 22:2).

8. This is the essence of the first of the twelve convictions of true worshipers

9. This was fulfilled in the simultaneous death of Eli's two sons (see 1 Samuel 4:11), the slaughter of the priests at Nob by Saul (see 1 Samuel 22) and the final deposing of Abiathar, Eli's last remaining priestly descendant, by Solomon (see 1 Kings 2:35); compare 1 Samuel 2:35 with 1 Kings 2:35.

Chapter 4: Early Landmarks

1. Although we do not know the specific number, we do know, according to Numbers 1:46, that there was at Sinai a total of 603,550 men who were twenty years of age and older and able to serve in Israel's army. Adding in the elderly men, the women and the children, some project the number to be between two and three million people.

2. Just for fun, try out these other terms on your friends: *teleological soteriology*, or perhaps, *salvific teleology*. (Have you ever wondered who comes up with these words?)

3. Remember the bumper stickers that said, "Smile—God Loves You!"?

4. That is changing, though—and I hope this book will make a difference.

5. I looked it up. It is in the dictionary. It refers to "something extraordinary," a "humdinger."

6. Mount Horeb and Mount Sinai are probably different names for the same mountain. If they *are* different mountains, they are located in the same area.

7. This is the origin of the "clergy-laity separation," in which many people tell their pastors, "You hear from God; we'll pay the bills."

8. See the discussion on priests in chapter 2.

9. As we will learn later in the story, Solomon came the closest to fulfilling this vision (although it was through an inferior priesthood to the one God offered at Sinai). Worship filled Israel's national life under his rule, and as a result, "all the kings of the earth sought audience with Solomon" (2 Chronicles 9:23).

10. Lewis, 79–80.

11. God spoke these words to Elijah on the very same mountain.

12. We know of Abraham's sacrifices. Isaac built an altar for worship in Genesis 26:25. Jacob offered a sacrifice in Genesis 31:54, and Moses in Exodus 17:15.

Chapter 5: Later Developments

1. These sons lorded over those they were supposed to serve, forcing offerings that benefited themselves and having sex with women who were involved in the ministry with them (see 1 Samuel 2:12–22).

2. This R-rated story (for sexuality and violence) is told in Numbers 25:1–13. It is not until we read in Numbers 31:15–16 that we learn Balaam, a counselor to the king of Moab (see Numbers 22–24), was behind this strategy.

3. Tracing lineages is not meant to suggest that we are helplessly locked into the patterns of our forebears. Jeremiah himself was probably a descendant of Abiathar; and Gentiles can become "sons of Abraham." The value of following lineages is that they can show the deep-seated nature of our motivations and habits.

4. This god of self-promotion, which is the official deity of modern-day humanism, is the ancient spirit of Babel. Its mantra is found in Genesis 11:4: Let's "make a name for ourselves." It contrasts with God's promise to His followers found in Genesis 12:2: "I will make your name great, and you will be a blessing."

5. The chronicler of the kings used this phrase twelve different times to describe the various kings of Israel: See 1 Kings 16:31; 2 Kings 3:3; 10:29, 31; 13:2, 11; 14:24; 15:9, 18, 24, 28; 17:22.

6. This amazing story is found in 2 Chronicles 32:1–22 and Isaiah 36–37. The miraculous intervention of God—a single angel slew 185,000 Assyrian soldiers—is in the same category as the deliverance from Egypt at the Red Sea.

7. Read about his worship revival in 2 Chronicles 34:1–35:19. The Book of the Law was rediscovered, and in it, they learned that idolatry was the cause of the curses that had come upon Judah.

8. One of Josiah's sons, Jehoahaz, was led in chains to Egypt, where he died. Another son, Jehoiachin, was taken prisoner by the Babylonians and later died there.

9. Also a son of Josiah (see 1 Chronicles 3:15).

10. The story of how God humbled this great king and made him a worshiper is something to tell your children and grandchildren. It is found in Daniel 4, and is surprisingly similar to the story in the Disney film *The Emperor's New Groove.*

11. The Liar had tried this before under Nebuchadnezzar's reign (see Daniel 3) and will try it again (see 2 Thessalonians 2:3–4).

12. Quoted in Winkie Pratney, *The Thomas Factor* (Grand Rapids: Chosen Books, 1989), 122.

13. "Every organization exists to serve people outside of that organization. When it exists to serve people inside the organization, it di·s" (Peter Drucker, qtd. in Leonard Sweet, *Carpe Mañana* [Grand Rapids: Zondervan, 2001], 28.)

14. He was fluent with the purposes of God, giving outline to the rise and fall of the kingdoms of man until the time of Christ's Second Coming (see Daniel 2, 7 and 8). He was especially informed regarding the Liar's ambition. He had seen it firsthand when Nebuchadnezzar, under the Liar's influence, commanded the worship of the image of gold in chapter 3. He knew that was a foreshadowing of a future, last-days attempt of the antichrist to own the worship that belongs to God (see 11:36–45). He referred to that event as the "abomination that causes desolation" (see 9:27; 12:11). Jesus confirmed its importance (see Matthew 24:15–16), as did Paul (see 2 Thessalonians 2:4) and John (see Revelation 13:14–15).

15. Jeremiah regularly told the exiles not to listen to those misguided prophets: See Jeremiah 23:16 and 29:8–9, for instance. The reference from chapter 29 follows up on his counsel to work and pray for Babylon's prosperity.

16. See Matthew 5:16. The end result of this kind of witness is that God is praised by those who see our good works.

Chapter 6: The Conclusion of the Matter

1. Today this is southern Iran.

2. In Jeremiah 33:11, Jeremiah gave us the lyrics of the song that would be sung. Ezra recorded that (see Ezra 3:11); in fact, that was what they sang. That particular song, by the way, had quite a history, stretching over many generations: Introduced when the Ark was brought back to Israel under David (see 1 Chronicles 16), it was sung at Solomon's dedication (see 2 Chronicles 5), Jehoshaphat's battle preparation (see 2 Chronicles 20) and finally at the laying of the foundation of Zerubbabel's Temple.

3. This is a great story for all those churches that take the first steps in worship renewal and then run into problems.

4. "The glory of the LORD entered the temple through the gate facing east. Then the Spirit lifted me up and brought me into the inner court, and the glory of the LORD filled the temple" (Ezekiel 43:4–5). "The Lord God Almighty and the Lamb are [the city's] temple" (Revelation 21:22). This Temple is not *of* God; it *is* God.

5. The Greek version of the word *Joshua*, a common name in those days, is *Jesus*. It means "the Lord saves."

6. See Isaiah 11:1. When Judah was cut down by the Babylonians, all that was left was a stump, but there was still life in the roots.

7. Could the fact that Antiochus' title, *Epiphanes*, means "God made manifest" indicate that the Liar and habitual usurper of praise might have been involved?

8. Compare 1 Maccabeus 2:1 with 1 Chronicles 9:10–11.

9. Do you remember his story from Numbers 25?

10. See 1 Maccabeus 2:54.

11. Read the amazing comparison between Sinai and Zion in Hebrews 12:18–24, and see, in verse 28, how we should respond as we are brought to this New Sinai: "Be thankful, and so worship God acceptably with reverence and awe."

12. Jesus' people are designated as a "holy nation" in 1 Peter 2:9.

13. Redemption is the buying back of "all things," not just humanity (Colossians 1:20). Redemption's end is that "in everything he might have the supremacy" (verse 18).

14. See 1 Peter 2:5. In both the Greek and Hebrew languages, the word *house* implies a household.

15. Remember, it is our ministry to the Lord that creates the power to bless others (see Deuteronomy 10:8).

16. The Duomo in Milan was begun in 1075 and completed in the mid-1700s.

17. The change of law (see Hebrews 7:12), termed the "New Covenant," was that the law would now be internalized, written on our minds and hearts (see Hebrews 8:8–10) and fulfilled by the power of the Holy Spirit (see Galatians 5:18, 22–23).

18. "In the same way, *after supper* he took the cup" (1 Corinthians 11:25, emphasis mine).

19. Some may object to the idea of becoming a kingdom of priests, saying that we already are just that. They may even quote 1 Peter 2:9—"you *are* . . . a royal priesthood"—emphasizing that it is a done deal. But looking more closely, we find that this is another example of the "already–not yet" tension found in God's way of speaking to us. Yes,

we *are* currently a royal priesthood; and yes, we *are becoming* what God declares us to be: "You . . . are being built into a spiritual house to be a holy priesthood" (1 Peter 2:5).

If you need some official-sounding names for these three models of worship, how about *Eucharistic, Kerygmatic* and *Leitourgistic. Eucharist* is another word for communion or the Lord's Supper, so *Eucharistic* would indicate the model of worship centered on the table. *Kerygma* is the Greek word for proclamation or preaching; *Kerygmatic*, then, would refer to the model of worship centered on the pulpit. *Leitourgeo* is a Greek word for worship or ministering to the Lord. It is used in Acts 13:2 where we find prophets and teachers in Antioch worshiping (NIV) or ministering to the Lord (KJV). *Leitourgistic*, then, would describe the third model of worship where we minister before the Lord's throne.

20. The most hideous persecution of the early Christians came to them under the folly and wickedness of Nero. As Philip Schaff records in his *History of the Christian Church*: "A 'vast multitude' of Christians was put to death in the most shocking manner . . . Christian men and women, covered with pitch or oil or resin, and nailed to posts of pine, were lighted and burned as torches for the amusement of the mob; while Nero, in fantastical dress, figured in a horse race, and displayed his art as charioteer" ([Oak Harbor, Wash.: Logos Research Systems, Inc., 1997], 382).

21. See Hebrews 7:20–24.

22. See Matthew 13:33.

23. "When this priest had offered for all time one sacrifice for sins, he sat down at the right hand of God. Since that time he waits for his enemies to be made his footstool, because by one sacrifice he has made perfect forever those who are being made holy" (Hebrews 10:12–14).

24. It seems that there is a parallel and simultaneous restoration of Israel and the Church. In light of that, Ezekiel's prophecy will probably have a dual fulfillment, involving a physical Temple and a spiritual one. As you read in the paper about the most contested real estate on earth, the Dome of the Rock, remember that there is also an invisible seat of power that is equally contested. The dual nature of God's purposes for Israel and the Church are not competing, but interdependent (see Romans 11:11–32). The challenge to ethnic Israel is to see beyond the natural; the challenge to the Church is to humbly accept that we are branches grafted into and supported by Israel's root.

25. "She is His new creation by water and the word." From the hymn "The Church's One Foundation," by Samuel Stone and Samuel Wesley (Charles' grandson).

26. From "All Hail the Power of Jesus' Name" by Edward Perronet (public domain).

27. Quoted in the introduction of *The Hymns of Martin Luther*, edited by Leonard Woolsey Bacon and Nathan Allen (public domain), distributed by The Project Gutenberg eText, www.gutenberg.org.

28. Philip Smith, ed., *The Autobiography of Benjamin Franklin* (Mineola, N.Y.: Dover, 1996).

29. Speaking of the twentieth century, the World Evangelical Alliance's Religious Liberty Commission reported that "more people have died in circumstances related to their faith in this century than in all the twentieth-century wars combined."

30. The word *revelation* means "unveiling."

31. Do you remember how Satan tempted Jesus with a shortcut to His own destiny? The destiny of the nations is to worship God (see Revelation 15:4). The Liar creates great confusion by appealing to mankind's innate desire to worship something greater than itself.

Chapter 9: Conviction #2

1. Since the same Greek word (*pneuma*) is used to refer to the human spirit and the person of the Holy Spirit, and since the Greek language does not capitalize as the English language does, the distinction between the human spirit and the Holy Spirit is not always clear. For the sake of our discussion, when we speak of worship in spirit, we are referring to worship that emanates in the human spirit by the power of the Holy Spirit.

2. George Barna, *The Barna Update*, October 8, 2002, www.barna.org.

3. On this point, I highly recommend Kevin Navarro's excellent book, *The Complete Worship Leader* (Grand Rapids: Baker, 2001).

4. W. E. Vine, *Vine's Complete Expository Dictionary of Old and New Testament Words* (Nashville: Thomas Nelson, 1996), *truth*.

5. George Barna, *Real Teens* (Ventura, Calif.: Regal, 2001).

Chapter 10: Conviction #3

1. Because the heart directs the mind and the body, *wholehearted* is the best single adjective to describe the total response of who we are.

Chapter 13: Conviction #6

1. James Strong, *Strong's Exhaustive Concordance of the Bible* (Nashville, Tenn.: Abingdon Press, 1970), #126.

Chapter 14: Conviction #7

1. The word *iconolatry* is sometimes used to refer to the worship of images of other gods.

2. The book *God at War*, by Gregory Boyd (Nottingham, U.K.: InterVarsity Press, 1997), provides a scholarly and provocative examination of the general subject of spiritual warfare and the specific subject of other gods.

Chapter 15: Conviction #8

1. David was anointed as king in 1 Samuel 16, but it was not until seventeen chapters later—covering many years—that he first took the throne over Judah, and it was even longer before he was installed as king over Israel. For much of the time between his anointing and his installation, David was a hunted man. He lived among the Philistines and in Adullam's cave for part of that time.

Chapter 17: Conviction #10

1. Most people have a hard time answering these two questions.

2. In the last days, "people will be lovers of themselves" (2 Timothy 3:2).

3. For some penetrating analysis on this subject, look at *The Connecting Church—Beyond Small Groups to Authentic Communities* by Randy Frazee (Grand Rapids: Zondervan, 2001).

4. One interesting development is the Global Day of Prayer that encourages unified prayer and worship around Pentecost Sunday each year. According to a report by WayMakers, in 2001, one stadium in Cape Town, South Africa, was filled with 45,000 people who came to pray. In 2002, it expanded to eight stadiums and 350,000 people. A year later, 2.5 million people gathered in 130 stadiums. In 2004, the movement exploded to nearly ten times the size. More than 22 million people rallied in prayer at more than two thousand sites throughout every single country on the continent of Africa (56 nations). Since then, the movement has spread to include many other nations, as well.

Chapter 18: Conviction #11

1. *Breakpoint with Chuck Colson,* May 17, 2005, www.breakpoint.org.

2. C. Austin Miles, "In the Garden," (1912), public domain.

Chapter 19: Conviction #12

1. Heaven's great "Holy, holy, holy, is the Lord God Almighty" is horizontal. And if you think about it, "Hallelujah," which means, "Praise

the Lord," is an instruction either to yourself or someone else. Therefore, it is horizontal.

Chapter 20: May All the Peoples Praise You

1. *Chronos* and *kairos* are two Greek words translated as "time" in the New Testament. Usually *chronos* refers to the duration or quantity of time, and *kairos* to the character or quality of time. For instance, Jesus came in the "fulness of the time" (*kairos*) (Galatians 4:4, KJV).

2. Many people think of liturgy as the antithesis of liberty in the Spirit. However, the word *leitourgeo*, from which it was derived, is a priestly term for worship, or ministry to the Lord (see, for example, Acts 13:2). In the best sense of the word, liturgy is about the divine protocol of coming before the Lord to worship. For instance, when we say, "We enter His gates with thanksgiving," we are talking about liturgy. A good worship leader will constantly be learning the art of entering God's presence. That makes him a liturgist.

3. The incarnation is God's act of becoming like us so that He could get through to us.

The Twelve Convictions of True Worshipers

Developing the heart and mind of worship

• •

1. **Worship and God's Love**
   Worship is a response to God's great love.

2. **Worship in Spirit and Truth**
   Acceptable worship springs out of life in the Spirit and love for truth and reality.

3. **Wholehearted Worship**
   A true worshiper engages the totality of his being in worship.

4. **Diversity in Worship**
   Practicing songs, hymns and spiritual songs enlarges our worship.

5. **Worship and God's Presence**
   Our praise opens the gates into God's presence.

6. **Worship and Prayer**
   Entering God's presence in worship, we can extend His purpose in prayer.

7. **Worship God Only**
   We must carefully guard against all forms of idolatry.

8. **Worship and Warfare**
   A true worshiper must become a warrior.

9. **Worship and Service to Others**
   Sacrificial service to others is fundamental to a life of worship.

10. **Worship and Community**
    True worshipers will be built together with other worshipers.

11. **Worship and Suffering**
    A true worshiper sings songs in the night.

12. **Worship and the Good News**
    Up-reach in worship leads to outreach to others.

• •
www.worshipschools.com

Developing the Twelve Convictions

How to develop the heart and mind of worship

• •

Jesus said that His Father is looking for worshipers.
In measuring growth, churches often count the number of members or attendees. But God is looking for worshipers. Does He find one in you?

What is a worshiper?
A worshiper is someone who is learning God's specifications for worship and worships accordingly. For instance, Jesus said true worshipers must worship in spirit and in truth. Those are two of God's specifications for true worship.

What exactly is a conviction?
Deeper than a belief, a conviction is something you are really convinced of. It's something you know that you know that you know! Convictions work from the inside out to affect our behavior; they become the governing principles of our lives.

How should I use this list of twelve convictions?
First, don't look at the list as a heavy burden of unattainable goals. Instead, bring to God your desire to be a true worshiper, and ask Him to help you develop the heart and mind of a true worshiper. Then let the twelve convictions be like a road map, showing you the ground to cover, the convictions to develop.

Lord, form these convictions in me so that I will become the kind of worshiper You are seeking!

• •
From *The Adventure of Worship*
(Chosen Books).
To request these bookmarks
for your small group,
go to www.worshipschools.com.

BIBLIOGRAPHY

Barna, George. *Real Teens*. Ventura, Calif.: Regal Books, 2001.

Boyd, Gregory. *God at War*. Nottingham, U.K.: InterVarsity Press, 1997.

Frazee, Randy. *The Connecting Church*. Grand Rapids: Zondervan, 2001.

Grubb, Norman. *Rees Howells, Intercessor*. Fort Washington, Penn.: Christian Literature Crusade, 1980.

Lewis, C. S. *The Lion, the Witch and the Wardrobe*. New York: HarperCollins Publishers, 1994.

Navarro, Kevin. *The Complete Worship Leader*. Grand Rapids: Baker, 2001.

Pratney, Winkie. *The Thomas Factor*. Grand Rapids: Chosen Books, 1989.

Smith, Philip, ed. *The Autobiography of Benjamin Franklin*. Mineola, N.Y.: Dover, 1996.

Stott, John, ed. *The Lausanne Covenant*. South Hamilton, Mass.: Lausanne Committee for World Evangelization, 1975.

Strong, James. *Strong's Exhaustive Concordance of the Bible*. Nashville, Tenn.: Abingdon Press, 1970.

Tolkien, J. R. R. *The Hobbit*. Boston, Mass.: Houghton Mifflin Company Publishers, 1997.

Unger, Merrill F., ed. *Unger's Bible Dictionary*. Chicago: Moody Press, 1973.

Vine, W. E. *Vine's Complete Expository Dictionary of Old and New Testament Words*. Nashville, Tenn.: Thomas Nelson, 1996.

Willard, Dallas. *Renovation of the Heart*. Colorado Springs: NavPress, 2002.

INDEX

It was in his college years at Florida State University that **Gerrit Gustafson** joined the adventure he is writing about. There, after coming to Christ, he encountered some wholehearted worshipers whose abandonment to God became a doorway into discovering his own calling as a worshiper.

During the next fifteen years, he was a pastor/teacher in Florida, Colorado, Mississippi and Alabama. In 1985 the church in Alabama where he was serving as music pastor started Hosanna Music, a ministry to resource churches with recordings of worship songs. Gerrit was part of the original creative team of this ministry, which was later named Integrity Music.

As the impact of the company grew, churches began requesting training to help them renew their own worship. This led Gerrit to develop a weekend seminar that eventually became known as Worship Schools. The next fifteen years found Gerrit offering encouragement and insight to worshipers in churches and conferences all over the world.

Along the way, Gerrit has worn many hats—church music director, songwriter, producer, publisher and pastor/teacher. But his greatest joy is seeing people and churches make the transition from passive worship to active worship, from halfheartedness to wholeheartedness in how they honor God.

According to Gerrit, "That transition requires a deepening of both experience and understanding. Two dangers exist: (1) that our understanding of worship is hefty while our experience is meager; and (2) that our experience of worship is not fortified by understanding."

Gerrit and Himmie, his wife of 31 years, have five children and live near Nashville, Tennessee, where they love to have invigorating conversation with guests around their table.

You can sample some of the products he has created at www.wholeheartedworship. com. And if your church needs to deepen its involvement in this adventure of worship, Gerrit would love to hear from you. You can contact him through www.worshipschools.com.